A TREASURY OF MODERN SMALL ARMS

A TREASURY OF MODERN SMALL ARMS

Edited by
JACOB BURK

GALLERY BOOKS
An imprint of W.H. Smith Publishers Inc.
112 Madison Avenue
New York, New York 10016

A Bison Book

Published by Gallery Books
A Division of W H Smith Publishers Inc.
112 Madison Avenue
New York, New York 10016

Produced by
Bison Books Corp.
15 Sherwood Place
Greenwich, CT 06830

ISBN 0-8317-6886-X

Printed in Spain

10 9 8 7 6 5 4 3 2 1

Editor's Note:

In general, we have attempted a survey of some of the major arms manufacturers in Europe, South America and the Middle East, concerning firearms which they now have in production. We hope that our selection is pleasing to you, since we think this Treasury of Small Arms will give the firearms buff a taste of the great variety of finely made firearms which are currently available in the world today.

All photos courtesy of the respective manufactures except:
Bison Books Corp: 24 (top), 29 (top), 56-57 (second from bottom, bottom)
Ruth DeJauregui: 110 (bottom), 192
Foto Zanoni: 61 (third from bottom, second from bottom, bottom)
Gun Review: 42-43 (right)
Steve's Photography, Inc: 20
TASS: 73 (top, second from top)

Designed by Tom Debolski

Page 1: Franchi SPAS-12 Semiautomatic Assault Shotgun

Pages 2-3: Remington's Model 870 Wing-master Shotgun

These pages: A-Square .500 Hannibal Magnum Rifle

TABLE OF CONTENTS

AUSTRIA

Josef Werndl founded the **Josef and Franz Werndl & Company Firearms Factory** some 120 years ago, and manufactured the Werndl bolt-action rifle, which was the first breechloader to be used by the Austro-Hungarian Imperial Army. Chief Engineer Ferdinand Mannlicher designed his famous straight-pull bolt-action repeater and the arms company was given the Imperial edict to manufacture the Mannlicher rifle. At the turn of the century, the arms factory branched out into a new mode of manufacture, and produced its first car, the 'Steyr.' In time, and as part of further permutations, the firm became part of a merger to form **Steyr-Daimler-Puch AG.** This firm has had many accomplishments over the years of its existence, and here we present the pride of Steyr-Daimler-Puch's present production of firearms.

The Steyr AUG (Army Universal Gun) is today the most highly modern personal weapon embodying the most up-to-date technology. The highly variable and versatile Steyr AUG weapons system is based on a total of six main assemblies comprising all individual parts of the various AUG versions. As a result it is possible to produce various AUG versions which, while basically differing from one another mere-ly as regards the length of the barrel, nevertheless cover a major part of the entire spectrum of small arms.

The basic AUG versions and their barrel lengths—which distinguish them—are as follows: Commando model, 14 inches; Machine Carbine model, 16 inches; Assault Rifle model, 20 inches; and the Light Support Weapon, 24.5 inches. However, all main assemblies and individual parts are fully interchangeable within the AUG weapons system. In addition there is a wide range of optional equipment, which can likewise be used for the entire AUG weapons system.

The Steyr AUG is engineered to the compact 'bullpup' design, and is rugged and durable—made to operate in a wide variety of conditions—from desert to artic, and in between. Weapons in which the magazine is located to the rear of the trigger are said to be of 'bullpup' design. This bullpup design makes for an extremely short overall length of the weapon, ie it is about 25 percent shorter than conventional designs.

The overall length with the 20 inch barrel is only 31 inches. With the 16 inch barrel, the overall length is even just 27 inches. In this way it becomes possible to dispense with a folding stock version, along with

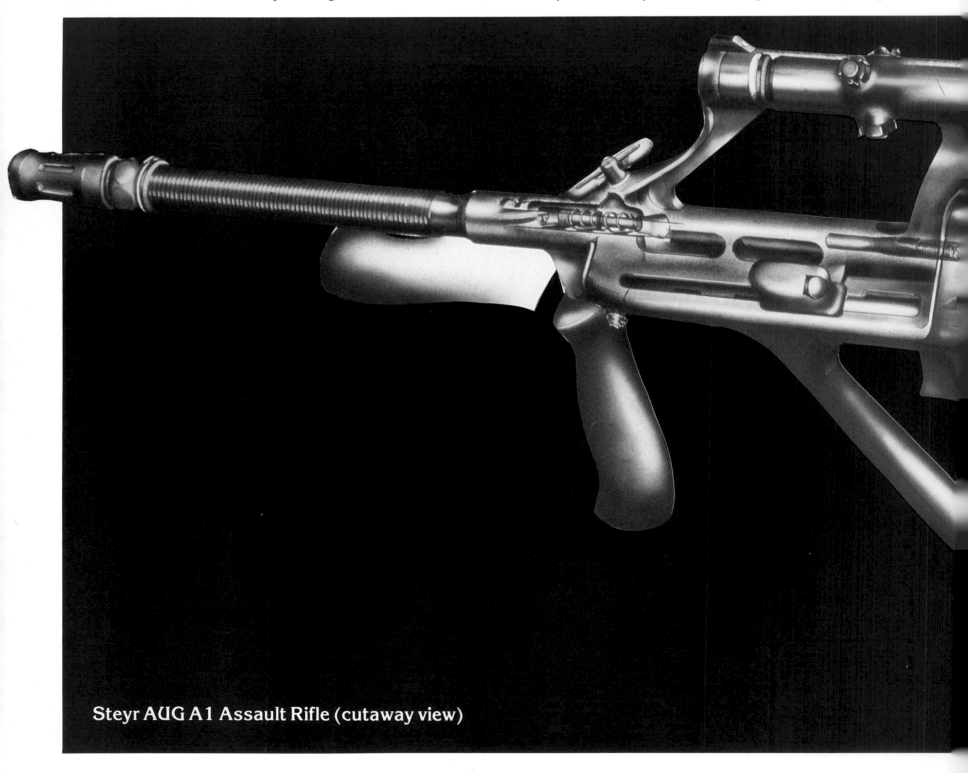

Steyr AUG A1 Assault Rifle (cutaway view)

Steyr AUG A1 Assault Rifle

all the drawbacks which that system entails. In addition to this, the AUG's quick-change barrel enables the swift, easy fieldstripping of this firearm. Fieldstripped, its longest component measures a mere 21 inches. Moreover, it is instantly possible to convert the assault rifle into any one of its machine carbine, commando weapon, light machine gun or heavy barrel automatic rifle configurations.

With the advent of the Steyr AUG, the first time in a military weapon, an optical sight has been integrated into the carrying handle and, thus, is housed in fully protected fashion. The optical sight offers a magnification of 1.5 times. This sight magnification means a wide field of sight; furthermore it is possible to fire with both eyes open (as the human eyes are able to adapt themselves from 1 to 1.5 ×). This optical sight features a standard ring reticule with a diameter of 1.8m projected on a distance of 300m.

The standard ring reticule offers a further advantage—it serves as an aid for range finding. Other reticules are offered optionally. An optical sight offers enormous advantages. For the average acquisition of a target via an optical sight, one reckons with 1.5 seconds (where two points must be lined up), versus open sights three seconds (where three points must be lined up).

In the hours of dawn or dusk and on overcast days, the target can be made out via an optical sight long after any hope of doing so with open sight has gone. The Steyr AUG fires 5.56mm (.223 caliber) ammunition. The advantages of this small, high-velocity round are many. For example, as compared to the tried-and-true 7.62mm (.308 caliber)

Steyr AUG A1 Assault Rifle
(with open sights)

Steyr AUG Assault Rifle

Steyr AUG Machine Carbine

Steyr AUG Commando Submachine Gun

9

round, the new ammo weighs approximately half of what the 7.62mm round weighs. And, because the ammo is lighter the weapon has a weight saving of approximately one-third.

Owing to the high muzzle velocity, the trajectory of the bullet is so flat that up to a range of 385 yards the soldier need not bother at all about the point of aim. There is no need for setting the sight. The small caliber also makes for exceptionally steady shooting, ie the gun will not jump, climb or swerve. Recoil is so slight as to be almost negligible. There is no flinching or fatigue.

The AUG features rapid changeover from single shots to sustained automatic fire and vice versa without any need for a lever, which means that no time is wasted looking for the selector.

The generously dimensioned, cold-hammered and internally chrome-plated barrel guarantees maximum service life. Minimum service life of the barrel will be 15,000 rounds provided a maximum temperature of 400° C is not exceeded (which means cooling after 150 rounds of fully automatic firing). The magazines are fracture-resistant and transparent: 30 and 42 round magazines are available. Cleaning is exceptionally easy, thanks to the chrome-plated barrel and the use of non-corrosive materials, such as aluminum and synthetics. No tools are needed to strip down or reassemble the weapon.

The AUG also has an adaptable receiver for night-sighting equipment or scope of more powerful magnification.

The six modular assemblies of the Steyr AUG are as follows. The barrel is hammer-forged of high-grade steel and features a chrome-plated bore. In all AUG versions, the barrel is connected to the receiver

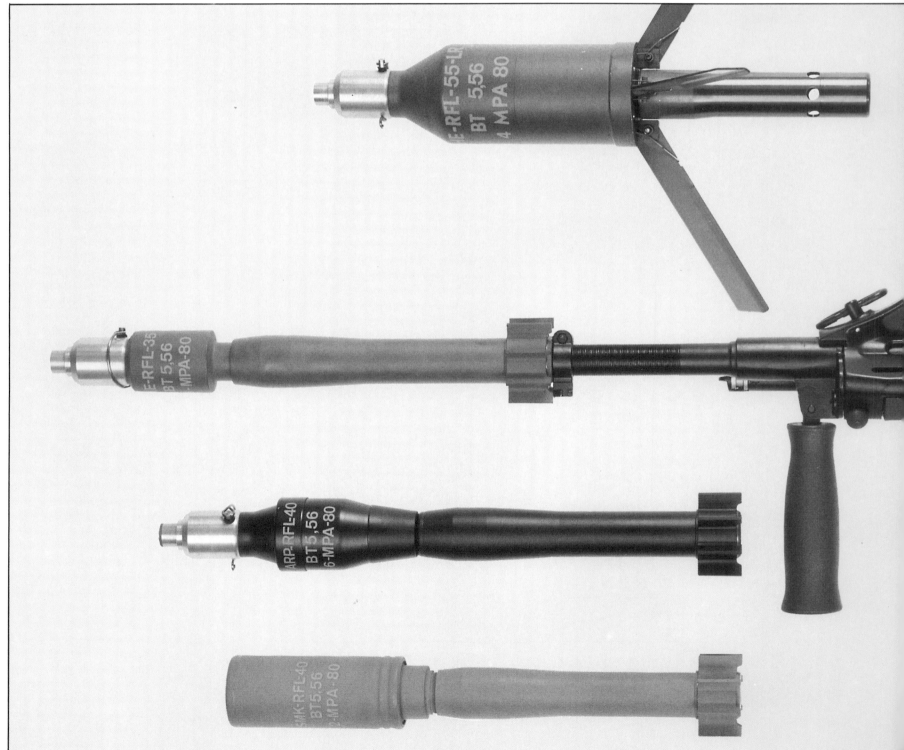

Steyr AUG/9mm Machine Carbine (with silencer)

Steyr AUG A1 Assault Rifle (with compatible grenade systems)

by means of locking lugs and, by a slight rotating movement, can be detached from it.

All AUG versions are equipped with a barrel-mounted handle. Except with the shortest barrel version of 14 inches length, this handle can be folded up and thus permits the weapon to be fired from the rest position. Apart from the barrel itself, this assembly also incorporates the gas pressure system consisting of the gas cylinder, the chrome-plated gas piston and the adjustable chrome-plated gas plug.

The bolt assembly is made of special high-grade steel. The well-tried rotary locking bolt action has been improved even further. The bolt locks following a rotation of 22.5 degrees in the receiver, with the rotation being controlled by means of a control pin via a cam in the bolt carrier. The latter, which houses the bolt, is equipped with two chrome-plated guide tubes.

The receiver, which is an aluminum die casting, combines all other assemblies into a single unit. For emergency use, the receiver is equipped with auxiliary mechanical sights as well as with an auxiliary night sight. The stock, which consists of glass-fiber reinforced polyamide 66, serves to accommodate the trigger—and real mechanism. The two halves are inseparably joined together by friction welding.

Owing to the adoption of the bullpup principle, the ejection lid, too, is located in the stock. So as to eliminate any problems for right handed or left handed shooters when firing from the shoulder, one ejection

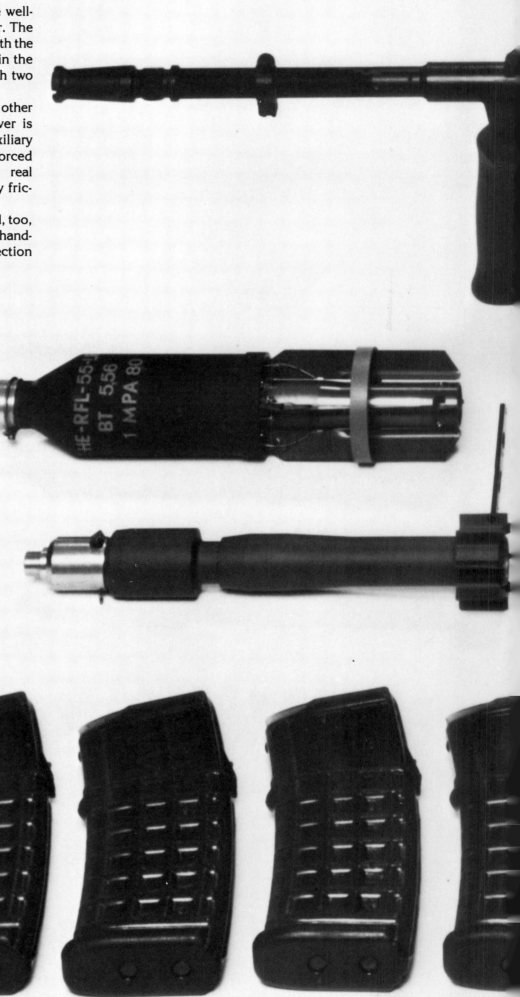

Steyr AUG A1 Assault Rifle (with ordnance)

lid each has been provided on the right and on the left. The port on the side facing the shooter is closed off in each case by an ejection cover that can be used on either side. Optionally, stocks with ejection ports on the right only or left only are available.

With the exception of a small number of minor parts, the trigger assembly, too, is made of synthetic material. The entire trigger mechanism has been designed as a compact assembly and, following the removal of the butt plate, can be readily withdrawn from the stock. It is controlled from the trigger via a sear lever located in the stock.

The magazine consists of transparent, highly impact-resistant synthetic material. In addition, the transparent material used enables the firer to check at a glance how many rounds are still left in the magazine.

The Steyr AUG A1—which designates the AUG's rifle configuration (named the Steyr Universal Automatic Rifle)—has been in use with the Austrian Federal Army for nearly a decade, and is the product of a cooperative effort between Steyr-Daimler-Puch AG and the Austrian Federal Army.

For all applications where optical sights cannot be used for some special reason or where their use is thought to be undesirable, STEYR also offers an AUG version with open sights. These open sights are also in accordance with all requirements of international standards and of NATO in regard to the length of the line of sight without foregoing the advantages of the bullpup principle or any other benefits offered by the AUG weapons system. Special attention has been paid to

**Steyr AUG A1
(with infra-red scope)**

**Steyr AUG Weapons Systems
(exploded view with
interchangeable barrel assemblies)**

Steyr AUG/Police Machine Carbine

Steyr AUG/9mm Machine Carbine

15

retaining interchangeability within the system. As a result this weapon can be readily re-equipped at any time for use with optical sights. The special receiver, which permits all optronic or sighting devices to be mounted, can be fitted quickly—and without tools.

The Steyr AUG P Police—as the model designation already indicates—has been tailored to the special requirements of law enforcement authorities. Its main distinguishing features compared with other AUG versions are: a black stock to provide an optical distinction from the military weapons; reticule with ring and a dot for more accurate aiming; and semiautomatic system which can, however, be replaced by a fully automatic trigger mechanism. Sustained automatic fire is actuated merely by pressure on the trigger. This safety feature can also be replaced by a center position device—a variant which is also available for all other AUG versions.

There is also a barrel that is shorter by 3.9 inches for the AUG version 407 in order to make the weapon even handier for use in built-up areas. However, if this should be required for operational reasons, it is also possible to use all other available barrel variants of the AUG weapons system. Similarly, an extensive choice of accessories is available, such as a special receiver, grenade launching system and low-light level image intensifier sight, which can be readily inserted in, or mounted on, this weapon.

The STEYR AUG HBAR (Heavy Barrel Automatic Rifle) and STEYR LMG (Light Machine Gun) reflect the consistent further development of the AUG weapons system. In carrying out this development work, Steyr-Daimler-Puch AG has succeeded in producing even this somewhat heavier weapon for the major part on the basis of the already available and well-tried assemblies and components of the AUG system. Moreover, the STEYR AUG HBAR and STEYR LMG also meet demands made on small arms by NATO.

The STEYR AUG LSW features the following components: a slightly heavier barrel with a length of 24 inches in order to cope with the high thermal stresses of a light machine gun; a special muzzle device which reduces recoil almost to zero and prevents the weapon from climbing when firing sustained bursts; an adjustable fold-up bipod fixture; and a magazine which contains 42 rounds but is also suitable for all other AUG versions.

Features of the STEYR variants AUG HBAR and LMG T are: the use of the well-tried Schmidt & Bender four power scope and of course any other type of scope; and the possibility of using night vision scopes on the same housing.

The four power scope has been optimally adapted by the manufacturer to the conditions encountered with 5.56mm cartridges. Every other type of optical device can, of course, also be fitted. As a result,

Steyr AUG LSW Light Machine Gun (with scope)

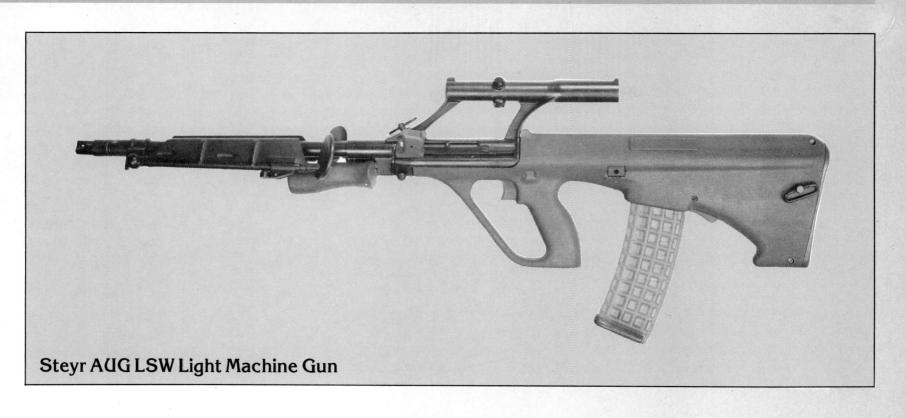

Steyr AUG LSW Light Machine Gun

the range of the AUG LSW's has been extended to more than 2600 feet against individual targets and to approximately 3937 feet against groups of targets.

Specifics of the four versions available in this Steyr genre are as follows: The AUG HBAR has a closed bolt system that is standard for all AUG versions and is equipped with the standard AUG optical sight; the Steyr Heavy Barrel Automatic Rifle AUG HBAR T is equipped with a rubber-covered four power scope that meets NATO standards; the Steyr Light Machine Gun AUG LMG features an open bolt to avoid cook off, and carries the AUG standard optical sight; and the Steyr Light Machine Gun AUG LMG T uses the open bolt to avoid cook off, and features a rubber-covered four power scope which complies with NATO standards.

What has been retained in all of the four versions is the economical bullpup design, the use of high-quality synthetic materials, the interchangeability of individual parts within the AUG weapons system and the simple design of these weapons. Together this results in low weight, a small storage and transport volume, simplification of maintenance work and modest time and expenditure requirements for training purposes in connection with the use of this weapon.

Finally, all STEYR AUG HBAR and LMG versions are also characterized by highest operational reliability under weather and environmental conditions of all kinds and descriptions. To change over from single shots to sustained fire, one must only modify the pressure exerted on the trigger.

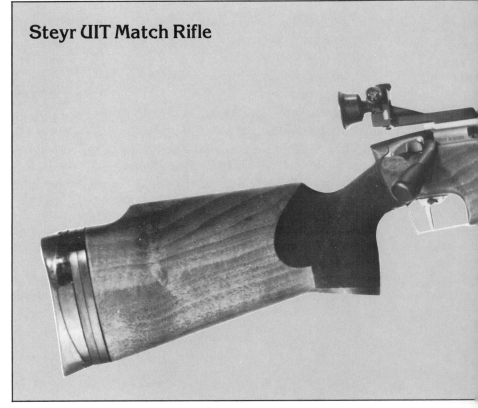

Steyr UIT Match Rifle

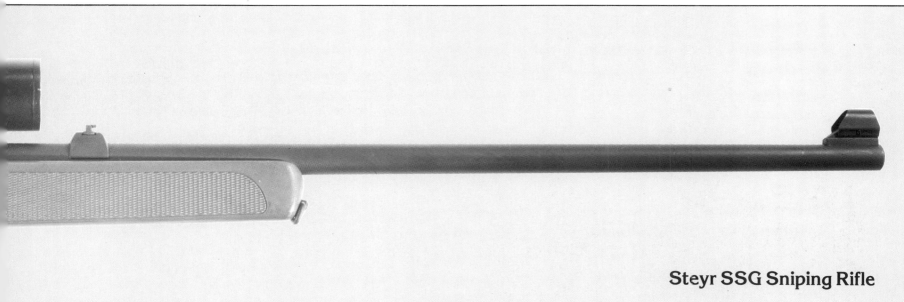

Steyr SSG Sniping Rifle

Steyr SSG/Police Sniping Rifle

Just like all other AUG models, the LSW versions can also be rapidly converted into an assault rifle with 20 inch barrel, a carbine with 16 inch barrel, or a paratroopers weapon with 14 inch barrel. This can be done—without impairing their operation—simply by changing the barrel.

The serially manufactured AUG special receiver can be called a special item of equipment, because no comparative products are available. Just like the standard receiver, the special receiver for all versions of the AUG weapons system is made of pressure die aluminum castings produced by the precision casting process. The special receiver is suitable for all AUG weapons.

Once the barrel has been sighted-in, the special receiver can be equipped and stored with any desired optical device, eg with a night vision sight. There is no need for renewed sighting-in when the weapon is used at some later time. In addition, the special receiver has been equipped with the standardized NATO mounts; however, it can also be fitted without difficulty with all other seats for any available mount. Also, in place of the standard receiver, a specially sealed receiver for water depths of nearly 230 feet is available.

To enlarge the AUG family , all Steyr Army Universal Guns can now be converted without the use of tools into a 9mm Parabellum Carbine. This conversion kit consists of barrel group, bolt group, magazine adaptor and magazine. The carbine handles like the AUG, but uses the 9mm Parabellum ammunition and still can take advantage of the built-in optical sight as well as any other features of the AUG family.

The Steyr SSG Sniping Rifle in 7.62mm (.308 Winchester) and .243 Winchester calibers would make an excellent sport rifle. Starting out from the Steyr line of hunting and sporting rifles, this weapon has been developed according to the requirements and advice of the Austrian Federal Army into a first rate sniping rifle. In doing so it proved possible to retain the operating comfort of the hunting rifles while the precision and ruggedness of the weapon had to be increased even further to fit it for military and police duties.

The receiver has been shrunk onto the cold hammer-forged barrel, which is 25.5 inches in length, in order to obtain an optimal connec-tion between the receiver and the barrel. For disassembly, a 10 to 20 ton press would be required.

For the stock, high-quality synthetic material has been used which facilitates cleaning and enables the use of this weapon in all weather conditions. In addition, the stock has been designed both for right and left handed shooters; and to accommodate marksmen of various builds, removable spacers have been built into the butt section of the virtually indestructible ABS Cycolac stock. Fast reloading is made possible by a bolt which is supported at six points and reduces the opening angle to no more than 60 degrees.

Total safety is ensured by a safety device working directly on the firing pin and locking the bolt handle as well as by a cocking indicator which can also be sensed at night. The trigger mechanism, which permits dual external adjustment, can also be replaced by a double set trigger.

A five round drum magazine ensures the optimal delivery of cartridges. Optionally a 10 round box magazine is also available. With both magazines, the supply of ammunition can be checked at a glance.

The standard scope is a 6 × 42 ZFM, which is characterized by particular luminosity and permits accurate aiming even under the most difficult conditions. In order to ensure the best possible connection and a line of aim that is as low as possible, this optical sight is mounted directly on the receiver (ie the seating socket has been milled into the receiver). At the same time, it is possible to mount all other day and night vision devices. In addition, open sights with sprung, adjustable front sight and adjustable rear sight notch, are also available. It is not by chance, therefore, that the high quality of the Steyr SSG has come to be fully recognized throughout the world.

The Steyr UIT Match Rifle in 7.62mm (.308 Winchester) and .243 Winchester is the top of the Steyr line of gunsmithing finesse. While even the predecessor of this sporting weapon was able to bag five world championship titles, the new Steyr match rifle significantly improved a great target rifle even further.

The UIT's new, well-contoured walnut stock not only meets all re-

Steyr GB 9mm Automatic Pistol

Steyr SSG/Police Sniping Rifle
(with double set trigger and scope)

Steyr SMG 9mm Submachine Gun
(fieldstripped)

quirements of weapons technology, but also provides the rifle with a characteristic appearance for which, in 1982, it was awarded the Austrian award for superior design; its new 10 round metal magazine has improved, optimum cartridge delivery; the UIT features full longitudinal and vertical adjustability of the butt plate; it has a straight, wider trigger for best possible distribution of the pressure from the trigger finger to the trigger proper; other improvements are the new design's adjustable trigger slack weight; and its newly designed bolt handle for speedier and safer reloading and repeating.

Additional 'news' items are the UIT's anti-glare strap, which repels the warm, shimmering air from the hot barrel and keeps the line of aim free of heat shimmer; and the possibility of simple conversion from a magazine fed to a single shot rifle by an inlay. Thanks to all of these improvements, the Steyr UIT Match now also conforms to the changed regulations of the UIT and is therefore suitable for all relevant competitions.

The Steyr SMG (Sub Machine Gun) in 9mm Parabellum caliber is a sturdy example of the breed, with semiautomatic and fully automatic capabilities. Magazines are available in 25 and 32 round capacities. In automatic fire, the SMG's cyclic rate is 550 rounds per minute. With its stock extended, the SMG measures only 18 inches in overall length. And it's feather-light, weighing in at only six pounds, which makes it even lighter than the Uzi. Need firepower quickly? Cock the SMG in a flash by pulling back on the sling or—both versions of the

SMG are available—cock the slide grip. Thanks to its selective trigger, the SMG can go from semiautomatic to fully automatic. Fieldstripping is a snap because of the minimum number of moving parts.

The Steyr GB Automatic Pistol in 9mm Parabellum is an excellent, easy-to-maintain sidearm. Few 9mm weapons offer as many features as the GB pistol. Accuracy in rapid fire is superb, thanks to the minimal recoil of its gas delayed blowback action. The GB has a 19 round capacity (18 in the magazine plus one in the chamber). And the GB's fast, trouble-free feeding of soft, hollow point or full metal jacketed rounds is always sure.

The unique firing pin and hammer safety are foolproof. It is absolutely impossible to discharge the GB with the hammer lowered. Drop it accidentally, and it won't go off. Although the GB will not need cleaning often (because the barrel has been designed to collect most of the powder residue on the outer surface), this unusual pistol can be completely disassembled in less than six seconds without compressing the main spring. Another feature is the GB's unique sighting system. The combat-type fixed sights are marked with luminous dots, assuring accuracy under conditions of low light or poor visibility.

Fixed to the frame, the 5.5 inch polygonal barrel of the GB eliminates any shot-to-shot variation because of barrel placement—you'll hit the same spot everytime. Thanks to its springloaded decocking lever, the GB is always ready to be fired in the double action mode. There's no fumbling or forgetting to activate a safety lever.

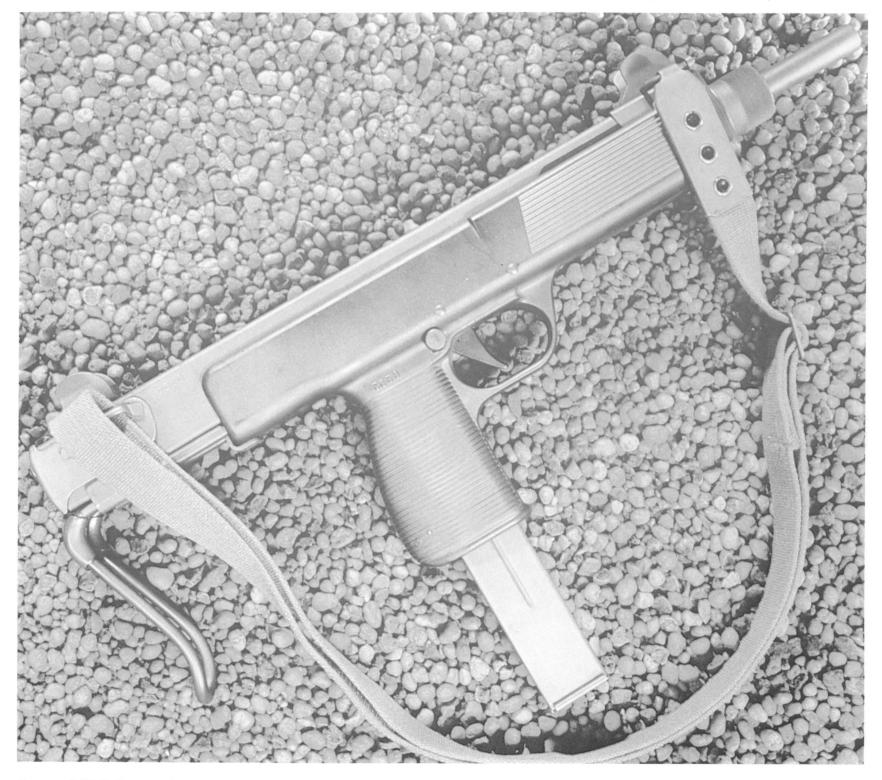

Steyr SMG 9mm Submachine Gun

Steyr SSG Sniping Rifle (in service)

BRAZIL

Amadeo Rossi, the first of southern Brazil's metalurgic companies, was established in 1889 in a pioneering development that became a renowned trade mark through its successful 94 years of dedicated technological development. A constant updating of its manufacture, through a restless development of new products highly controlled by an emphasis on superior quality, together with a philosophy of safe workmanship, has made Rossi's products a world wide famous brand in sport firearms and handguns. Rossi is now the largest Latin American manufacturer and the major Brazilian exporter of sport firearms, having already sold over five million guns to nearly 57 countries in the world, which is the fruit of almost one century of skillful and dedicated labor.

Rossi's .32 S&W Long Caliber Six Shot Revolvers pioneered all-steel construction, introducing a new technology in the manufacture of handguns. Rossi Six Shot models feature carbon steel forged frame construction; cylinder barrel, yoke and main parts made of processed alloy steel; single and double action; hammer block (safety) against accidental discharge, in case the revolver is bumped or dropped;

direct percussion; fixed or adjustable sights; wood grips checkered or plain; normal finish: blue, with optional finishes of matte blue, blue engraved, bright or satin nickel, chrome engraved or gold engraved.

Rossi models 20 and 69 have three inch barrels; Model 28 has a two inch barrel. Grips are checkered hardwood, and sights are fixed front and rear, excepting the Model 69, which has a windage-adjustable rear sight. Models 20 and 69 weigh 21.4 ounces; Model 28 weighs 19.6 ounces.

Rossi Stainless Steel Revolver models 87, 88, 89 and 881 feature stainless steel, corrosion resistant construction, stainless steel forged frame—all internal and external parts are made of polished stainless steel; single action and double action; hammer block safety against accidental discharge, in case the revolver is bumped or dropped; direct percussion; fixed and adjustable sights; checkered hardwood or rubber anatomic grips; and matte polished finish.

The Model 89 is in .32 S&W caliber, and Rossi models 87, 88 and 881 are in .38 Special caliber. Model 89 is a six shot firearm, the other Rossi Stainless Steel Revolvers are five shot firearms. Model 881 is

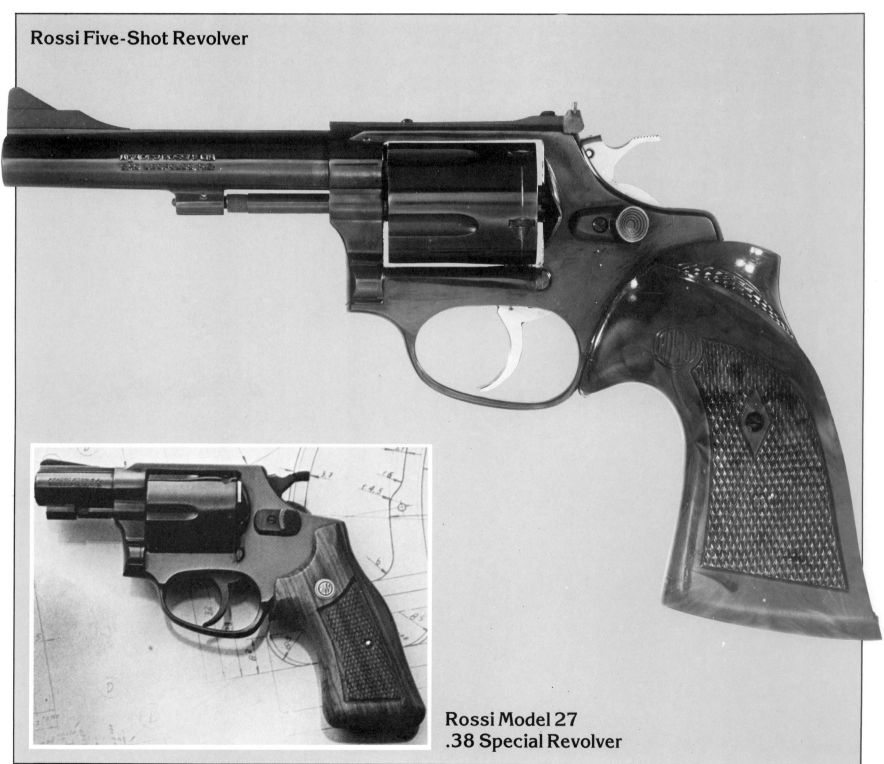

Rossi Five-Shot Revolver

Rossi Model 27
.38 Special Revolver

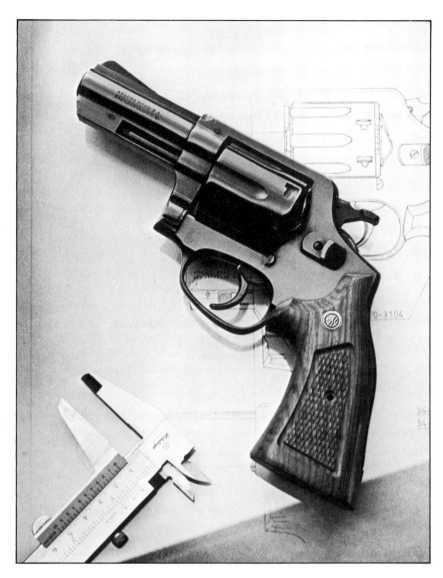

Rossi Model 94
.38 Special Revolver

Rossi Model 851
.38 Special Stainless Steel Revolver

Rossi Model 69
.32 S&W Long Revolver

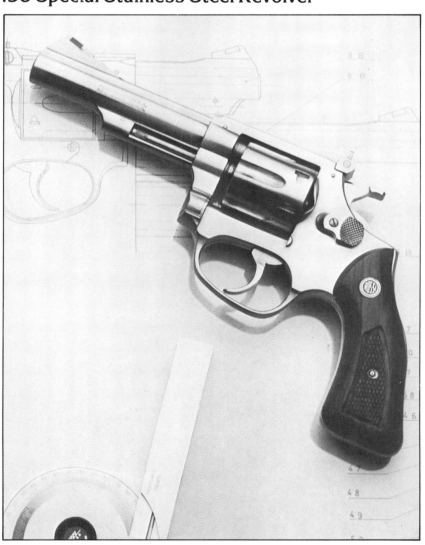

Rossi Model 511
.22 LR Stainless Steel Revolver

equipped with a four inch barrel, models 88 and 89 have three inch barrels, and Model 87 has a two inch barrel. Weights are comparable to the Rossi .32 caliber six shot series; and sights, excepting the Model 87, are windage-adjustable rear, fixed front.

Rossi .38 Special caliber Six Shot Revolvers feature carbon steel forged and hardened frame construction; cylinder, barrel, yoke and main parts made of processed alloy steel; double action; hammer block (safety) against accidental discharge, in case the revolver is bumped or dropped; direct percussion; semianatomic wood grips, checkered or plain; barrel with protection for extractor rod; checkered thumbpiece; hammer with checkered spur; serrated anatomic trigger; normal finish: blue, with optional finishes of matte blue, blue engraved, bright or satin nickel, chrome engraved or gold engraved.

Model 94 weighs 27 ounces; Model 941 weighs 30.4 ounces and Model 944 weighs 26.8 ounces. All have fixed sights.

Rossi's .38 Special caliber Five Shot Revolvers feature excellent handling, as well as carbon steel forged frame construction: cylinder, barrel, yoke and main parts made of processed alloy steel; double action; hammer block safety; direct percussion; fixed or adjustable sights; wood grips checkered or plain; normal finish: blue, with optional finishes of matte blue, blue engraved, bright or satin nickel, chrome engraved; and gold engraved.

Barrel lengths for Rossi models in this mode are: Model 27, two inches; Model 31, four inches; Model 33, three inches; and Model 68, three inches. Model 68 has a windage-adjustable rear sight, and all of the above models have a fixed front sight with serrated ramp.

Rossi .38 Special Stainless Steel Six Shot Revolvers comprise models 85, 851, 853 and 854. Barrel lengths for these models are, respectively; three, four, six and two inches. All of these models, save Model 853, have a fixed front sight with plastic insert. All have micrometric, click adjustable, rear sights.

Rossi models 42, 43 and 511 are .22 long rifle caliber six shot revolvers. They feature carbon steel forged frame construction; cylinder, barrel, yoke and main parts made of processed alloy steel; single and double action; hammer block (safety) against accidental discharge; floating firing pin; fixed or adjustable sights; checkered Brazilian wood grips; normal finish: blue, with optional finishes of matte blue, blue engraved, bright or satin nickel, chrome engraved or gold engraved. Model 511 features a rear sight which is adjustable for both windage and elevation. Its standard front sight is fixed, with a serrated ramp, and insert.

Standard features for these models are: fully anticorrosive stainless steel contruction, barrel with ventilated rib; double action; hammer block safety; direct percussion; checkered hardwood grips; matte polished finish; and protected extractor rod.

Rossi Puma Lever Action Carbines feature 10 shot capacity, 20 inch barrel length, high-quality heat-treated steel construction, precision fitting, and a heritage that comes from America's Old West and the Winchester lever action saddle carbine upon which this handsome design is based.

Included in this design is the Rossi hammer-block safety; adjustable rear sight; authentic saddle ring; a standard, handsome blue finish, and optional finishes including gold, blue and chrome engraved finishes, not to mention the 'Puma' medallion, which can be engraved upon the carbine's receiver. The four models of Puma carbines are: Model 77, a domestic production, in .38 Special; Models 65, 65M and 67—all of which are for export only—in, respectively, .44-40 Winchester, .44 Magnum and .38 Special/.357 Magnum.

Rossi also produces fine shotguns. The Overland Model 11 Side-by-Side will surely be a favorite with shooters around the world, with its Old West flavor: this is just the type of gun favored by old-time Western lawmen and stagecoach guards—hence its name, 'Overland.'

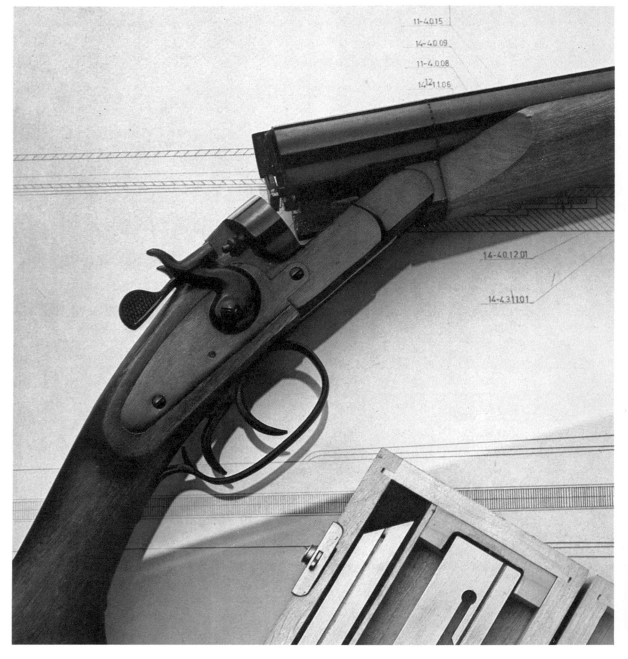

Rossi Overland Side-by-Side Shotgun Model 11

Rossi Puma Carbine

Rossi Model 88
.38 Special Stainless Steel Revolver

Rossi Model 87
.38 Special Stainless Steel Revolver

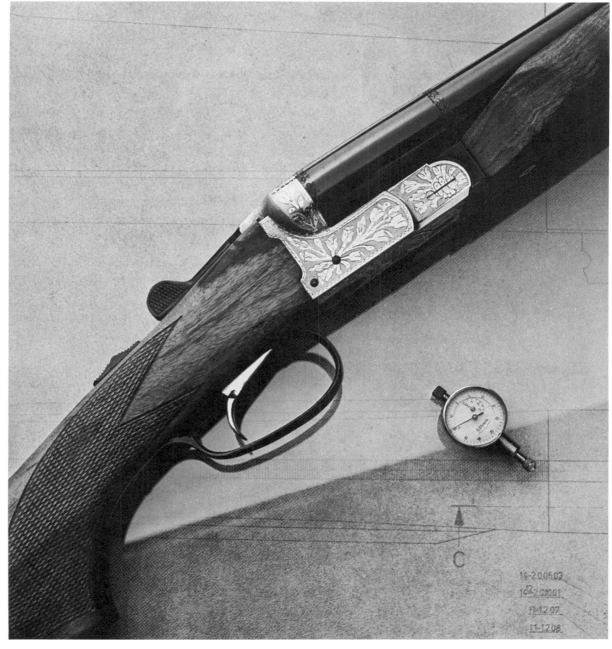

Rossi Royal Bonanza Side-by-Side Shotgun Model 75

The Overland Model 11 features breech assembly and monobloc made from forged carbon steel; barrel and other component parts made from processed alloy steel; double clamping; safety device against accidental discharges; pistol grip type hardwood stock and fore end; and standard blue—or optional blue engraved, chrome (plain or engraved) or gold engraved—finishes. Additional engraving, custom finishes, chokes, complementary barrels, and stocks are available upon request. The Model 11 comes in .410, 32, 28, 20, 16 and 12 gauge, and comes in a variety of barrel lengths and choke fittings. This is a fine line of classic, traditional sporting shotguns.

Rossi's Overland Security and Bonanza Security model shotguns feature new designs and features adapted to traditional models. These models are ideal guns for the performance of police activities, with breech assembly and monobloc made from forged carbon steel (models 99 and 100); internally and externally polished barrels; barrel and other component parts made from processed alloy steel (models 99 and 100); double clamping (models 99 and 100); safety device against accidental discharges caused by drops or shocks (model 99); automatic safety system (operation of trigger block device synchronized with opening of the gun) (model 100); and pistol grip type and special fore end, with handle made from hardwood.

The basic difference between the Overland—Model 99—and the Bonanza—Model 100—Security Shotguns is the use of exposed hammers in the former design, and the use of hidden hammers in the latter. Both are designed to chamber, in their side-by-side double barrels, three inch 12 gauge shells. Both have 13 inch barrels and a standard blue finish.

The Model 14 Bonanza Hammerless Side-by-Side Shotgun features a variety of barrel lengths from 20 inches to 28 inches; a variety of choke settings; complementary barrel sets; custom finishes and engraving over and beyond the standard and optional finishes regularly supplied—which include blue, blue engraved, chrome engraved and gold engraved.

This fine, traditional design is great for hunting and for skeet shooting. Its breech assembly and monobloc are made from forged carbon steel, and it has a trigger block device to prevent accidents while opening the shotgun's double clamping breech.

Rossi Slide Action Rifles and Carbines include models 37 and 59 (rifles) and Model 57 (carbine). Models 37 and 57 are made for .22 short, long and long rifle ammo, and Model 59 (made for export only) is made to fire .22 Magnum ammunition. Rifle barrels are 23 inches long, and the carbine barrel is 16.5 inches long. These fine slide-action repeaters feature the full range of Rossi finishes, hammer-block safety and hardwood stocks.

The Rossi Model 75 Royal Bonanza is a finely-finished side-by-side hammerless double barrel shotgun which has a **single** trigger. It is chambered for three inch 12 gauge shells, has a standard 28 inch barrel (other lengths upon request) with a modified full choke (other chokes upon request). Standard finish is chrome engraved, with optional choice of blue engraved and gold engraved—other finishes are available upon request. Also, complementary barrel sets are available for this 7.7 pound shotgun. Checkered hardwood stocks are standard.

The Rossi Pomba Single Barrel Shotgun models 22–26 and 23–30 feature chamberings for 2.75 and three inch shells, with a variety of gauges from .410 to 12. Barrel length is 28 inches and chokes are set at full.

Other features of this fine shotgun line are high-quality steel, heat treated; hammer-block safety; perfect balance; pistol grip type hardwood stock and fore end; mechanism modified to permit a smoother opening; redesigned stock and butt plate; standard blue finish, and optional finishes including blue engraved, chrome engraved, and gold engraved.

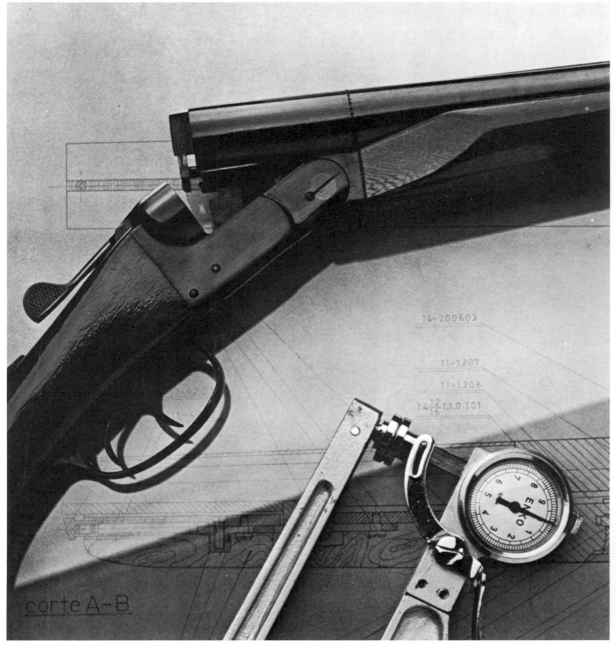

Rossi Bonanza Hammerless Side-by-Side Shotgun

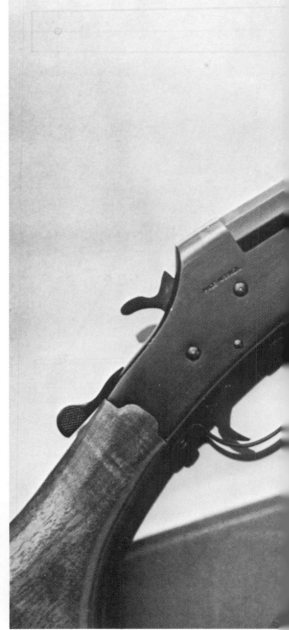

Rossi Pomba Shotgun

Rossi Overland Side-by-Side Shotgun

Rossi Overland Security Model Shotgun

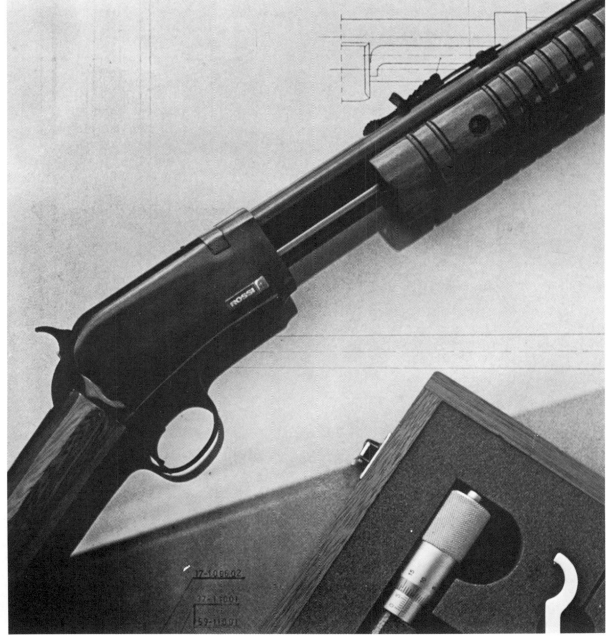

Rossi Gallery Slide Action Carbine

FINLAND

The **Valmet** M76 Rifle is an adaption of the Soviet Kalashnikov design. A gas operated, selective-fire rifle with 16.5 inch barrel in 7.62 Soviet caliber, it has an optional magazine capacity of 15 or 30 rounds and an automatic rate of 650rpm. Valmet, a Finnish firm, has given this product a fine finish, despite the fact that most of the four versions' stocks are plastic coated steel.

Front and rear sights are hooded adjustable and protected aperture, respectively. The rear sight is situated behind the chamber for a better sight line. Both sights have Tritium beads for night aiming.

The M76T has a rigid tubular butt stock; the M76F has a folding skeleton butt; the M76M has a conventional-looking plastic coated metal butt; and the traditionalist of the lot, the M76W, has wooden stocks. A sportier version of this latter is available in the United States. This has checkered stocks and is available with scope mounts. A hinged lever is fitted just between the trigger guard assembly and the magazine; this lever precludes the accidental release of the magazine. Another Valmet design is the Model 255-470 Bullpup, a plastic Stock Assault Rifle in the familiar bullpup design.

The Valmet 412 Shooting System has a firearm that offers the options of superposed double rifle, rifle-shotgun, over-and-under or superposed double barrel shotgun. This system has four interchangeable buttstocks and a very expansive variety of barrels. The shotgun barrels tend to be in 12 or 20 gauge, and in combination shotgun/rifles, the rifle barrels range from .22 Hornet to 9.33mm. Double rifle barrel sets range from .243 Winchester to .375 Winchester. You can buy the system, or just keep adding on to it. For cheap plinking, adaptors are available to allow the use of .22 rimfires in all rifle barrels. Barrel assemblies are doubles, and combination guns and double rifles have two adjustments to "harmonize" the two barrels. All in all, the Valmet 412 Shooting System is extremely versatile.

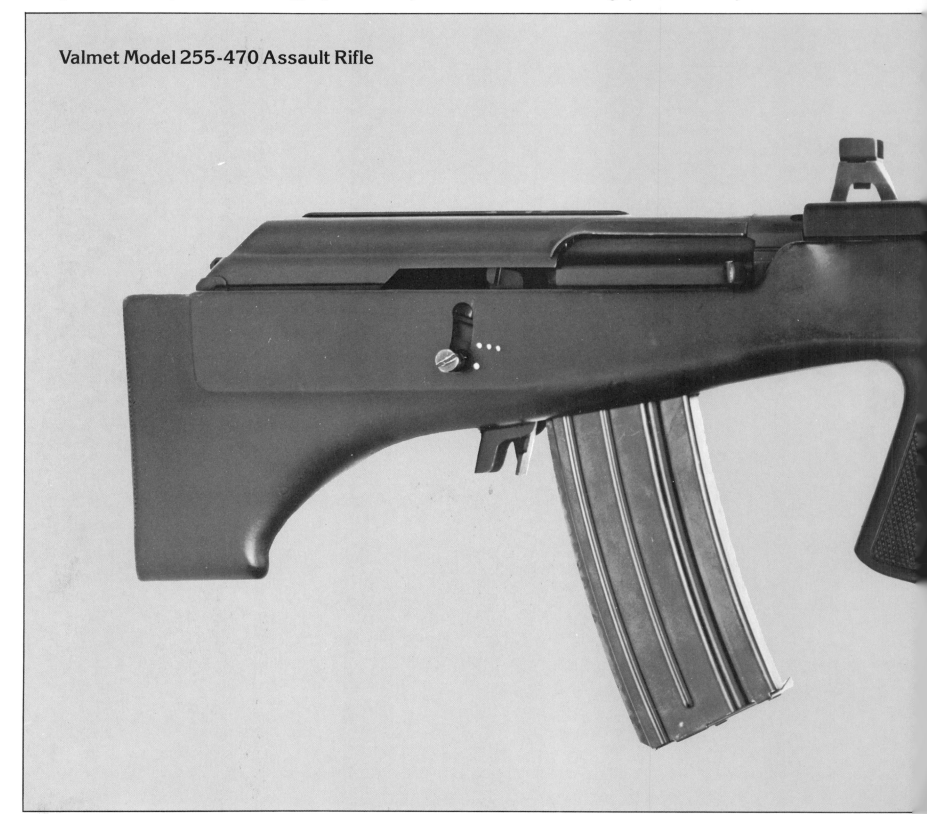

Valmet Model 255-470 Assault Rifle

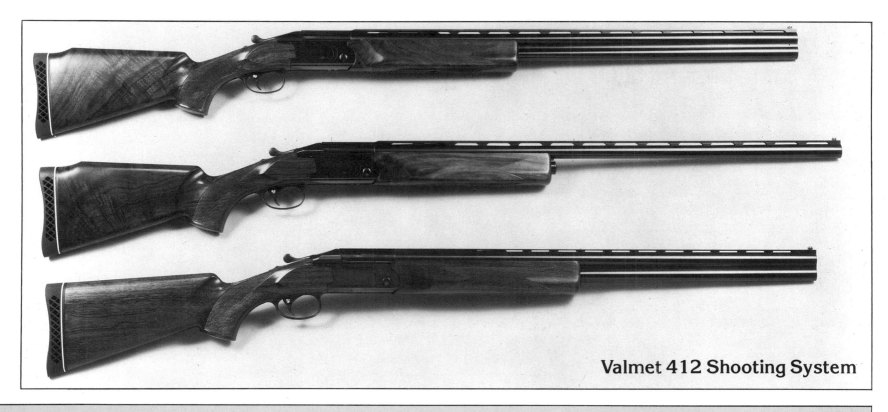

Valmet 412 Shooting System

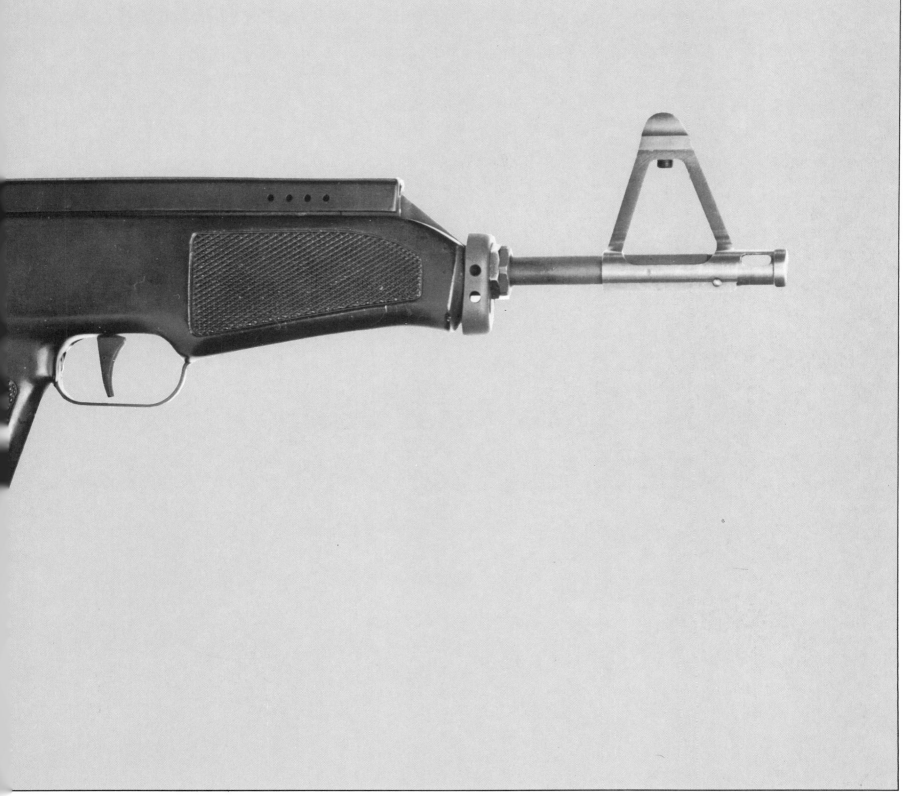

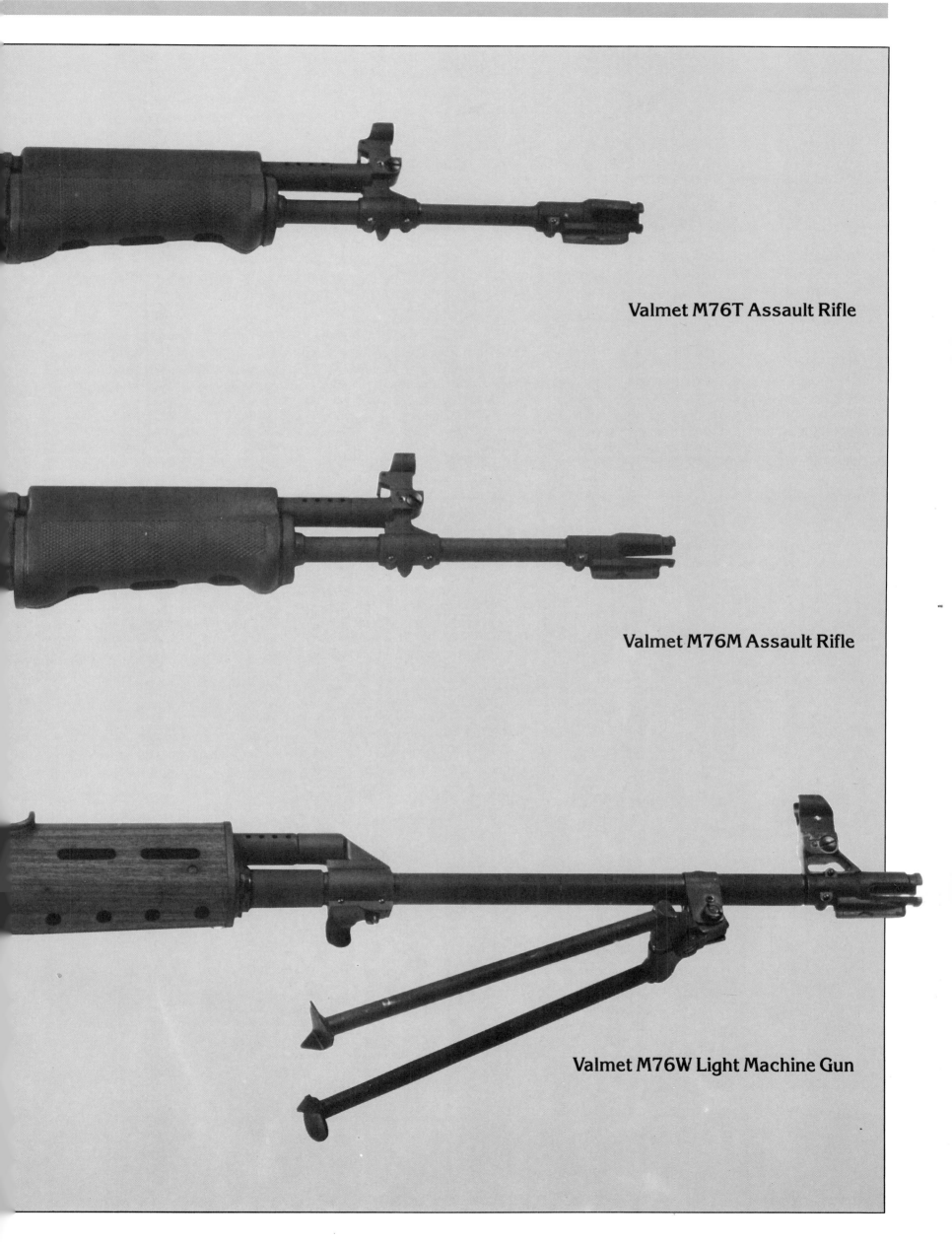

Valmet M76T Assault Rifle

Valmet M76M Assault Rifle

Valmet M76W Light Machine Gun

FRANCE

M anufacture d'Armes des Pyrenees Francaises manufactures the 'Unique' line of excellent firearms.

The Mikros automatic pistol is the latest creation of the Manufacture d'Armes des Pyrenees Francaises, whose Unique arms are well known throughout the world. Because of its long experience in arms manufacture, its modern tools, and first class workmen, this firm has endeavored, in creating the Mikros, that it shall be the most accurate, safest, improved and most modern of all small pistols, while retaining good taste in the pistol's design.

This pistol is carefully made of the finest special alloys and combines accuracy, strength, safety and elegance and features an external hammer, side safety and magazine safety—which prevents reloading accidents.

This 6.35mm (.25 caliber) pistol fits literally in the palm of your hand, and weighs—depending on your choice of steel frame or alloy frame, respectively—0.8 pounds, or 0.6 pounds. At 2.25 × 4.43 × 2.93 inches, the Mikros is a handful of shooting genius.

The Model L is available in three models: the seven shot Model Lc, in 7.65mm (.32 caliber); the six shot Model Lf in 9mm (.38 caliber);

and the 10 shot Model Ld in .22 long rifle caliber. Total lengths for these pistols are identical at 5.8 inches each. Height and width match also, at 3.9 inches and 1.1 inches, respectively. A very handy pistol in three popular models.

The Model L automatic pistol is also available in either steel or light alloy frame designs. This pistol features elegant lines and careful finish, accuracy, strength, safety, lightness, ease of use and maintenance, exterior hammer (now required by most users), simple and rapid dismantling, strict control of the raw materials used, and excellence of manufacture.

The Bcf model is specially produced for, and fully satisfies, the strict requirements called for in a firearm for defensive purposes: accuracy, strength, safety and ease of use and maintenance under all circumstances. Unique pistols are used particularly by the French police forces and others abroad.

Due to design incorporating interchangeability of parts, and manufacturing precision, it is simple to change the Model Bcf from caliber .380 (9mm short) to caliber .32 (7.65mm), by merely changing barrels. The pistol can be supplied with either thumbrest grips or with

Matra Manurhin Defense MR 73 Sport Revolver with scope

Custom gold plated Matra Manurhin Defense MR Long Range Revolvers with ivory grips

plain checkered grips. The plain grips are especially useful for left handed shooters.

The Unique Model Bcf owes its excellent accuracy to the manufacture of the barrel, in treated steel, perfectly rifled and polished both exteriorly and interiorly: it can withstand thousands of shots without a trace of wear. The firing pin and firing pin stop, the sear, the hammer, the extractor and etc, are also of specially treated steel and have the same guarantee of strength. The hand grips are of brown unbreakable plastic. All the springs in the pistol are checked and measured. The firearm balances perfectly in the hand. A ring is provided on the left side of the firearm for the fitting of the lanyard.

The intentional simplicity of the pistol allows its immediate dismantling into only four parts for cleaning, which makes maintenance easy, without the risk of losing parts. The firearm, before leaving the factory, undergoes a test of precision firing and functioning, and a test of resistance made by the Paris Proof House.

The exposed hammer of this pistol is very practical; the slide stop holds the action open after the last round is fired; and the pistol is equipped with multiple safeties: a magazine safety, which prevents loading accidents; a thumb safety near the slide; a safety which prevents firing unless the slide is altogether closed; and a hammer-notch safety which allows the pistol to be carried with a round in the chamber.

Unique models D2, D4, D6 and E4 are manufactured with fixed barrel and external hammer, in two calibers—the designation 'D' stands for .22 long rifle, and the designation 'E' stands for .22 short. This is an excellent 'plinking' pistol design, and for competition shooting, the addition of an optional counterweight improves the design's already good balance even further on models D4 and E4.

Models D4 and E4 are equipped with a muzzle brake which lessens the kick at the moment of firing. The greatest possible measure of safety is given to the shooter, on all models, by the exterior hammer and two safeties; one free, the other automatic.

The barrel is made of special steel, perfectly rifled and polished. It can stand tens of thousands of shots without trace of wear and still shoot accurately. A special light alloy of high strength has been used to make the slide of the model E (caliber 22 short). The other parts, except the unbreakable plastic grips, are machined from best quality steel, carefully selected and examined. The springs are all tested for compression before fitting and ensure a smooth and even working.

Besides the many checks during manufacture, all pistols are individually submitted to a firing test before they leave the Works. Every pistol is tested by Paris Proof House, and bears the corresponding marks. The official certificate is supplied with each arm.

These pistols also feature: normal thumb safety, plus a second automatic safety operated by the magazine; sights adjustable vertically and laterally by screws; extreme simplicity of dismantling without tools; a slide safety such that the slide remains open after firing the last round in the magazine; and unbreakable plastic grips with thumbpiece (or flat plastic grips for left handed shooters).

Unique models Rr-51 Police and Fr-51 Police automatic pistols are produced specially for police requirements: accuracy, strength, safety, and ease of use and maintenance under all circumstances. The Rr pistol and the Fr pistol differ only in caliber and magazine capacity, which are respectively, nine shots, 7.65mm (.32 caliber), and eight shots, 9mm (.38 caliber).

The barrel of each of these pistols, made of treated steel, is perfectly rifled and polished both exteriorly and interiorly and can withstand thousands of shots without a trace of wear. The firing pin and firing pin stop, the sear, the hammer, the extractor and etc are also of special treated steel, and have the same guarantee of strength. The grips are in black unbreakable plastic.

The firearm balances perfectly in the hand. Its dimensions, exceptionally reduced for a pistol of this capacity, and the absence of sharp angles on the exterior profile, make its carrying and handling extremely easy. A ring is provided on the left side of the firearm for the fitting of a lanyard. The intentional simplicity of the pistol allows rapid dismantling into only four parts. The firearm, besides multiple checkings during manufacture, undergoes a test of precision and functioning before leaving the factory.

These pistols, the Rr and the Fr, feature an action safety which locks the breech open after the last shot is fired. In addition, when the chamber contains a cartridge, the extractor projects over the exterior surface of the slide, indicating immediately to the eye or to the touch,

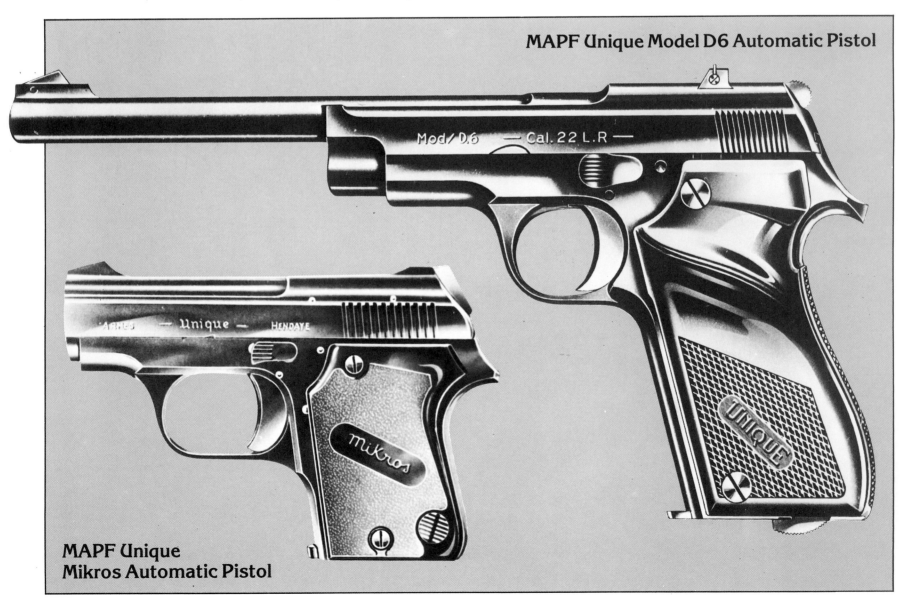

MAPF Unique Model D6 Automatic Pistol

MAPF Unique Mikros Automatic Pistol

MAPF Unique Model DES69 Target Pistol

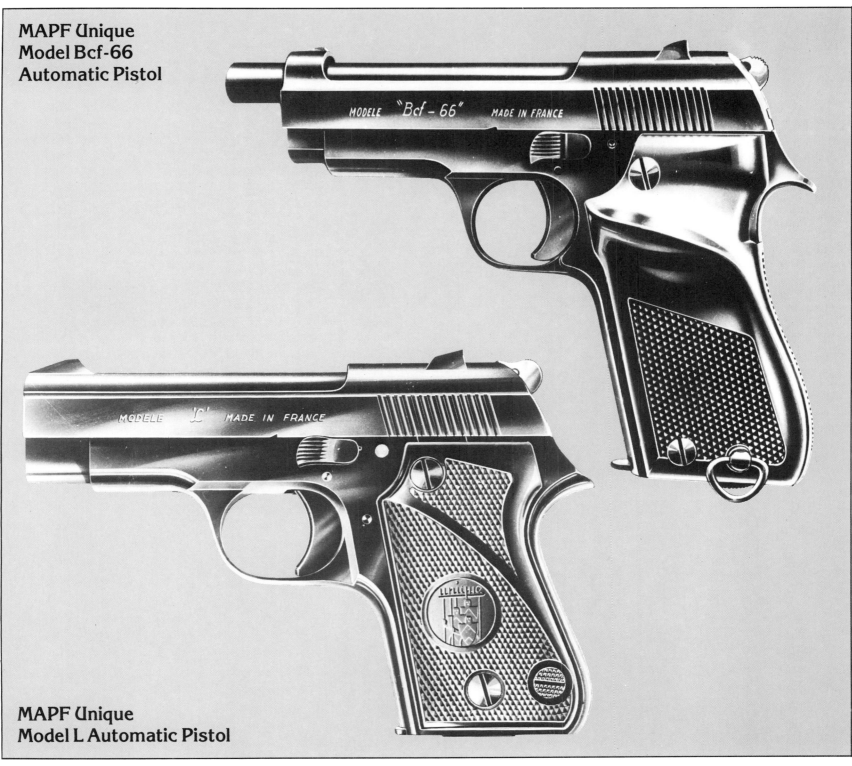

MAPF Unique
Model Bcf-66
Automatic Pistol

MAPF Unique
Model L Automatic Pistol

Matra Manurhin Defense MR 73 Silhouette Long Range Target Pistol

that the firearm is loaded. Additional safety mechanisms are those which are described on the models D2 through E4 pistols. Both models Rr and Fr are 5.7 inches long by 4.7 inches in height.

The Unique DES69 .22 long rifle target pistol features an adjustable backlash-type trigger mechanism. This fine pistol has a magazine capacity of five shots. The DES69 comes with a variety of optional barrel counterweights in gradations from 3.5 ounces to 12.4 ounces. Also, there is now a barrel sleeve-type counterweight.

With its all-steel construction and handsome design, which includes French walnut anatomical grips, the DES69 will be a welcome addition to any target shooter's pistol collection. With dry-firing capability and full adjustable rear sight, this is a fine target pistol.

Unique rifle models include the .22 long rifle caliber G21 autoloader with yardage, vertical and horizontal adjustable peep sight and solid, protected front sight. Magazines for the G21 hold two, five, 10 and 20 shots. Its 17.5 inch barrel and 33.5 inch overall length make the G21 a handy target arm. Dovetail receiver grooves admit the fitting of a scope, in addition. The G21 has a trigger safety and a cocking indicator. Altogether, with its French walnut stock, this is a fine 'plinking' arm. Various scope, sight and other options are available.

Unique bolt action repeating rifle models T Audax and T Dioptera both feature micro-groove rifling, 6.6 pound weight, five and 10 shot magazine and dovetail receiver grooves for the mounting of an optional scope. Insert ramp front sight with bead and fully adjustable rear sight—plus optional micro-match peep sight—completes the package for these well-rounded sporting firearms.

The T Audax features single lock bolt, sear safety, two stage trigger and French walnut sporter stock. This rifle is available in .22 long rifle caliber and will also, for cheap plinking, fire .22 shorts. T Audax has a 21.6 inch barrel.

The T Dioptera features double lock bolt, firing pin and sear safeties, adjustable trigger and right or left handed French walnut Monte Carlo style stock. The T Dioptera is available in .22 long rifle/.22 short caliber or .22 Magnum caliber. T Dioptera has a 23.6 inch barrel.

Unique has been making automatic weapons for more than forty years and was appointed supplier to the French and foreign police forces for their requirements in automatic pistols for defense. It was the first in France to manufacture .22 long rifle caliber automatic weapons for hunting and target shooting.

The Unique X 51 - X 51 bis Rifle is the fruit of this long experience. The latest in modern perfection, it is nevertheless light, easy to handle, simple and tough. The Unique automatic and semiautomatic rifle is manufactured in two versions: X 51 and X 51 bis: The standard American-type rack rearsight on the model X 51 bis is replaced by an improved sight on model X 51, with windage and elevation adjustment by means of a precision screw. The foresight, of the copper bead type, is mounted on a grooved ramp with steel protection.

The hundreds of thousands of automatic arms of Unique which are now in use in France and abroad, are the best form of advertisement and have increased the use by sportsmen of the caliber .22 long rifle for hunting and target shooting amazingly. We think a word about this may be useful.

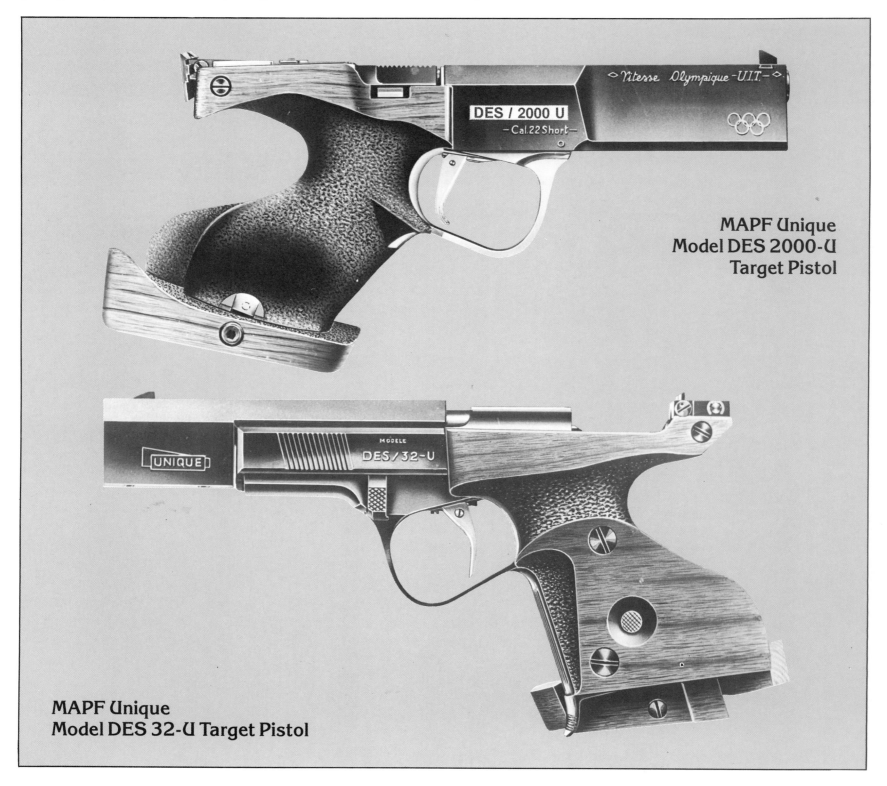

MAPF Unique
Model DES 2000-U
Target Pistol

MAPF Unique
Model DES 32-U Target Pistol

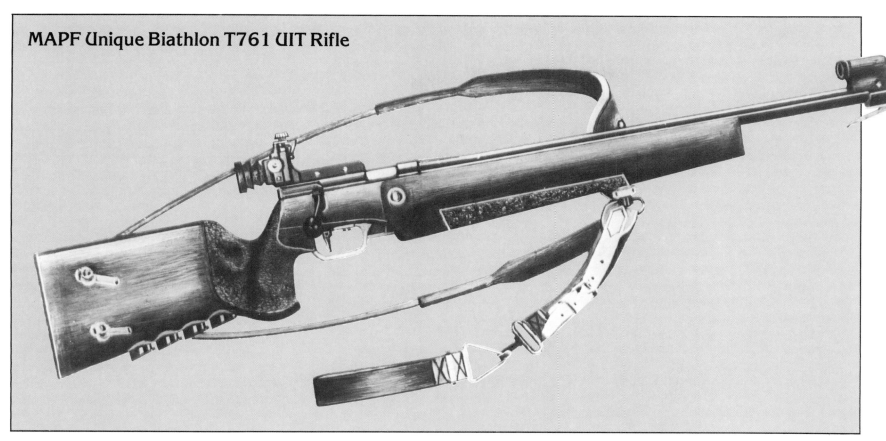

MAPF Unique Biathlon T761 UIT Rifle

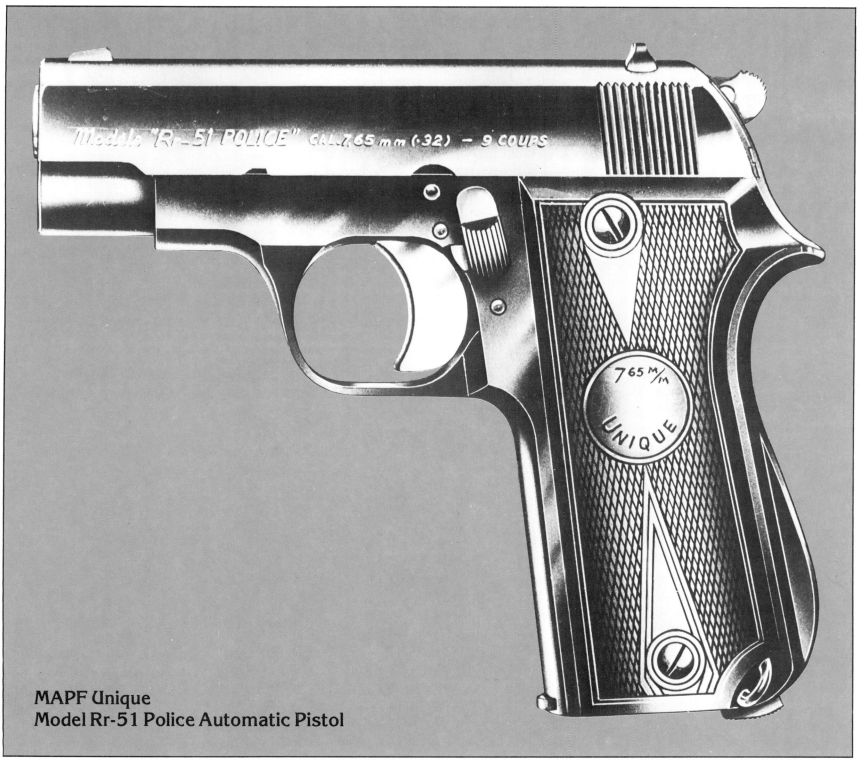

MAPF Unique
Model Rr-51 Police Automatic Pistol

The X51-X51 bis models are 'hammerless' .22 long rifle caliber rifles which have selective automatic/semiautomatic fire. The rifle components are few in number; dismantling takes five seconds. The safety system is extremely simple and accessible. The piston used for semiautomatic firing can also be used to lock the slide in the rear position, thus enabling the barrel to be cleaned without difficulty. All components of the weapon are manufactured from the best selected steel. The perfect blueing and the beauty of the luxuriously polished walnut stock give the X51-X51 bis rifle a fine finish. The rifles have their own case with separate compartments for the barrel and stock. It is stamped by the Paris Proof House whose official certificate is supplied with each rifle. A Works test-firing target (all weapons are individually adjusted on the bench) is enclosed.

The Unique X51-X51 bis rifle has an automatic magazine safety: removal of the magazine causes automatic locking of the trigger mechanism. The rifle is normally supplied with a five shot magazine, but a 10 shot magazine is available.

The optional safety catch, simple and well within reach of the hand, has an ingenious cocking indicator which is a small lever appearing in front of the shooter's finger when the hammer is not cocked. This triple safety system, together with the automatic or semiautomatic firing device, makes the Unique X51-X51 bis one of the safest rifles. Two receiver grooves enable the mounting of an optional telescopic sight. The X51 is available in two barrel lengths, 19.5 inches and 23.5 inches. With the longer barrel, the X51 weighs 5.8 pounds. The X51 bis has one barrel length, which is 23.5 inches, and this rifle weighs six

Matra Manurhin MR .32 Match Revolver

**Matra Manurhin Defense
MR Convertible Revolver**

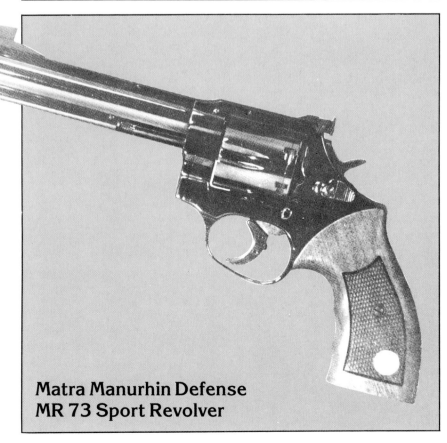

**Matra Manurhin Defense
MR 73 Sport Revolver**

pounds. The X51 bis has advanced sights. Both of these are fine, multi purpose firearms and advance Unique's pioneering work one step further in the world of .22 caliber sporting rifles.

The F.11 Unique is the only licensed .22 long rifle caliber replica of the FAMAS, the French military rifle which is now the standard issue arm in the French Army. Cocking and cartridge feed are automatic after the first shot. This handy little autoloader weighs 8.1 pounds and has an overall length of 33.1 inches. Sights are windage and elevation click-adjustable, and 10 or 20 shot magazines are available.

Safeties featured in the F.11 are a trigger safety, a magazine safety and a stock safety—the weapon cannot be fired sans its stock. All principal metal parts are made of steel, and the stock and grips are polyamide high-strength plastic. A variety of options for this model, which comes with its own handy carrying sling, are available.

The characteristics of accuracy, reliability and solidity have built the international renown of Unique. Every Unique rifle is tested and stamped by the Official French Proof House of Saint-Etienne. The corresponding certificate is supplied with the rifle.

The **Matra Manurhin Defense** MR 73 Defense pistol is a fine double and single action revolver chambered for .38 Special or .357 Magnum, with an interchangeable cylinder for 9mm Parabellum. The MR 73 has fixed sights, and optional barrel lengths of 2.5, three and four inches. This fine sidearm comes from a long line of Matra revolvers going back to 1892. A full range of accessories is available.

The MR 73 Gendarmerie is based on the MR 73 Defense, and bears modifications tailored to police work, including barrel lengths of 2.5,

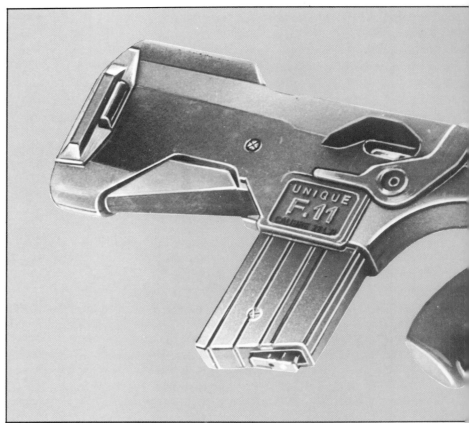

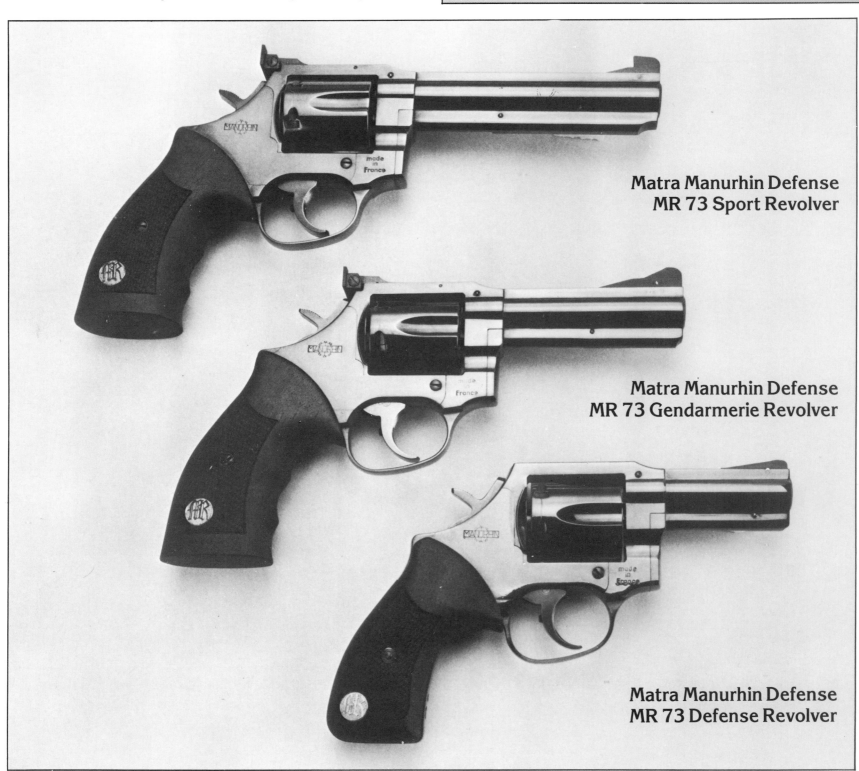

Matra Manurhin Defense
MR 73 Sport Revolver

Matra Manurhin Defense
MR 73 Gendarmerie Revolver

Matra Manurhin Defense
MR 73 Defense Revolver

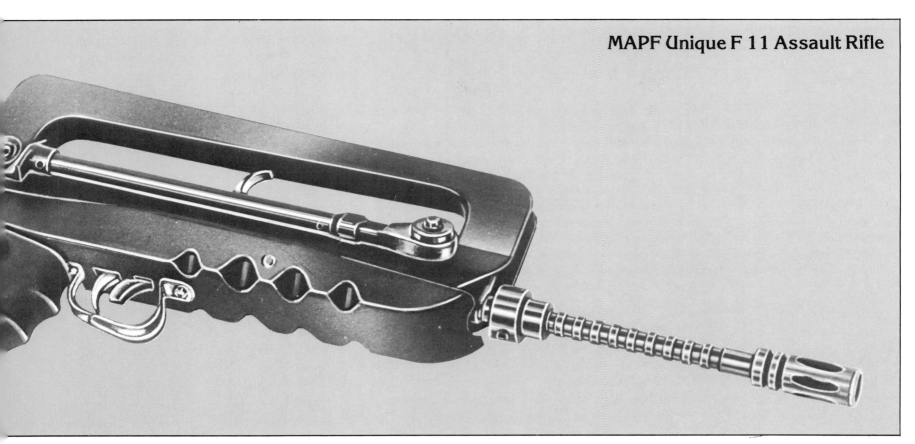

MAPF Unique F 11 Assault Rifle

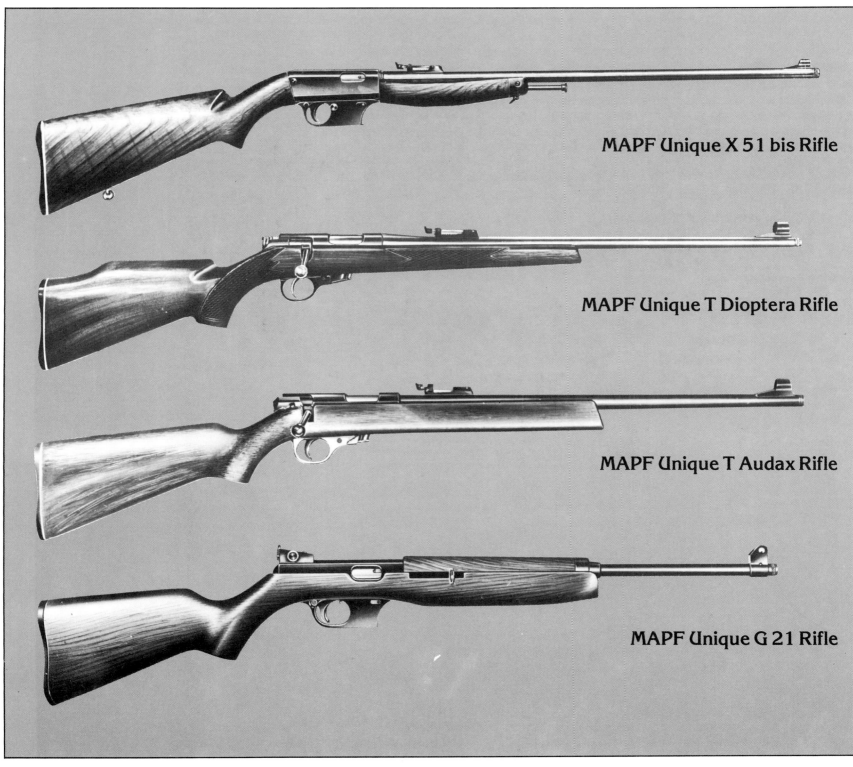

MAPF Unique X 51 bis Rifle

MAPF Unique T Dioptera Rifle

MAPF Unique T Audax Rifle

MAPF Unique G 21 Rifle

three, four, 5.75, six and eight inches; micrometric-adjustable rear sight; ramp front sight; single and double action; the same caliber selections **and** interchangeable cylinder as the MR 73 Defense; a wide range of optional holsters; five optional grips; a speed loader; and various carrying cases.

The MR 73 Sport features great stability, minimum hammer stroke, micrometric-adjustable rear sight and adjustable, free-release trigger. This fine sport model comes with four, 5.25, six and eight inch barrels; chambering for .38 Special or .357 Magnum, with interchangeable cylinder for 9mm Parabellum. Its single and double action mechanism leaves the choice up to the sportsman. The MR 73 Sport comes to you complete, but a wide array of accessories is available for the discerning pistol hunter and and/or target shooter. These accessories include five grip styles for the utmost in shooting comfort and stability.

MR Convertibles come in two variations—.38 Special/.22 long rifle caliber and .32 long/.22 long rifle. Barrel lengths for these are: .38 Special, 5.75 inches; and for the .32 long and .22 long rifle variants, six inches. The cylinders for these conversion pistols each hold six rounds, and swing out to the left and feature hand ejection of empties. The MR Convertible trigger is of the adjustable backlash type, single action. Sights are interchangeable front, and micrometric-adjustable rear. Grips are standard, with an optional choice of anatomical grips. A trigger shoe and adjustable counterweight are also available.

The MR Long Range Silhouette pistol is perfectly suited for shooting at metallic and long range targets, as laid down by the international rules of the IHMSA (International Handgun Metallic Silhouette Association) and by the IHLRA (International Handgun Long Range Association). Its features include stabilized heavy barrel, rifling twist to meet the ballistic requirements of long range shooting with heavy

160 to 220 grain bullets (180 grain MR-MEGA-MATCH ammunition).

Two models of this advanced pistol are available: the 'Long Range' and the 'Silhouette.' Both are single action, six shot firearms, and feature an adjustable backlash trigger. The cylinder swings out to the left, and ejection is by hand. Both versions are in .357 Magnum caliber. The Long Range model has a nine inch barrel, and the Silhouette model has a 10.75 inch barrel. Both have counterweights mounted within the pistol grips, between the grip panels. Grip styles are virtually unlimited. Sights are adjustable micrometric rear and interchangeable front. The Long Range weighs 49.2 ounces, and the Silhouette weighs 53.9 ounces.

The excellent MR Match pistols come in three advanced high precision models. The MR 38 Match is in .38 Special caliber, the MR 32 Match is in .32 long caliber and the MR 22 Match is in .22 long rifle caliber. Barrel lengths are, respectively, 5.75 inches, six inches and six inches, and sights are interchangeable front, with adjustable micrometric rear. Cylinder capacities are six rounds, and cylinders swing out to the left, with hand ejection. Options include anatomical grips, trigger shoe and adjustable counterweight. High accuracy rifling, excellent balance and stability, and fine finish complete these finely engineered examples of the gunsmiths art. Highly accurate, these pistols will help the match shooter garner the highest of scores.

In particular, the MR 32 Match has been France's best sport handgun and has won several awards abroad; the MR 32 MATCH model is set to become the world's top handgun in its field. Its features include: extended and underlying rear sight; aiming notches and reduced free flight, stabilized groove mounted front sights.

The MR 22 Match is a very good ladies' and juniors' match pistol, and also provides inexpensive ammo practice for the heavier caliber match events.

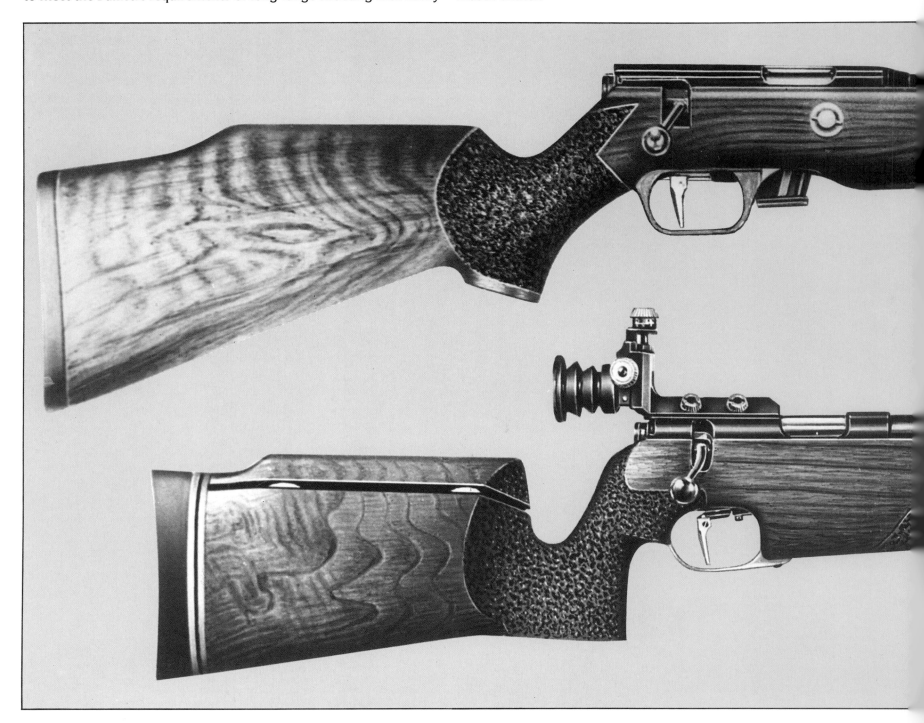

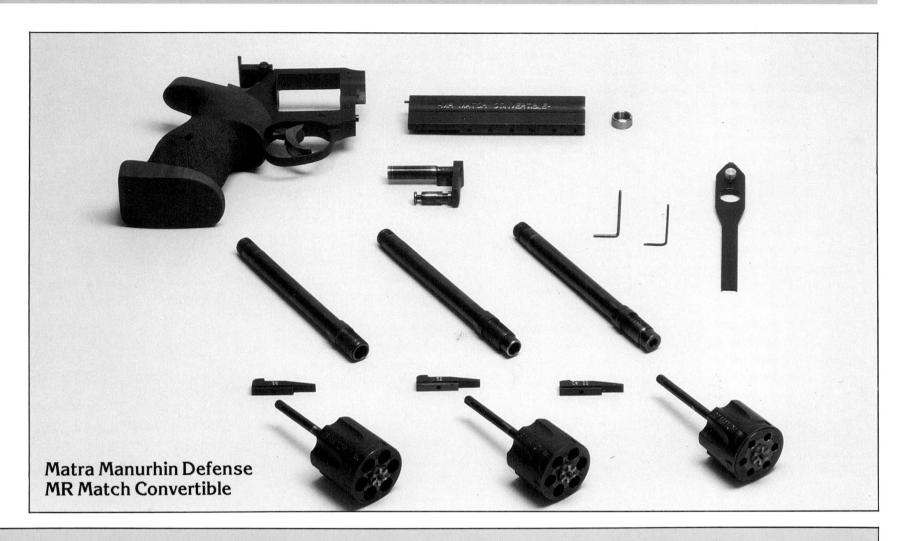

Matra Manurhin Defense MR Match Convertible

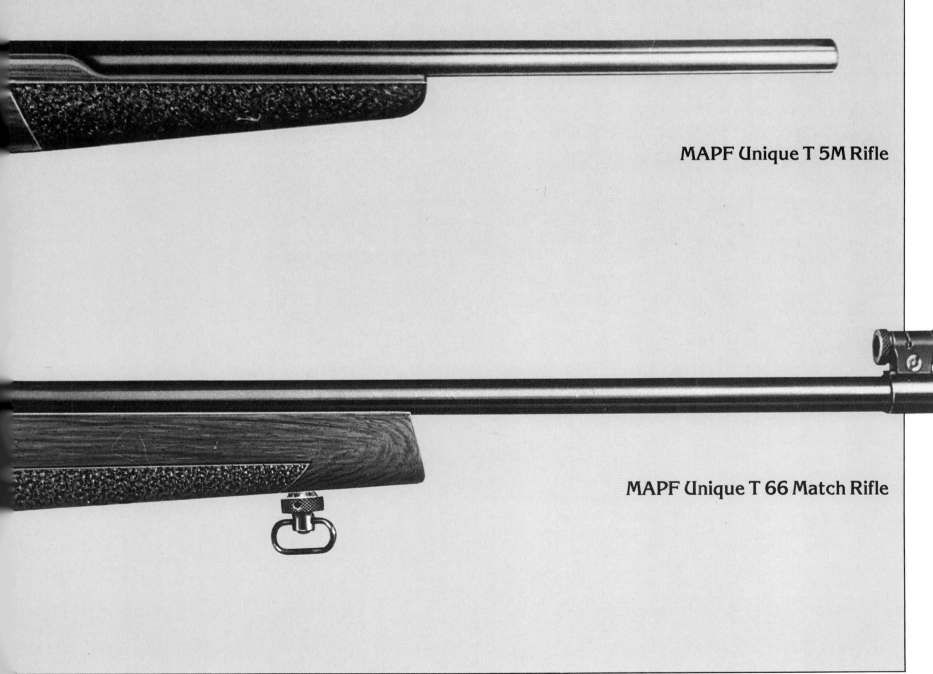

MAPF Unique T 5M Rifle

MAPF Unique T 66 Match Rifle

ISRAEL

Israel Military Industries manufactures a world-famous family of light weapons. The newest member, the Desert Eagle .357 Magnum semiautomatic pistol, is gas operated with a rotating bolt for positive lockup. In addition to its high accuracy and low recoil, the Desert Eagle offers the convenience of firing standard rimmed .357 Magnum cartridges, widely available as revolver ammunition: semi-jacketed and jacketed ammunition may be used. A new .44 caliber version of this pistol is also available. A full range of 'Samson' cartridges, cases and bullets is offered from IMI.

The Desert Eagle pistol is supplied with a standard six inch barrel. A 14 inch barrel is also available and can be interchanged without tools. The trigger guard is combat type, for two handed grip. The safety catch is operable by right and left handed shooters. When in safe position it provides double safety against accidental firing by immobilizing the firing pin and disconnecting the trigger from the hammer mechanism at the same time. Extensive tests in accordance with military specifications include drop tests and show that the Desert Eagle is safe from accidental firing, even when dropped on the hammer. The

Desert Eagle pistol is equipped with open combat sights; the Bomar De Luxe BMCS adjustable rear sight is optional. The barrel of the Desert Eagle is designed to accommodate a telescopic sight.

Hundreds of thousands of Uzi submachine guns have been manufactured by Israel Military Industries and thousands more go into service every year in armies, security forces and law enforcement agencies the world over.

The Uzi is lightweight, air cooled and magazine fed and can be fired in either full automatic or semiautomatic mode, from hip or shoulder. Three independent safety features make the Uzi among the safest of all automatic weapons. A thumb operated fire selector blocks the trigger when in 'Safe' position. The grip safety, at the rear of the pistol grip, must be depressed before the weapon will fire, thus preventing accidental discharge. A retracting safety ratchet keeps the bolt from sliding forward and the weapon from firing, even if the operator's hand should slip off the cocking knob while cocking.

Famous for its accuracy and safety, the Uzi is even more famous for its reliability. Battle-proven in thousands of engagements in environ-

**IMI Galil 5.56mm
Model AR Assault Rifle**

**IMI Galil 5.56mm
Model ARM Assault Rifle**

**IMI Galil 5.56mm
Model SAR Assault Rifle**

IMI Mini Uzi 9mm Submachine Gun

IMI Desert Eagle Semiautomatic Pistol

ments ranging from snow to desert, the Uzi's ability to keep firing in the presence of sand, dust and water has made it the standard against which other weapons are judged.

The Uzi is designed for operation with equal ease by left or right handed shooters. For greater versatility, 20, 25 and 32 round magazines are standard and available. Stripping and cleaning are quick and easy and maintenance is simple. Only five parts are involved in stripping the Uzi and the entire operation is routinely accomplished without tools in ten seconds. A complete inventory of spare parts is always available.

With metal stock, the Uzi weighs 125 ounces, and is 25.6 inches long with stock extended; 18.5 inches long with stock folded. Although the total length of the weapon (stock folded) is only 18.5 inches, the unique sleeved bolt of the Uzi allows it to accommodate a 10.25 inch barrel. The Uzi's 10.25 inch barrel is rifled right hand, one turn in 10 inches. Rate of fire for this 9mm Parabellum submachine gun is 600rpm.

The Uzi 9mm Semiautomatic Carbine was specially designed for sportsmen, marksmen and hunters. It is manufactured by Israel Military Industries to the same exacting standards as the world-famous Uzi, used by military men the world over. This carbine will continue firing in rain, snow, sandstorms, desert heat or sub-zero weather. In addition to its safety catch, the Uzi carbine has a safety grip that has to be squeezed all the way, or the carbine won't fire. It's just about child-proof too, because a child's hand isn't big enough to squeeze the safety grip and pull the trigger at the same time or strong enough to pull

IMI Mini Uzi 9mm Submachine Gun

IMI Micro Uzi 9mm Machine Pistol

back the cocking knob. The Uzi carbine is pre-zeroed at the factory and will give you 2.9 inch groups at 109 yards. Adjustment of the rear sight for windage and the front sight for elevation (or individual eyesight) is simple: the optionally available sight adjustment tool does the job in seconds. Sight guards protect both sights against accidental knocks. The Uzi Semiautomatic Carbine weighs just 9.5 pounds, and is 31.5 inches long, with metal stock extended.

The Uzi carbine conversion kit allows one to fire .22 caliber long rifle ammunition without any modifications to the carbine itself. All you have to do is insert the .22 caliber barrel, replace the bolt with the bolt housing assembly and magazine provided and you're all set. You will then be able to practice firing on enclosed ranges using inexpensive ammunition. The kit includes the following main parts: .22 caliber carbine barrel; bolt housing/striker assembly, including the bolt housing and ejector; and the magazine assembly—this is a carbine magazine housing, modified to take the special .22 caliber magazine.

Israel Military Industries has now produced the Mini Uzi Submachine gun. With stock folded, the Mini Uzi measures just over 14 inches in length. It can be fired full or semiautomatic from the hip or, with stock extended, from the shoulder. Its perfect balance makes it easy to control during automatic fire, permitting sustained accuracy, even at a high rate of fire. The weapon has three safety features: fire selector, grip safety, and retracting safety ratchet. These safety features are independent of each other and positively eliminate the possibility of accidental firing.

The new Micro Uzi offers the police and security officers the advantages of the Uzi submachine gun in pistol form. Specially designed for police and security use, the Micro Uzi can be fired either full or semi-

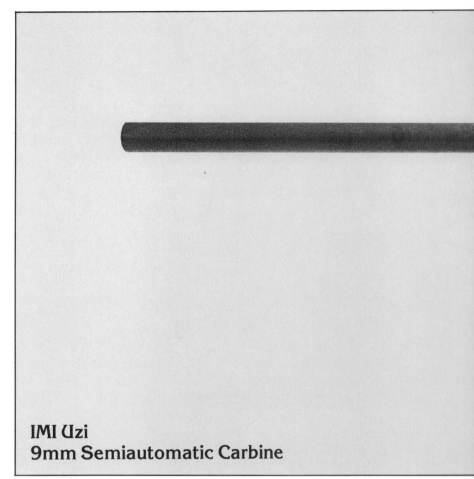

**IMI Uzi
9mm Semiautomatic Carbine**

**IMI Galil 7.62mm
Semiautomatic Sniper Rifle**

IMI Galil Model ARM 7.62mm Assault Rifle

automatic and has a folding stock, for firing from the shoulder. Perfect balance and a deviation compensator on the muzzle which reduces 'ride' make control under full automatic fire relatively effortless. Two independent safety features make it one of the safest as well as one of the most powerful security arms you can own. Just 19 inches long with stock extended, the 9mm Micro Uzi weighs just 4.4 pounds.

The new Uzi 9mm Semiautomatic Pistol offers the sportsman, hunter and security officer the advantages of the Uzi Semiautomatic Carbine, in pistol form. The Uzi pistol has perfect balance; control while firing a series of shots in rapid succession requires little effort. In addition, the Uzi pistol has an effective range of 198 feet and its 20 round magazine gives it fire power unusual in a semiautomatic pistol. The overall length of this pistol is 9.45 inches, including its 4.5 inch barrel, which is rifled right hand, one turn in 10 inches.

In addition to the Uzi's well-known ability to continue firing under the most adverse conditions and roughest handling, the new Uzi pistol shares with the other Uzi weapons great simplicity in cleaning and maintenance. Only seven parts are involved in stripping and no tools are required. An extremely important feature of the new Uzi pistol is its high degree of safety in handling. In addition to a standard safety catch, the Uzi has a grip safety; unless the weapon is securely held by the user and the grip safety depressed, the weapon will not fire.

The Galil 5.56mm Assault Rifle in all its models has been tested and proven by thousands of infantrymen, paratroopers and members of tank crews. The Galil has shown that it will continue firing when other rifles quit. The Galil Assault Rifle is lightweight, air cooled, gas

IMI Galil 7.62mm Model AR Assault Rifle

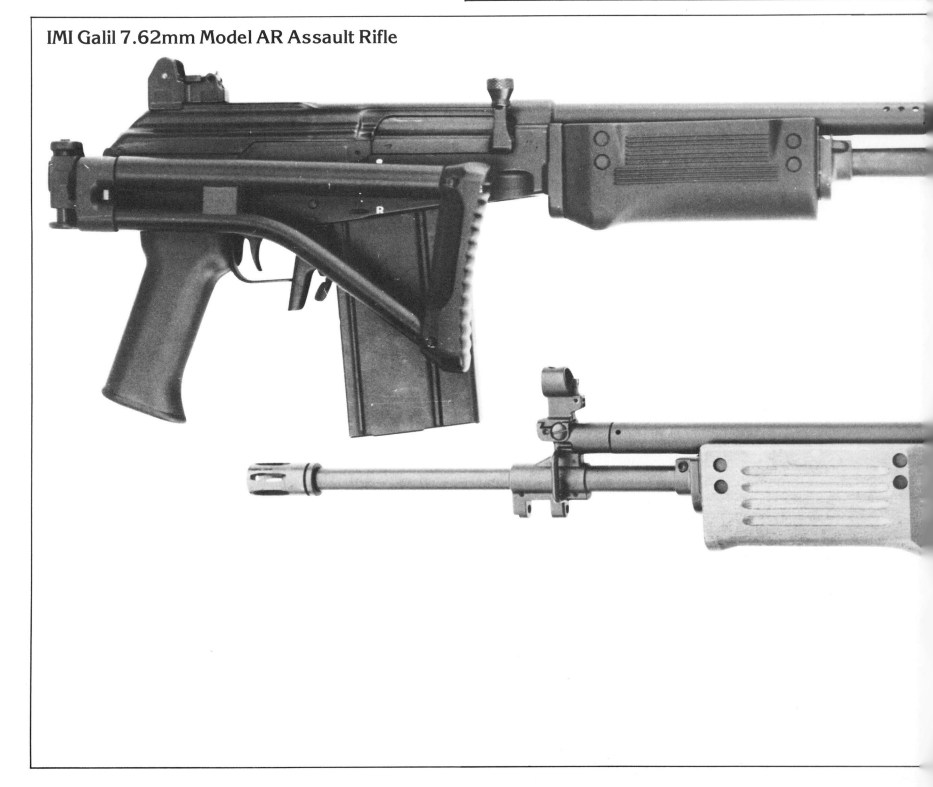

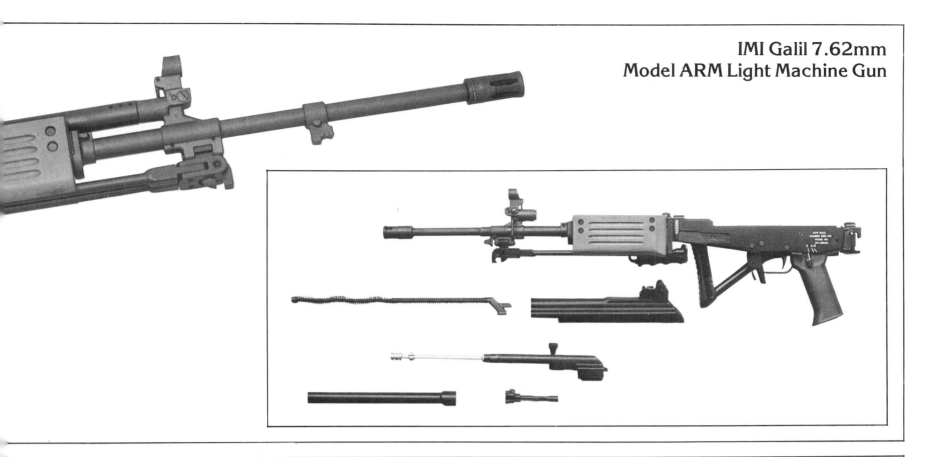

**IMI Galil 7.62mm
Model ARM Light Machine Gun**

**IMI Galil 5.56mm
Model SAR Assault Rifle**

operated and magazine fed. It can be fired from hip or shoulder in automatic or semiautomatic mode. All three models of the Galil are available for use with the new NATO-recommended SS109, 5.56mm cartridge.

The Galil 5.56mm—Model ARM is an assault rifle and light machine gun with bipod and carrying handle; the Galil 5.56mm—Model AR is a fully automatic assault rifle: the basic infantry weapon; and the Galil 5.56mm—Model SAR is a fully automatic short barreled assault rifle; ideal for tank crews, airborne troops and commandos. The Galil Model ARM is one of very few assault rifles with a built-in bipod. The Galil's bipod is strong, won't break or deform when slammed on the ground and contains a wire cutter.

Galil alone among the major assault rifles has foldable night sights (tritium light); in addition, only the Galil has a built-in base for accomodating almost all types of sight and SLS mounts. A special night safety catch, featured only on the Galil, permits the shooter to retract the cocking knob and open the receiver without putting a round in the chamber from the magazine. The chamber is directly in front of the ejection port, allowing the shooter to finger check (in the dark) for the presence of a round and close the receiver, leaving the chamber empty. The Galil breaks down into a mere five parts with no pins or other small parts (easily lost in the dark).

Overall lengths for the ARM, AR and SAR, respectively, are: 38.6 inches, 38.6 inches and 33.1 inches. The maximum rate of fire for all three is 650rpm. Rifling for these three Galil models is right handed, one turn in 12 inches.

The Galil has a three position fire selector lever: safe, semiautomatic, and fully automatic. When in safe position the fire selector lever completely blocks the trigger and covers the slot in which the cocking handle travels, thus preventing cocking of the weapon and preventing dirt from entering the mechanism.

The Galil 7.62mm Assault Rifle is a version of the Galil 5.56mm in service throughout the world and in combat use since 1973. It is operable in a range of extreme environmental conditions and fires successfully even after exposure to sand, dirt, snow and water.

The new weapon fires standard 7.62mm NATO ammunition and retains all the advantages of the 5.56mm model with added range and impact, with only a weight increase of only 100 grams (3.5 ounces). The Galil's front sight is post type; rear sight is L flip type, set for 328 and 546.8 yards. Overall lengths for the 7.62mm Galil ARM, AR and SAR models differ slightly from their 5.56mm counterparts: respectively, these are 41.4 inches, 41.4 inches and 36.1 inches. The Galil 7.62mm Semiautomatic Sniper Rifle was developed in close cooperation with the Israel Defence Forces.

The Galil Sniper Rifle is a semiautomatic, gas operated rifle with a rotating bolt, fed from a 20 round magazine and firing M-118, F.N. Match or any other standard NATO 7.62 × 51mm ammunition. The shot grouping possible with this very accurate firearm is within a circle of 4.7 to 5.9 inches diameter at 328 yards. This is possible thanks to three important features: a special heavy barrel; location of the bipod on the receiver; and the design of the telescopic sight mount and its attaching slide on the receiver.

IMI Uzi 9mm Semiautomatic Carbine

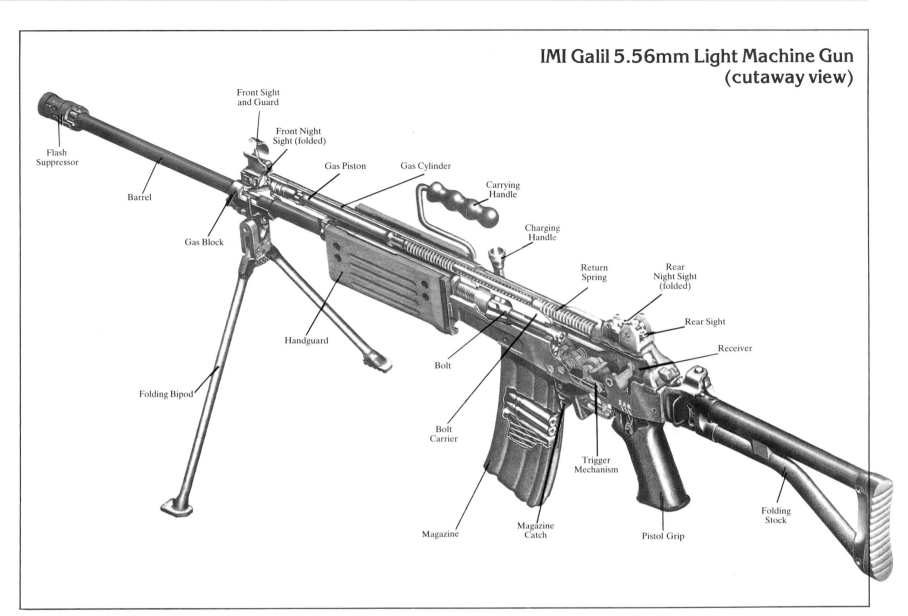

IMI Galil 5.56mm Light Machine Gun
(cutaway view)

Flash Suppressor

Front Sight and Guard

Front Night Sight (folded)

Barrel

Gas Piston

Gas Cylinder

Carrying Handle

Gas Block

Charging Handle

Return Spring

Rear Night Sight (folded)

Handguard

Rear Sight

Receiver

Bolt

Folding Bipod

Bolt Carrier

Trigger Mechanism

Magazine

Magazine Catch

Pistol Grip

Folding Stock

IMI Micro Uzi 9mm Machine Pistol

ITALY

The renowned firm of **Beretta—Armi Beretta SpA** and **P Beretta SpA**—have been producing robust, dependable and accurate firearms for some years now. The following is an incomplete compendium of recent Beretta models.

Beretta Models 81 and 84 are blowback semiautomatic double action pistols. The Model 81 comes in 7.65mm ACP caliber, and the Model 84 is available in .380 caliber (9mm short).

Barrels are 3.8 inches—the Model 81 weighs 23.5 ounces and holds 12 rounds; the Model 84 weighs 22.5 ounces and holds 13 rounds. Both are directly related to the famous Model 1934 Beretta, having fixed barrels and the Beretta 'cutaway' slide. Design modernizations include double action mechanism, handier grips, bigger magazines, and better finish. Sights are fixed front, with a dovetail notch windage rear sight; walnut grips are standard. The extractor is machined with a safety protrusion which indicates when a round is in the chamber.

The Beretta Model 92 is a locked-breech semiautomatic double action pistol in 9mm Parabellum caliber. The Model 92's barrel is 4.9 inches long, and it has a magazine capacity of 15 rounds. At 33.5 ounces, it's a handy military pistol. The Italian Army has adopted it, and has been followed in doing so by several other armed forces.

Its locking breech operates on the same general 'dropping block' principal as that of the Walther 38. The Beretta Model 92 features the same 'chamber loaded' safety extractor indicator as the Beretta Models 81 and 84—a handy device which can be easily seen and felt—if one is in the dark. The front sight is fixed, with a windage-adjustable dovetail notch groove arrangement in the rear.

The Beretta Model 92S is identical to the Model 92, except that it has a slide mounted firing pin safety which blocks the firing pin from the hammer blow, releases the hammer and disconnects the trigger bar/sear connection. The 92S is rated very high for safety and reliability.

The Beretta Model 93R Machine Pistol is a locked-breech double action semiautomatic pistol with burst firing capability. The Model 93R fires 9mm Parabellum ammo, holds 20 rounds, has a 6.1 inch barrel and weighs 41.2 ounces.

Based on the Model 92, the Beretta Model 93R features a muzzle break integral with its barrel, which protrudes markedly unlike the Model 92; it also has, unlike the Model 92, a folding front grip attached to the trigger guard. Also an appearance 'giveaway' is the lengthened, protruding magazine, and the detachable folding metal stock.

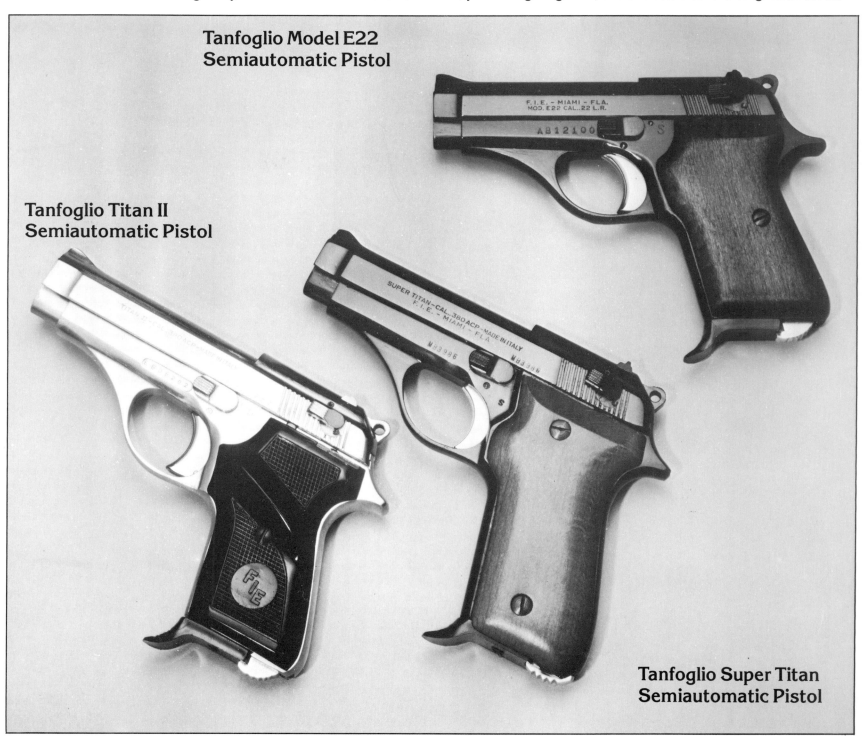

Tanfoglio Model E22 Semiautomatic Pistol

Tanfoglio Titan II Semiautomatic Pistol

Tanfoglio Super Titan Semiautomatic Pistol

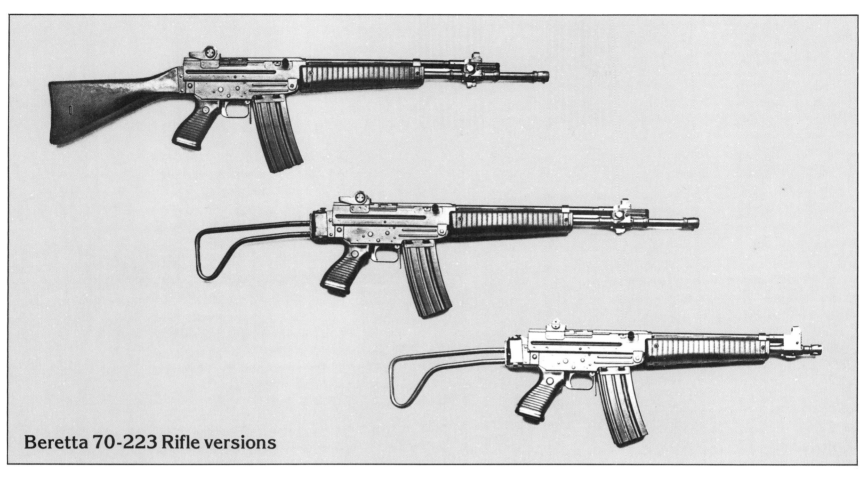

Beretta 70-223 Rifle versions

**Beretta Model 93R
Machine Pistol**

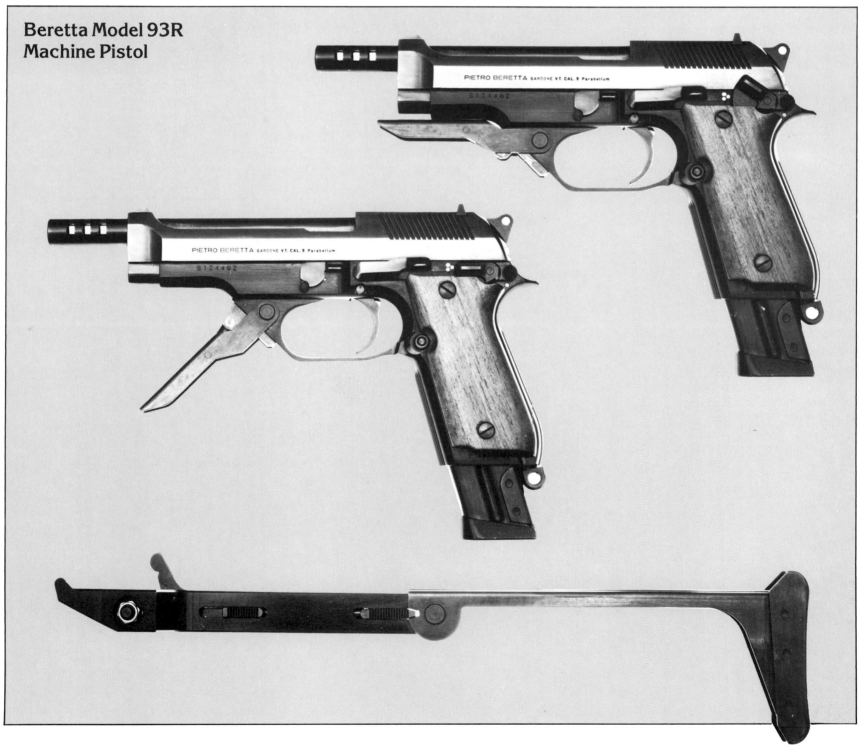

The frame mounted safety can be set for safe, semiautomatic and three round burst. In this latter mode, the forward grip, shoulder stock and muzzle break combine to cut automatic fire muzzle climb to almost nil.

The Beretta Model 12/12S is a blowback, selective-fire 9mm submachine gun having a 7.9 inch barrel and alternate magazine capacities of 20, 32 or 40 rounds. The basic Model 12 has been in military use for some 30 years. It is a durable, dependable arm in the classic sheet steel 'burp gun' design. With a safety in the pistol grip, this 550rpm weapon cannot fire unless it is held in the 'firing ready' position. Most of the barrel is inside the receiver of this very smooth working 'smg.' This, and its comparatively low rate of fire lend the Model 12 to good fire control.

The Model 12S is an adapted version, with a combination fire selector and safety catch, instead of having two levers; the folding metal stock has been given a positive locking action, and other improvements including a windage and elevation-adjustable front sight.

The Beretta BM-62 is a gas operated semiautomatic .308 Winchester/7.62mm NATO retooling of the legendary Garand service rifle.

Shortly after World War II, the Italian Army adopted the US M1 Garand, and Beretta was granted a license to manufacture M1s for the Italian and other armies.

The BM-59 Beretta military version of the BM-62 evolved from the M1 when updated firepower was demanded by NATO forces. With a detachable 20 round magazine, fire selector, grenade launcher and flash suppressor, Beretta modified the M1 into the Italian Army's standard arm since 1962. For sport shooters, Beretta modified the BM-59—chiefly by eliminating its automatic fire capability. For fans of the fabled M1, this could be the ideal sporter.

The Beretta 70-223 Rifle is a gas operated, selective-fire 5.56mm/.223 caliber rifle with 30 to 40 round capacity, 17.7 inch barrel and a 650rpm rate of fire. Four versions are available: The first is the AR70

**Tanfoglio Titan 25
Semiautomatic Pistol**

**Tanfoglio Titan 25
(with gold plating)**

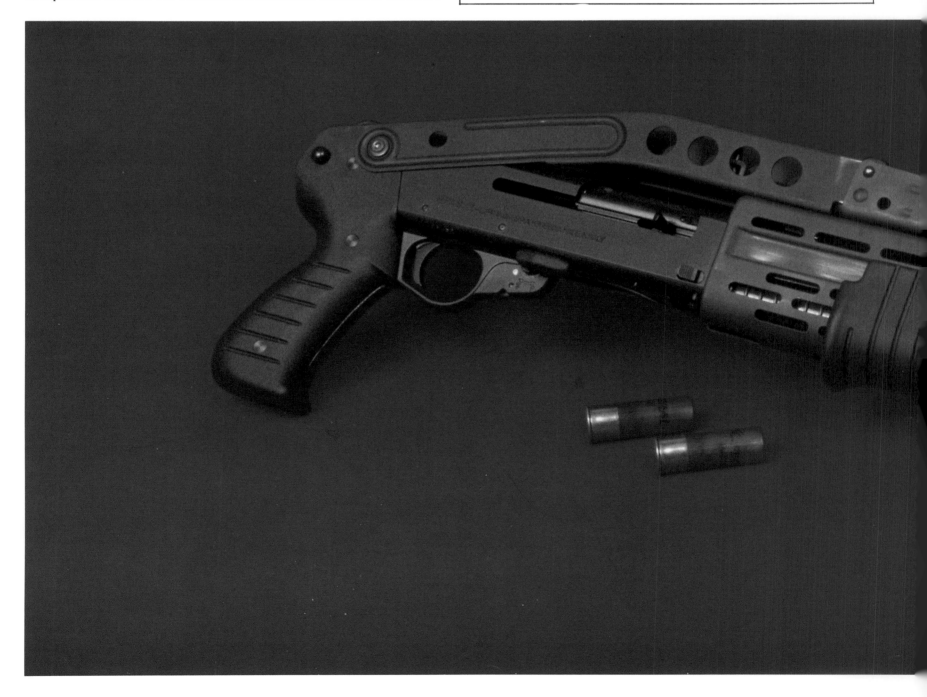

Beretta Model 92F Semiautomatic Pistol

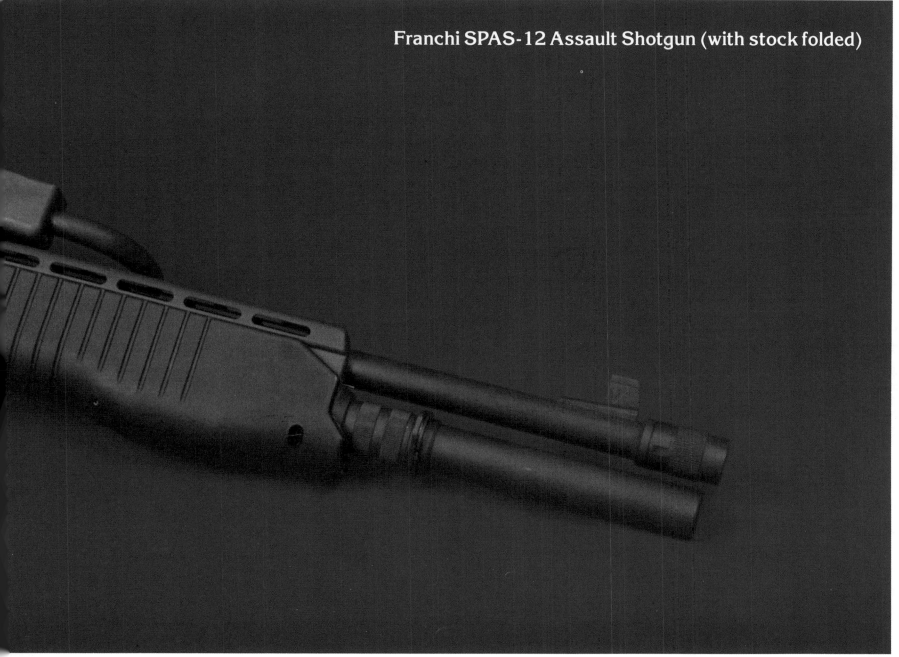

Franchi SPAS-12 Assault Shotgun (with stock folded)

Beretta Model 12S 9mm Submachine Gun

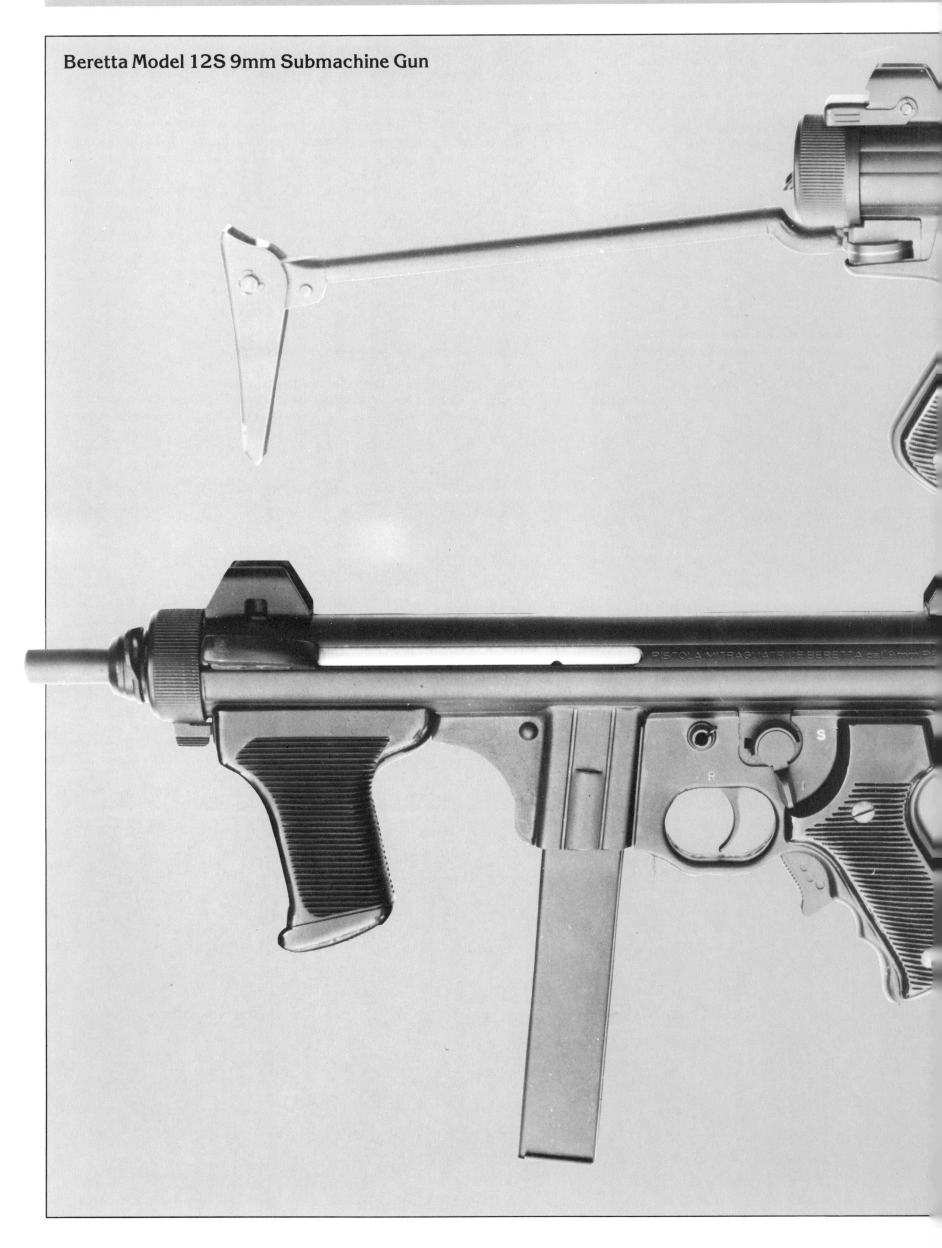

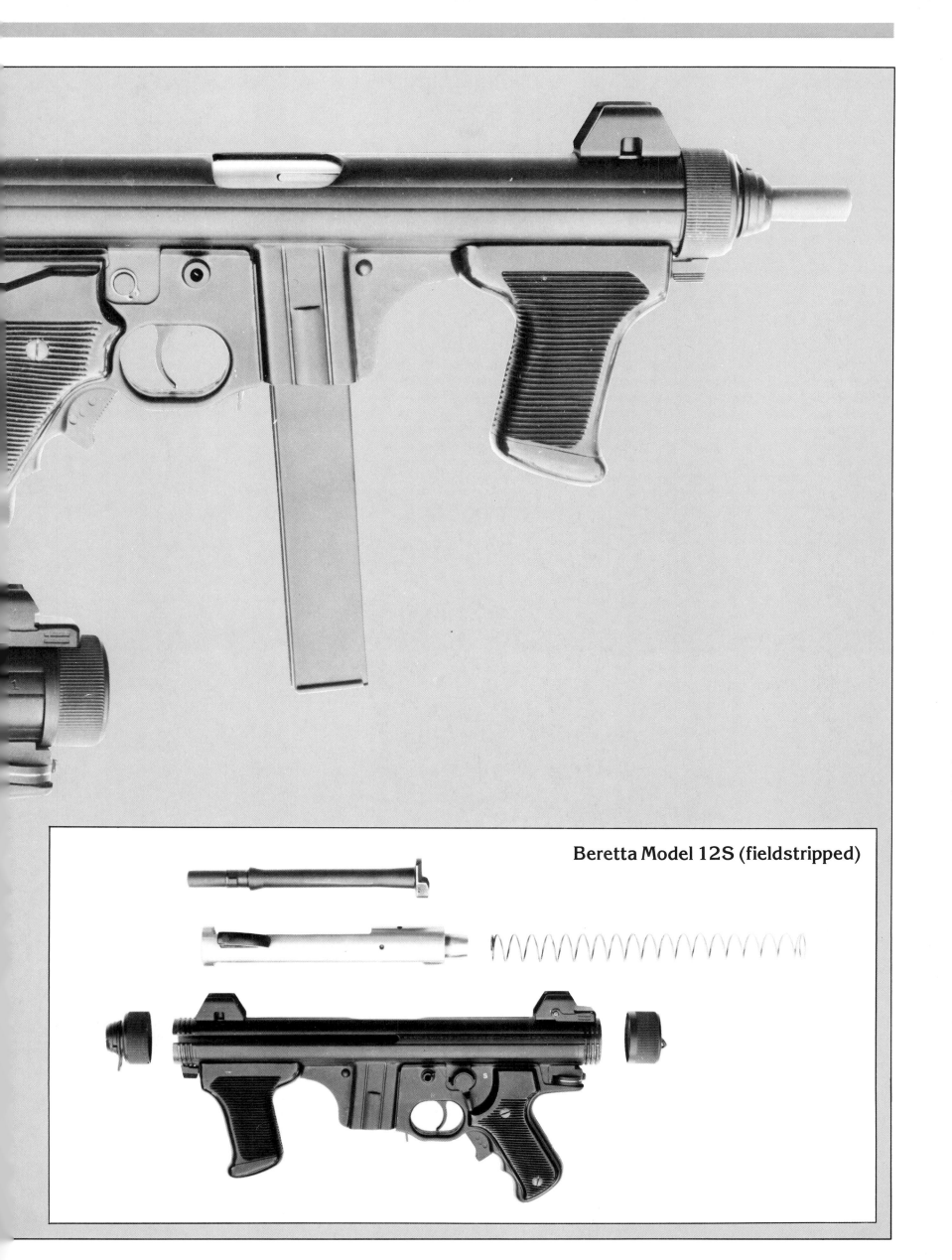

Beretta Model 12S (fieldstripped)

Assault Rifle, with rotating bolt, plastic stocks, gas magazine, range and windage-adjustable front sight. Sight mounts are available for scopes or night sights.

The SC70 Special Carbine has a folding metal stock, and features the same as the AR70, including optional folding bipod. The SC70 Short has a 12.6 inch barrel and folding metal stock. The 70-78 Light Machine Gun has an extra heavy interchangeable 17.7 inch barrel and a standard 40 round magazine. Altogether, the various versions of this firearm serve several armed forces, and no doubt will continue to do so.

Beretta also manufactures—among other products, the finely tooled RS-202P Police and Security Shotgun, a hammerless pump action with folding metal stock, rubber butt plate and bead front sight.

Beretta is one of the renowned arms manufacturers of the world—known for expertise and finesse.

While Luigi Franchi SpA is an old, established arms family with a high reputation for manufacturing fine sporting shotguns which are sold the world over, another Italian arms manufacturer has, since the 1950s, made commercial inroads on the world arms industry in the field of semiautomatic pistols. This manufacturer is **G Tanfoglio** (aka 'Tanfoglio and Sabotti') of Gardone Val Trompia.

Tanfoglio's Super Titan semiauto is 3.9 inches long, and is available in .380/(9mm short) and .32 ACP(7.65mm) calibers.

This blowback semiautomatic features two manual safeties—one which locks the firing pin, and one which locks the trigger. This is a middling quality, but reliable pistol with fixed front and rear sights and an open-topped slide. The magazine of the Super Titan holds 11 rounds of .32 ammo. Super Titan models are also aka 'Titan II,' and in this configuration have a slightly different slide locking catch.

These models are imported into the US by FIE, Inc, of Florida, and are stamped with that company's name on their slides. They are available in a number of finishes and grip configurations.

The Super Titan's predecessor is the Titan—a semiauto that was nearly ubiquitous in the 1950s. This little pistol fires .25 caliber ammo and is available in a number of finishes—blue, chrome, matte and combinations of these, and are made for self-protection and for those shooters who enjoy trying to achieve accuracy with small firearms such as these. If you enjoy busting cans, bottles and close-range paper targets, the Titan is the pistol for you.

Tanfolgio Model T2-75 Double Action Pistol (in chrome and blue finishes)

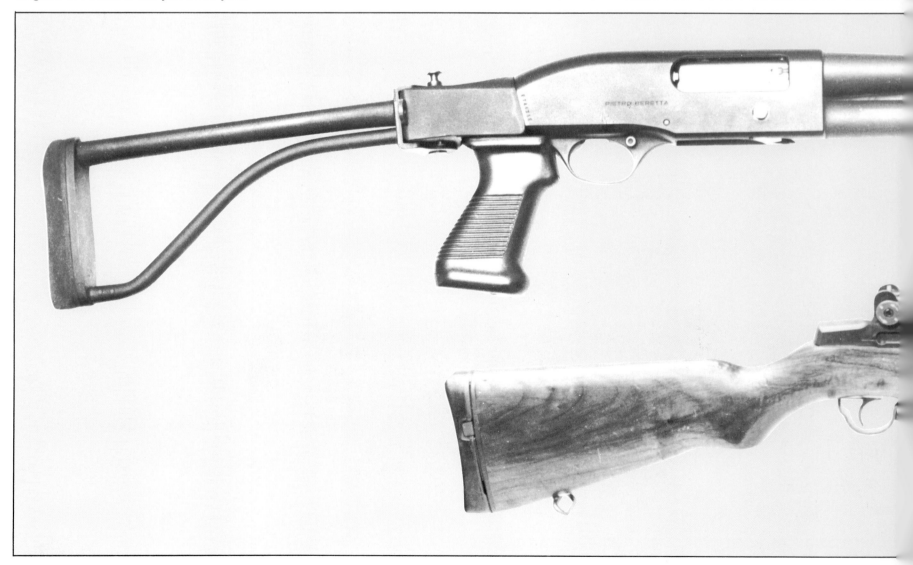

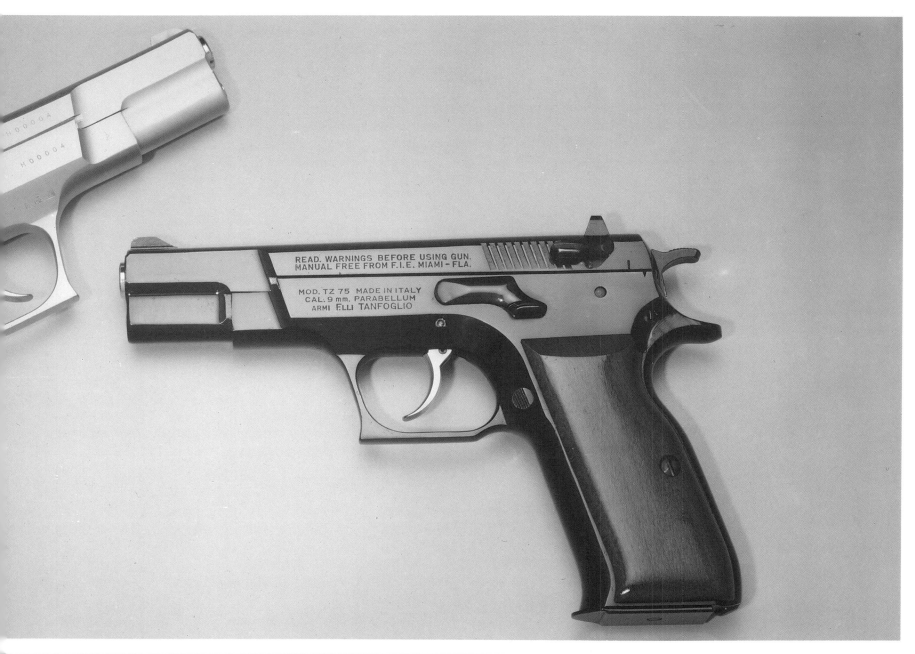

READ. WARNINGS BEFORE USING GUN.
MANUAL FREE FROM F.I.E. MIAMI – FLA.

MOD. TZ 75   MADE IN ITALY
CAL. 9 mm. PARABELLUM
ARMI F.LLI TANFOGLIO

Beretta Model 202P Police and Security Shotgun

Beretta Model BM-59 Military Rifle

JAPAN

Miroku manufactures the Browning Bolt Action Rifle for the Browning Company of Morgan, Utah in the USA. Miroku also manufactures the Browning slide action BPS Shotgun.

Located in Kochi, Japan, Miroku is one of Japan's most respected arms manufacturers. Insofar as the Browning BBR is concerned, Miroku has given it a fine finish and excellent workmanship. Available in calibers from .25-06 Remington to .300 Winchester, the BBR is capable of 1.5 inch groups at 100 yards. A bolt action, four round magazine rifle, the BBR has a 24 inch barrel and weighs eight pounds.

No sights are provided with the rifle but the receiver is drilled and tapped for telescope mounts. The BBR's Monte Carlo walnut stock, complete with cheekpiece, features beautiful checkering and a thumbrest. The action cocks as the bolt is closed, and the bolt has nine locking lugs. All in all, a fine firearm with a beautiful finish.

Among their other projects, Miroku manufactures extremely fine grade shotguns. Beginning with the Miroku 3800 Series shotguns, these are fine finish superposed doubles, with hammerless action, vent rib barrel bead front sight, and engraving. Some of the models in this series are the 3800 Trap II and Trap III, and the 3800 Skeet Models SK1 through SK14.

The trap models feature a heavy rubber shoulder pad, and the skeet models are equipped with a thin shoulder pad, but all models feature finely polished stocks, blued barrels with chrome receivers, and fine checkering on the stocks. Trap and skeet models both also feature finger grooved forestocks and pistol grip buttstocks with thumbrests. All feature the traditional thumb lever break top action, and are very well designed and machined, with smooth action.

The Miroku 6000 series features trap and skeet models plus the GM1 and GM3 model line. The Miroku 6000 series shotguns are extremely fine finish firearms with polished wood stocks which are beautifully checkered on the pistol grip—and in the 6000 trap and skeet models feature finger grooved forestocks, with heavy shoulder pad on the trap models. The 6000 series are all superposed doubles featuring blued barrels, chrome receiver and gold plated trigger. In the 6000 Trap and GM1 models, the forepart of the break action and the thumb lever are blued, while in the 6000 Skeet model and the GM3 model, these parts are chrome. The 6000 Trap model features an extremely high vent rib to prevent overheating.

The GM1 and the GM3 have finely checkered forestocks without finger grooves, but with a gracefully bobtailed fore end.

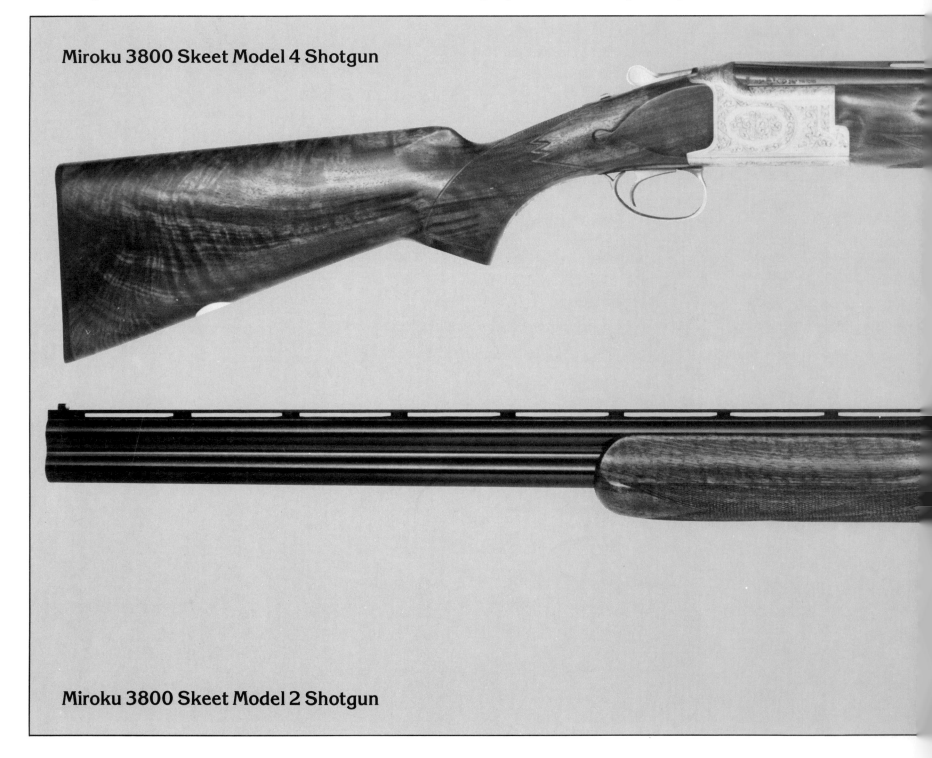

Miroku 3800 Skeet Model 4 Shotgun

Miroku 3800 Skeet Model 2 Shotgun

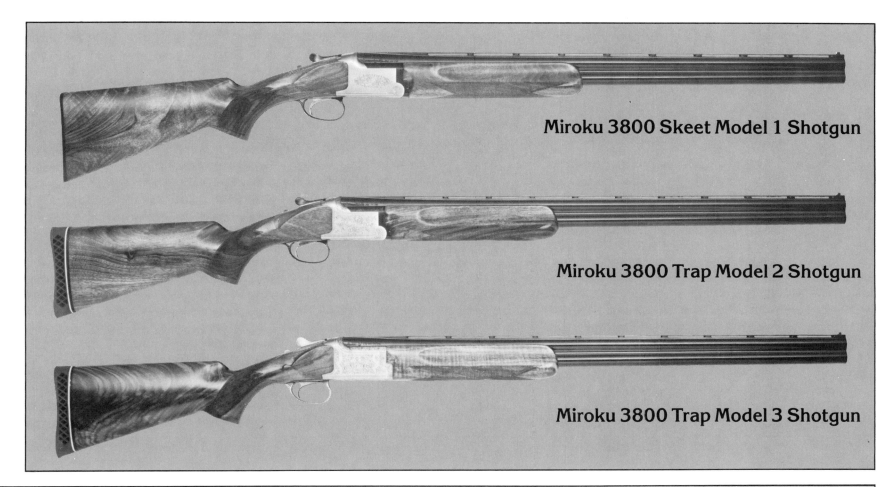

Miroku 3800 Skeet Model 1 Shotgun

Miroku 3800 Trap Model 2 Shotgun

Miroku 3800 Trap Model 3 Shotgun

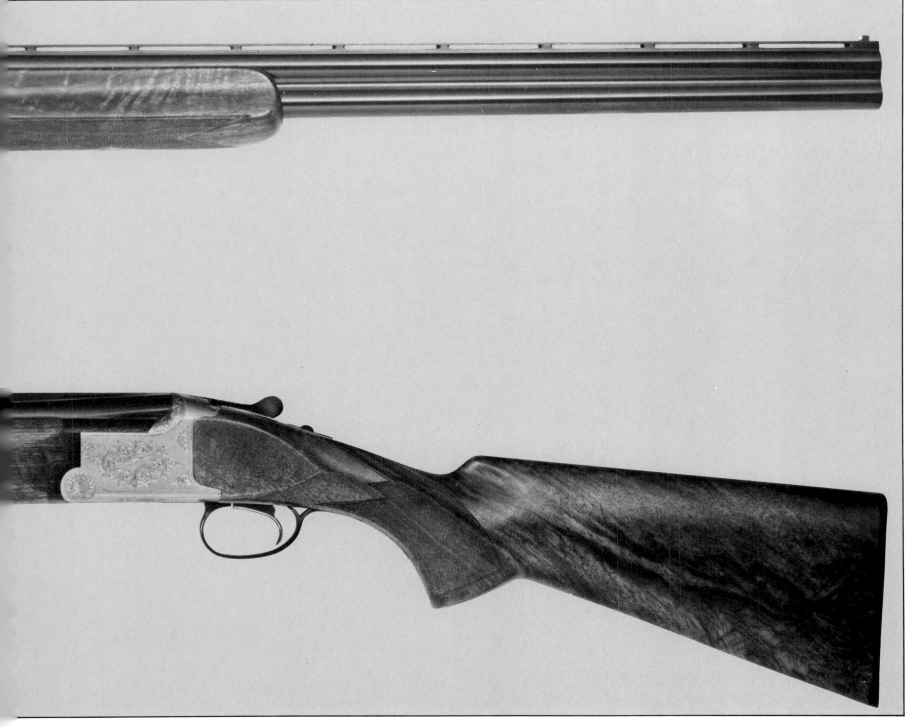

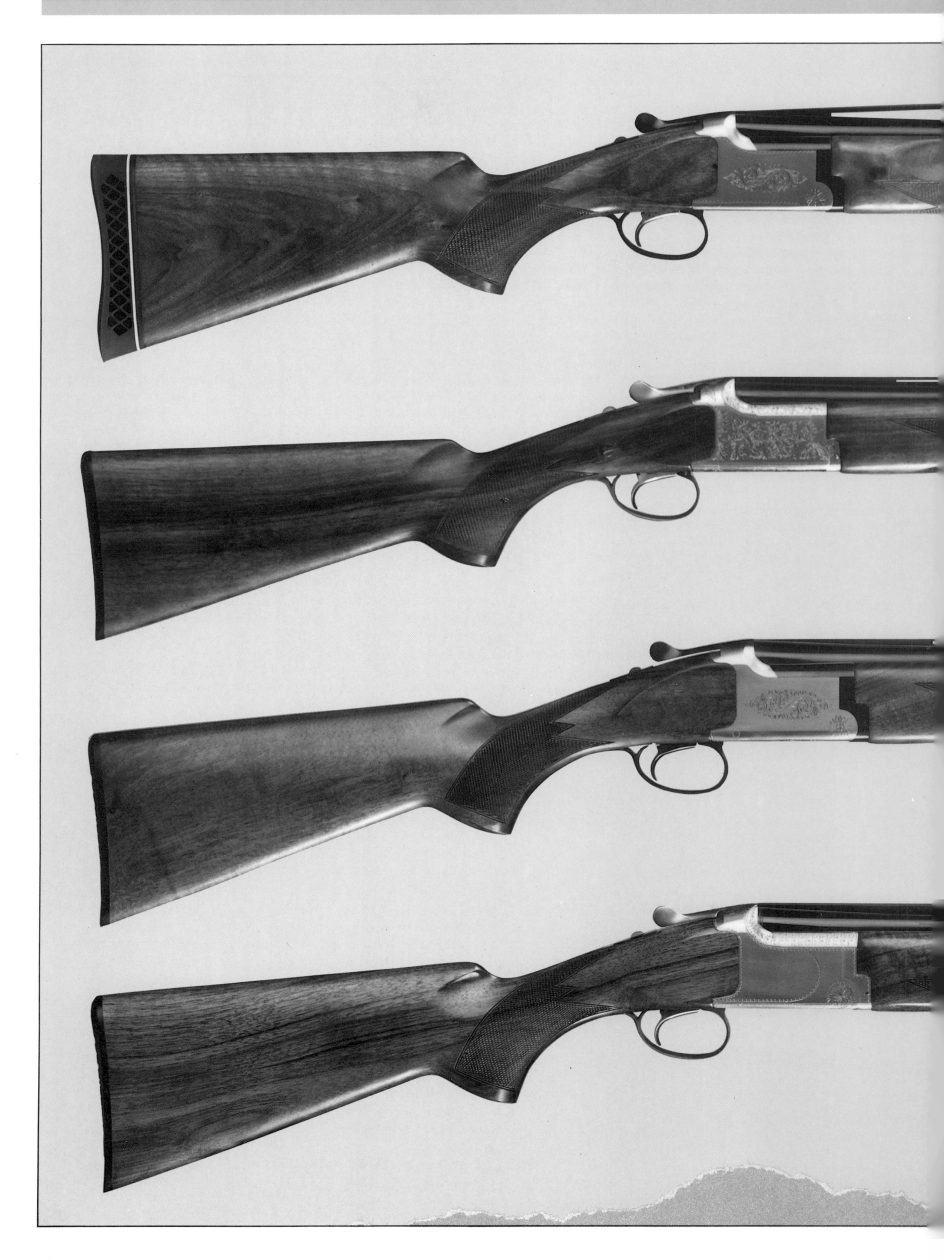

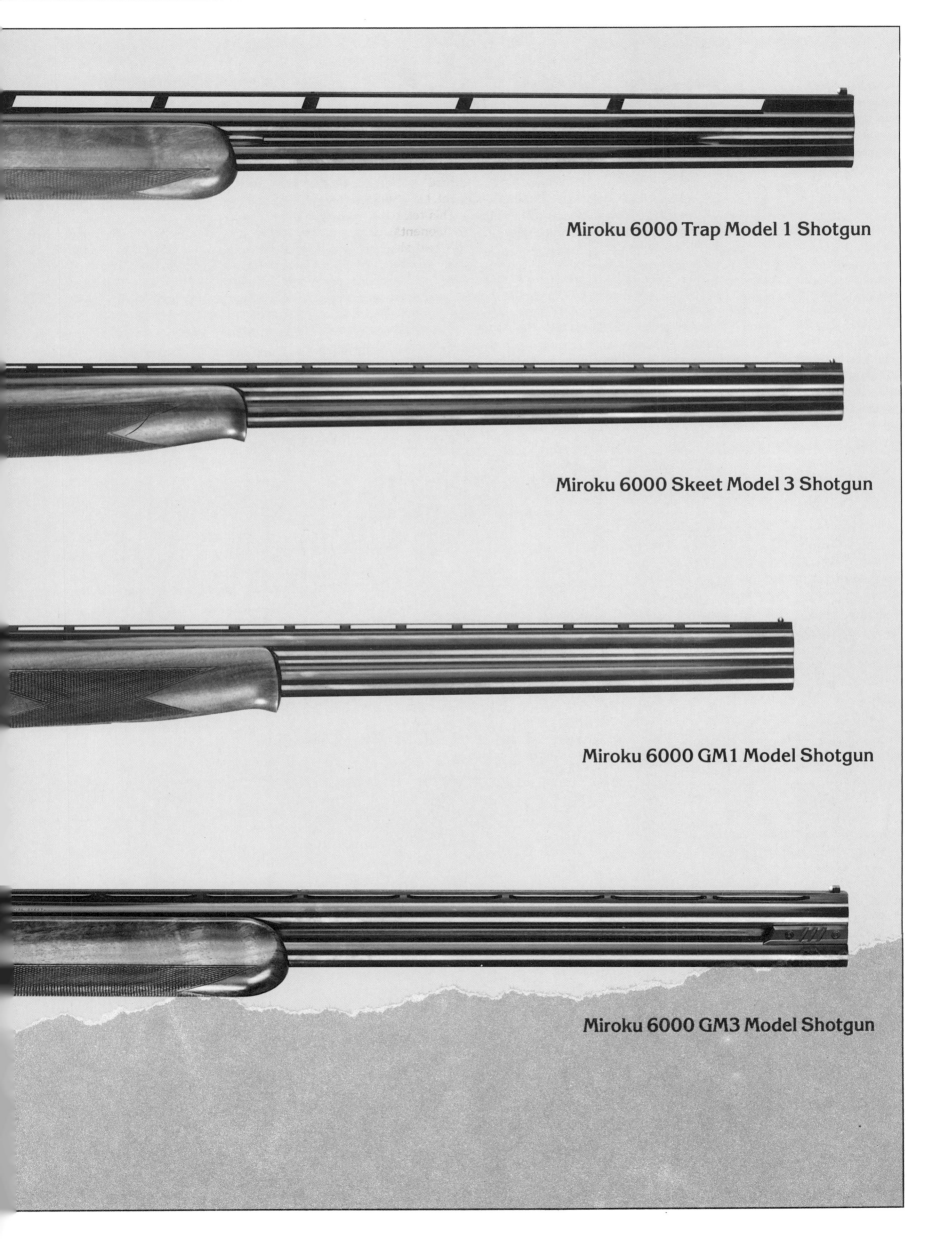

Miroku 6000 Trap Model 1 Shotgun

Miroku 6000 Skeet Model 3 Shotgun

Miroku 6000 GM1 Model Shotgun

Miroku 6000 GM3 Model Shotgun

SOVIET UNION

In the late 1930s, when Germany's arms companies were searching for a better military cartridge, it had been seen from the various gruesome lessons of World War I that the infantryman was equipped with rifle and ammunition to attack targets at distances nearly four times as distant as any he was likely—or even capable, given wartime infantry training—to attack.

This led to the desire for a lighter, less powerful round of ammunition, which would enable the soldier to knock off targets at up to 500 yards, and would still weigh less than the existing ammo, actually easing the infantryman's physical burden.

This less powerful round—after various convolutions in its development—turned out to be shorter than the then-standard ammunition, and thus allowed a shorter, more compact rifle action. The Haenel Company developed a suitable rifle to fit this bullet, and it was designated, actually, as a machine pistol—this was to evade its development being quashed by Adolf Hitler, who was at the time encouraging the development of submachine and machine guns, and was discouraging the development of rifles. So this 'machine pistol' sneaked through the German wartime assembly lines, and proving itself in combat, Hitler was made a convert to this new idea in rifle development. Hitler dubbed the new weapon 'Sturmgewehr,' or 'Assault Rifle.'

This relatively compact, lightweight weapon with its pressed steel components was the subject of much curiosity. The Soviet State Arsenals had already been developing their own version of a short cartridge for much the same reason that the Germans had, and after the war, they began developing the weapon to suit the cartridge—as the Germans had (with lots of design help from captured Sturmgewehrs).

This short Soviet round evolved into the now-standard Warsaw Pact cartridge, the 7.62 × 39mm, which is actually longer than the 7.92mm German round, but still is shorter than any other medium-caliber round. These developments led to the now-globally ubiquitous Kalashnikov rifles—the AKM AK-47 and the AK-74, which are distributed, and produced in various knock-off copies, around the world. These weapons are simple and easy to maintain, and have for some years been the chief means of intimidation used by terrorists and insurrectionists worldwide.

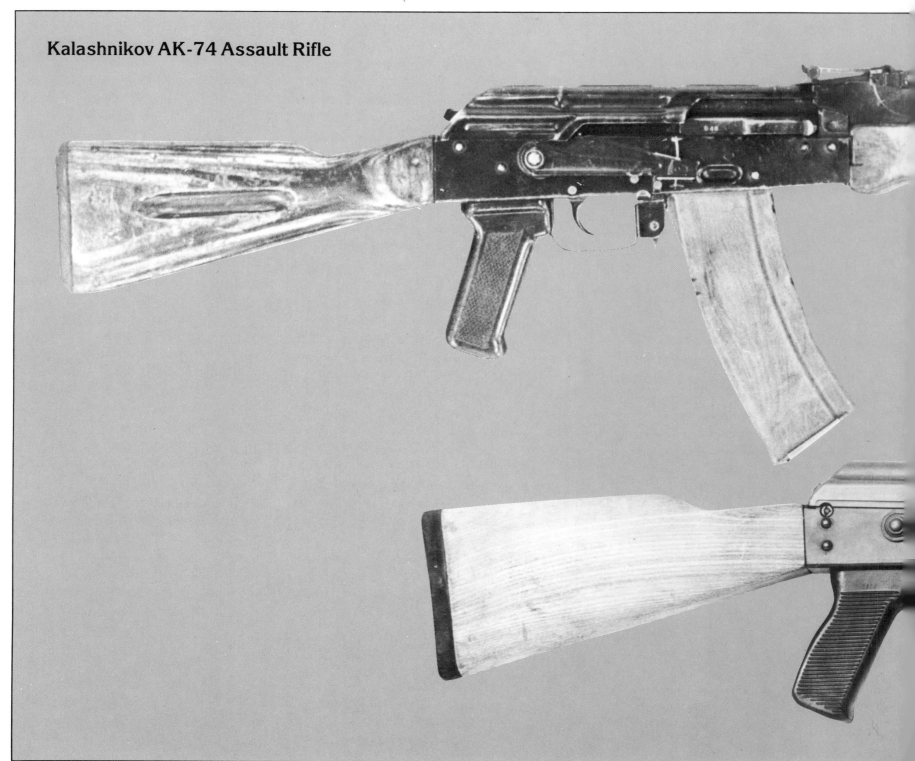

Kalashnikov AK-74 Assault Rifle

Kalashnikov AK-47S
Assault Rifle

Kalashnikov AK-47 Assault Rifle

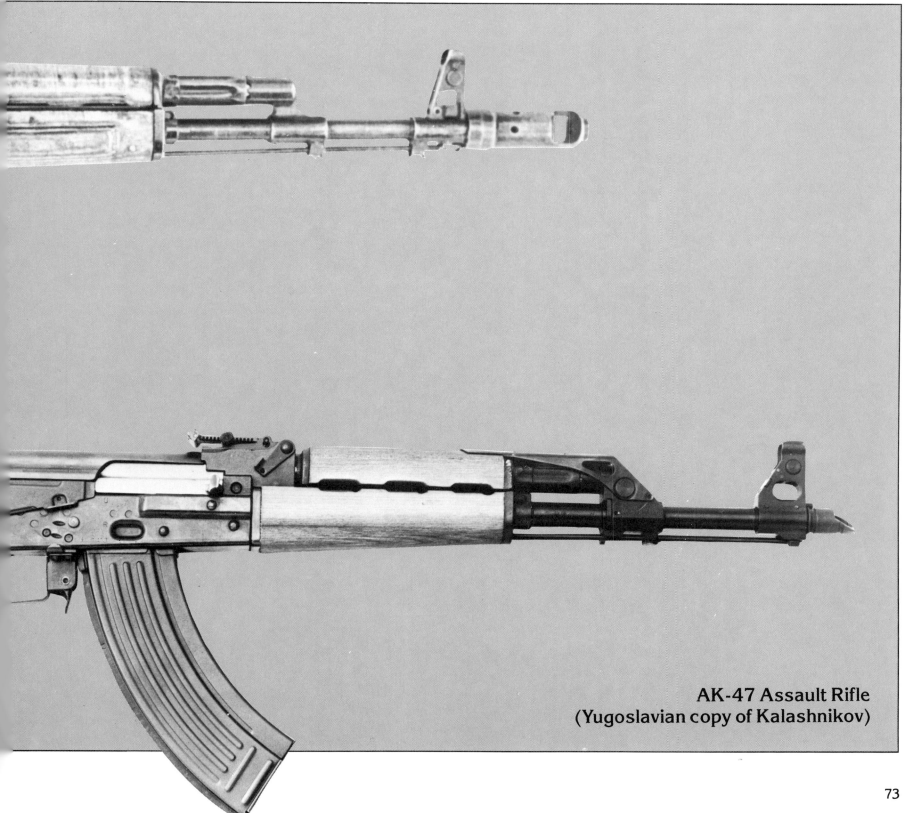

AK-47 Assault Rifle
(Yugoslavian copy of Kalashnikov)

In the 1960s the **Soviet State Arsenals** had developed a 5.56mm necked-down version of their 7.62mm caliber round, but this small bullet served mainly in research toward development of the 5.45mm bullet, upon which their improved infantry arm, the AK-74, is based.

The old, reliable AK-47 was an improved submachine gun having a selective mode of firing, and an automatic rate of over 600rpm. Simple and rugged, this short-range weapon was ideal for the suppressive fire role for which it was designed: basically, you made the enemy keep their heads down until you could take their position.

The basic firing system for the Kalashnikov family of automatic weapons is a gas operated rotating bolt mechanism. The AK-74 is a modified AK-47: the pistol grip, receiver, bolt carrier, gas piston, stock and trigger mechanism are the same, and the rifle's overall configuration is obviously 'familial.' The bolt and chamber are shorter, due to the ammo used by the AK-74: the 5.45mm round could be described as a short, fat version of the .223.

The AK-74 also has a muzzle break which ejects excess gases to the sides of the firearm. This improves its 'pointability'—it doesn't jump around as much as it might without the muzzle break, and the weapon's recoil truly is minimized. On the bad side of this, however, is the fact that those unfortunates standing beside the persons firing the AK-74 are likely to have a ringing in their ears—and potentially powder burns on their faces—from the rifle's muzzle blast. This has been ameliorated somewhat by the design of the muzzle break itself, which has two small, asymmetrical vents dorsally, these release jets of gas upward, the two large side vents cut at a forward angle—this obviously being intended to push the majority of the blast forward, and out of the faces of one's companions.

The AK-74 has supplanted the AK-47 in the Soviet military lists. At least two versions have so far been noted—one with nonfolding wooden stock, and one with a foldable metal wire stock. Its barrel is rifled at the rate of one caliber in 26, and the rifling is beveled on its leading edge. This is a technique thought by some to reduce the rifling's 'drag' on the bullet, while retaining its ballistically beneficial influence on the bullet's centrifugal motion. The AK-74, for the record, is a selective-fire weapon having a barrel length of 15.75 inches, weighing 7.93 pounds, with a standard magazine capacity of 40 rounds (10 over the AK-47, which used longer ammo) and having an automatic rate of fire of 650rpm.

As an offshoot of the Kalashnikov family of arms is the Soviet PK Machine Gun, which is a design spinoff from the basic Kalashnikov design. This machine gun is designed for the old (circa 1891) Nagant 7.62 mm cartridge. The PK ('Pulyemet Kalashnikova') uses much of the mechanism of the infantry rifles, and borrows some parts from previously existing designs—thus it has the advantage of parts availability and the additional benefit of partaking of a well-known tradition. The Soviets followed through on this design in their established 'incremental' design methods—this same weapon appears in a variety of roles, including bipod and tripod mountings for service as light and heavy squad machine guns; with sights, stock, pistol grip and trigger removed, and with an electric firing mechanism installed, the PK becomes the coaxial gun for a tank.

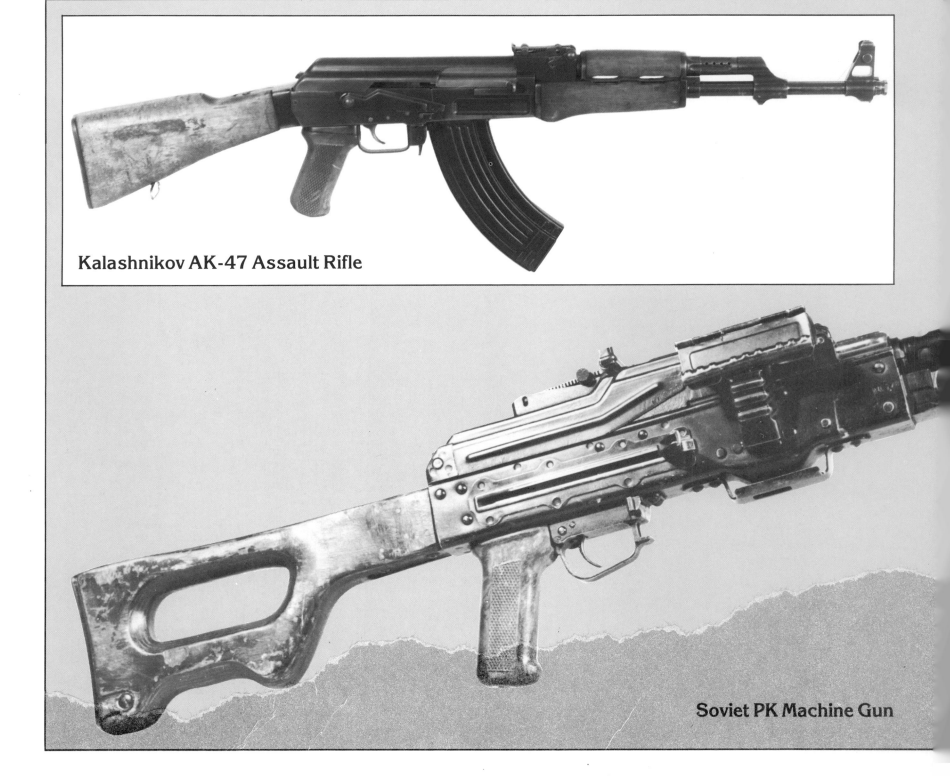

Kalashnikov AK-47 Assault Rifle

Soviet PK Machine Gun

Soviet RPK-74 Light Machine Gun

AK-74 (in action)

SWITZERLAND

SIG, of Neuhausen-Rheinfalls, Switzerland, sells by licensing agreement with other manufacturers, a variety of well-made firearms for personal, sport, military and police purposes. One of SIG's most frequent sales collaborators is JP Sauer & Son of Eckenford, Federal Republic of Germany, who also manufactures SIG firearms—also by licensing agreement.

The SIG-Sauer Model P230 Auto Pistol is a blowback semiautomatic in 7.65mm/.32 ACP, 9mm short/.380 and 9mm Police calibers. With a 3.6 inch barrel, eight round capacity and 16.2 ounce empty weight, this is a compact firearm which enjoys wide usage by many European police departments, and is popular with many private owners as well. It has a double action mechanism with a decocking lever which allows the gentle letdown of the hammer on a loaded cylinder. The firing pin is locked—to be released only at the moment that the hammer is dropped by action of the trigger.

In its smaller calibers, this pistol has a lightweight alloy frame, but in 9mm Police, the P230 has a heavier steel frame to bring the total weight (unloaded) for this version to 24.3 ounces.

Other SIG automatic pistols are the P210-6, the P226, and the super fine quality 210 de luxe, available in numbered runs and commemorative editions, with various platings and engraving styles, inlaid grips and fine finish.

The SIG-Sauer P226 is a double action semiautomatic with an optional 20 shot magazine, which, when fitted into the pistol, protrudes a bit, rather like the Beretta Model 93R machine pistol.

SIG has in times past sold this pistol in the US, under the auspices of the Maremount Corporation, which calls the pistol the SIG-Maremount P226. SIG weapons have become Swiss Army standards: SIG produces assault rifle models such as the Stgw 90, a gas operated rifle capable of selective fire and full automatic cyclic fire of approximately 750rpm.

With folding bipod and optional side-by-side magazine clips for faster reloading, the Stgw 90 is a versatile weapon. Sights are aperture rear and blade front, with luminous dots for night fire. The butt stock folds alongside the receiver when not in use. Stocks are plastic, and the weapon weighs in the neighborhood of eight pounds.

SIG also makes the Stgw 57, a full automatic rifle/machine gun with bipod, barrel cooling sleeve and fully adjustable sights.

SIG-Sauer P226 Semiautomatic Pistol

SIG-Sauer P230 SL Automatic Pistol

SIG-Sauer P210 Deluxe Automatic Pistol

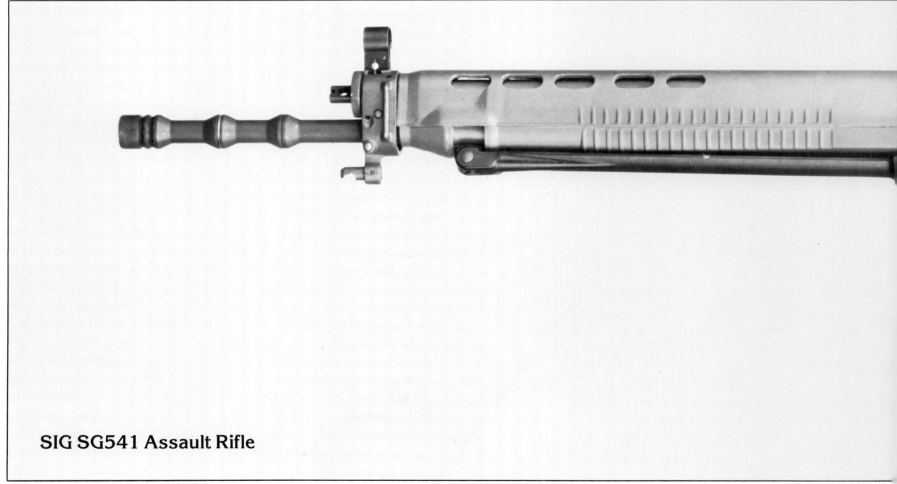

SIG SG541 Assault Rifle

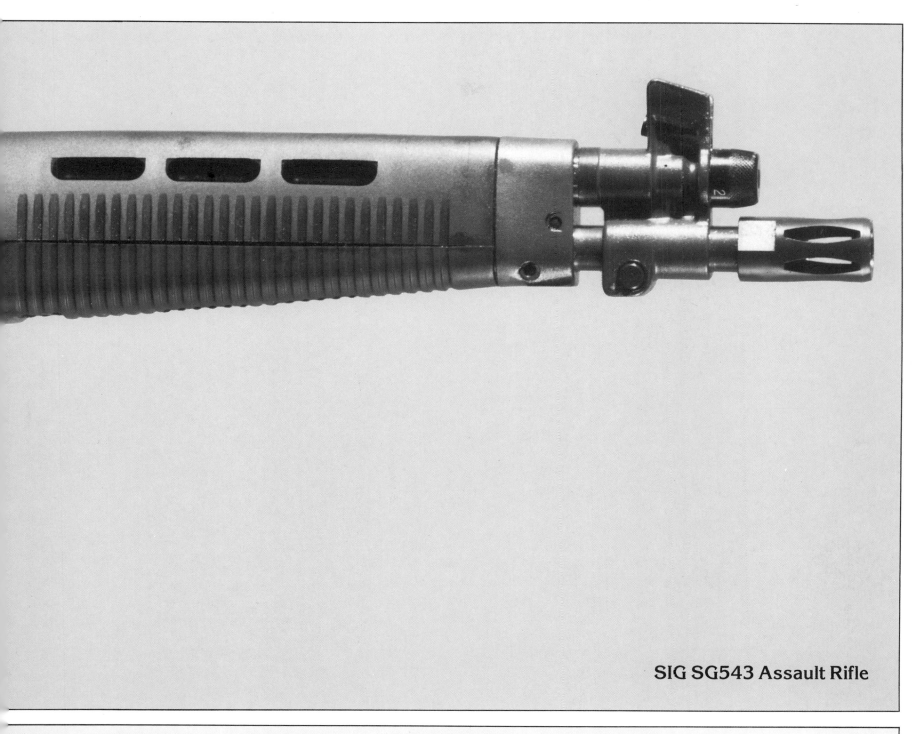

SIG SG543 Assault Rifle

UNITED KINGDOM

England has acquired a reputation for producing fine, handmade shotguns, and indeed, many British shotguns are excellent examples of the gunmaker's art. With its 'cottage industry' gunmaking background, Great Britain has a natural claim to this distinction: you got your hammers from the fellow who made good hammers, the springs from the springmaker's, the stock from the woodsmith's, the barrels from the blacksmith's and engraving from the master metalsmith's. All materials had an exact value: no scrimping, no cutting back. The type of wood and metal used amounted to the craftsman's very belief that it was the best for its particular purpose; and this belief was born of the accumulated knowledge passed down for generations—for many of these craftsfolk were doing what they were because their family had been doing that sort of thing for generations.

Times have changed, but the craft of the handmade gunmaker has changed only slightly: time, patience, precision and the utmost care are cornerstones of the handcrafter's art.

In various places on the globe, this art lives on—at the Perigini & Visini Firm of Brescia, Italy, for instance. But it is only in the British Isles that the crafting of handmade shotguns is most prevalent. We here present a few examples of the work of an excellent handcrafting firm.

W and C Scott, of Birmingham, England, possibly makes some of the finest shotguns in the world. Their extra fine grade Chatsworth model is, of course, handmade and could be called the Rolls Royce of shotguns. Smooth, firm action and a finish that only handwork can produce is the hallmark of the Chatsworth. These are classic side-by-side double barrel guns, with hammerless double trigger action and smooth yet positive break open design.

Scott does its own engraving, and produces designs and motifs that are reminiscent of the great presentation arms of the 17th and 18th centuries. Yet Scott has used a good sense of moderation, producing with these beautiful designs a firearm that carries a deep, traditional richness with a balancing sense of moderation and taste: an exquisite and nobly executed, decorative—and supremely functional—fine classic shotgun.

Stocks are checkered front, and subtly carved rear; both are buffed and polished to a soft, deep luster. The rear stock is subtly shaped and checkered, producing an effect of slightly altered standard design that on closer inspection is revealed to be a joyful, harmonious example of wood sculptor's art: no fancy designs here, but extremely fine cuts are performed. These are beautiful weapons, and will bring much pleasure to the dedicated sportsman.

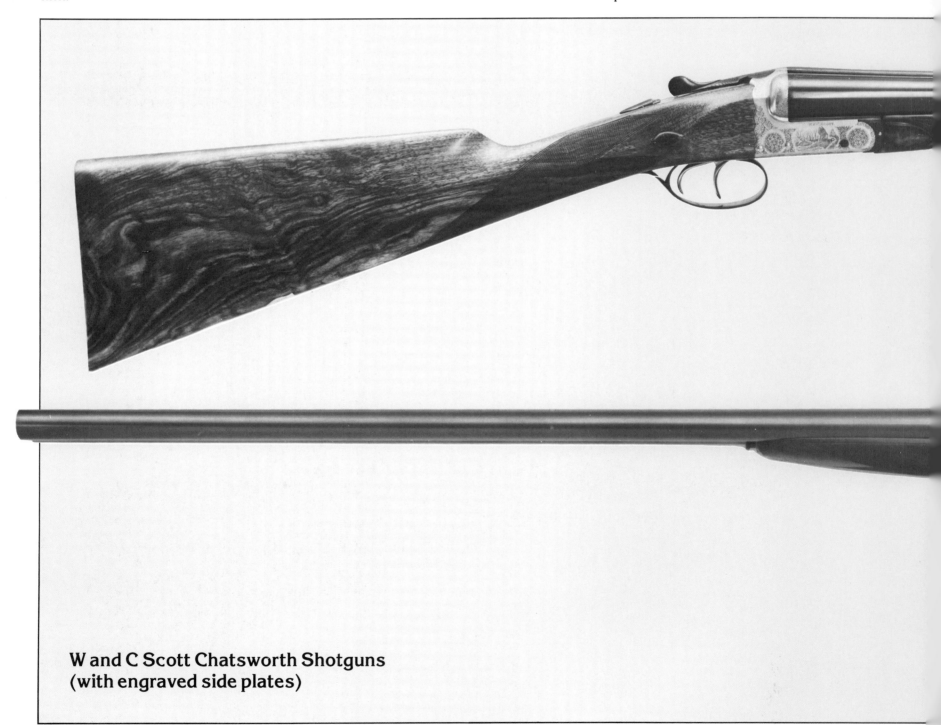

**W and C Scott Chatsworth Shotguns
(with engraved side plates)**

W and C Scott Chatsworth Shotgun
(side plate detail)

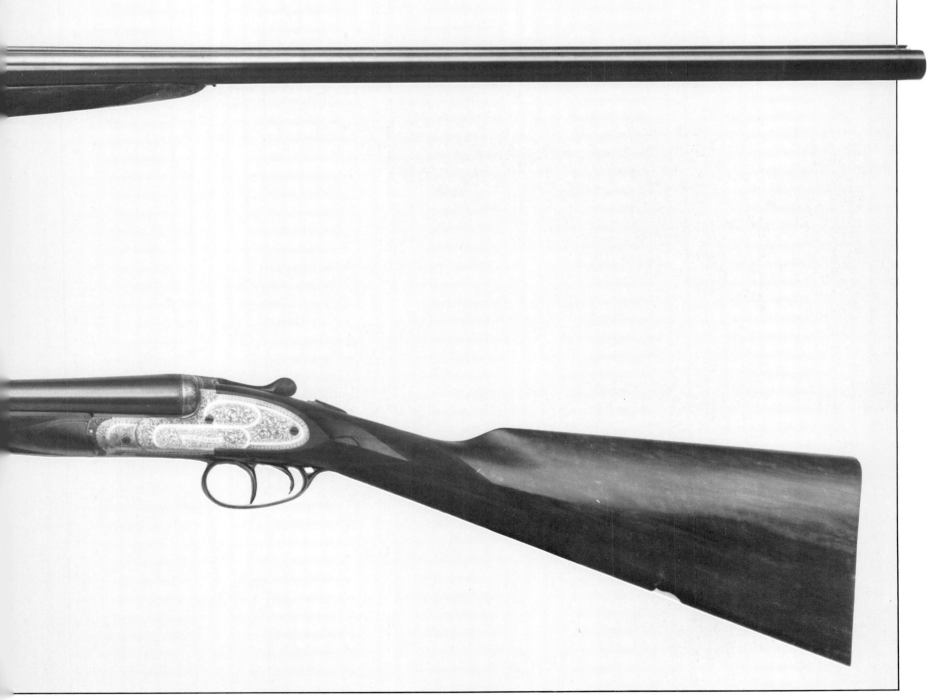

UNITED STATES

Since the United States is arguably the most diverse, and probably the most ubiquitous, producer of small arms in the modern world, this section is a sampling of the many quality firearms—both well known and not so well known—which are in production in the US.

Historically, the United States arms industry brought the world of weapons making into the modern era—witness Samuel Colt's 'assembly line' of craftsmen, and the many innovations brought to bear on arms making by Colt, Remington, Winchester, Smith & Wesson and many other American gunsmithing establishments.

Therefore, this section is intended to be an informative gloss of the current world of United States arms manufacturers. The information in this section is of necessity fragmentary, for, in a book of this size, if such information were of length comparable to that afforded manufacturers in other venues, the sheer number of models produced by American manufacturers would be guaranteed to crowd out all others. Here then is a sampler of contemporary American small arms.

Daniel Boone relied heavily on his trusty 'Kentucky Rifle'—an American innovation—as did most early frontiersmen and settlers. The constant threat of Indian attack, and the need to have a reliable means of bringing home meat for the winter led to the rapid sophistication of American small arms. American Indians often traded furs for rifles and muskets in the 18th century. Alliances with whites in their wars, and wars with the whites themselves, brought gunpowder into the lives of many tribes.

American Derringer Corporation's 15 ounce Derringer is available in calibers ranging from .22 long rifle to .44 Magnum—quite a handful! The large hinge, part of the Remington-originated 'top-hinge' barrel, also forms the Derringer's rear sight.

The Alaska Survival model of the ADC Model 4 Derringer combines .45 Colt/.410, and (rare for a pistol) .45-70. The Model 6 has a six inch barrel. Available in three models, the **Arminex** Trifire Pistol has a recoil spring guide which reduces muzzle lift.

The **Auto-Ordnance** 1911A1 Government Model Pistol is designed to the same specifications as the standard US military model made famous by Colt Industries, and is replete with slide lock (above trigger), thumb safety (at rear of receiver) and grip safety (on backstrap). The 'Thompson' logo on the slide evidences the fact that Auto-Ord-

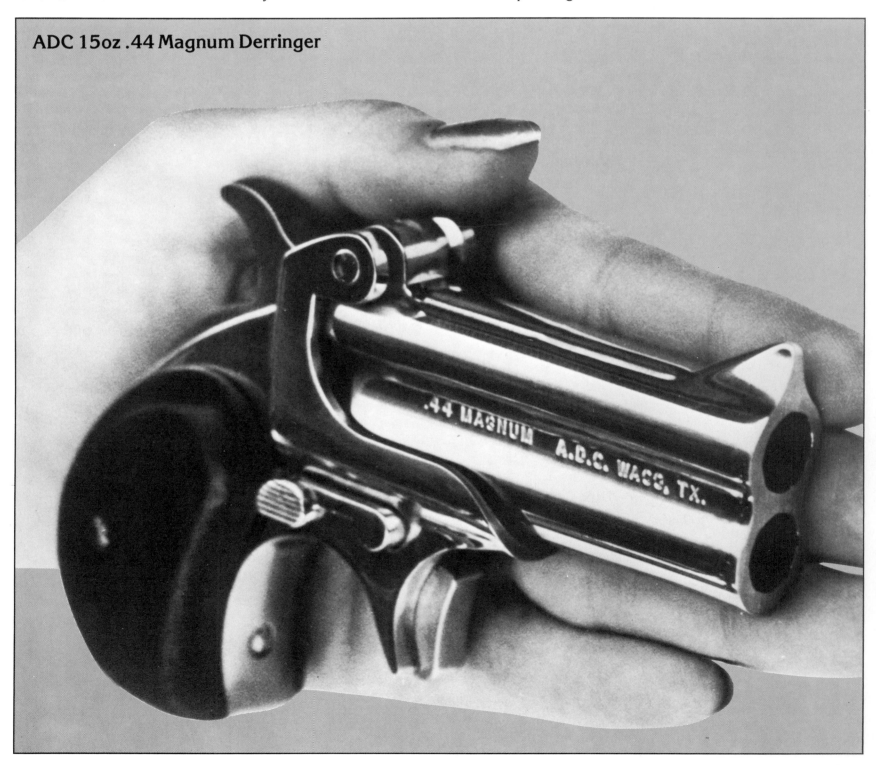

ADC 15oz .44 Magnum Derringer

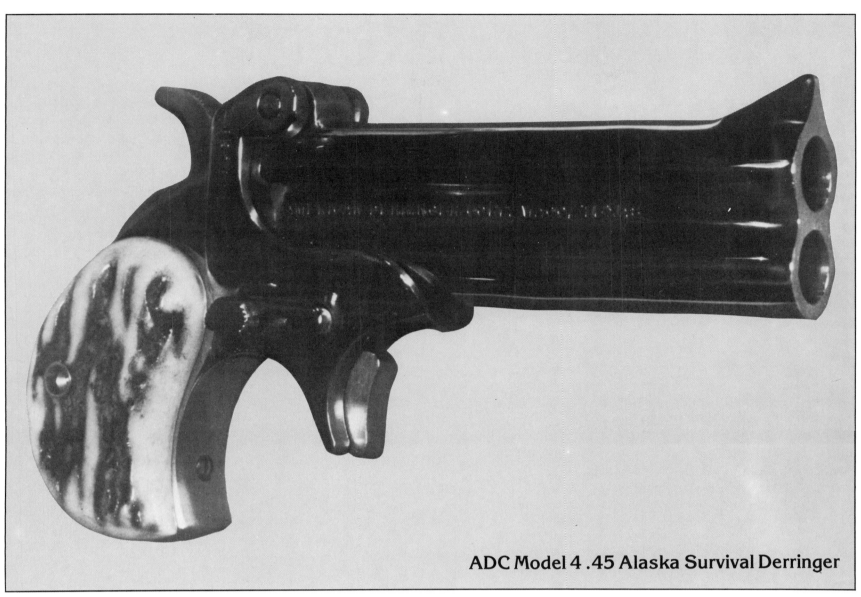

ADC Model 4 .45 Alaska Survival Derringer

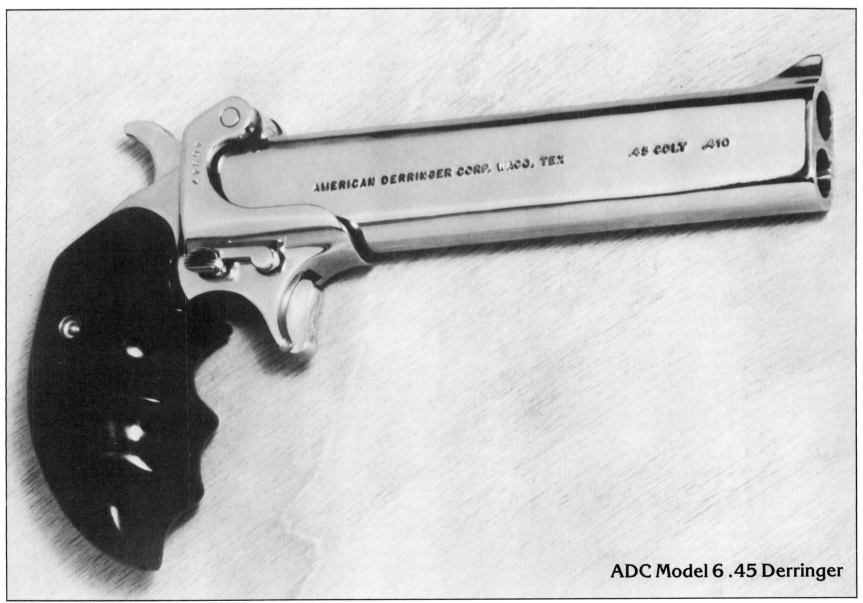

ADC Model 6 .45 Derringer

nance was founded by John Thompson and continues to produce the Thompson Submachine Gun.

The Auto-Ordnance Thompson 1927 A-1 semiautomatic carbine and the full or semiautomatic 1927 M-1 Military Assault Rifle are revivals of the originals in all but those design characteristics which have been modified to comply with contemporary firearms legislation. The A-1 is made of solid milled steel and burnished metal parts. Auto-Ordnance also makes a lightweight model—the 1C—having the same appearance but made of lightweight alloys. Both the A-1 and M-1 are .45 caliber and saw extensive World War II service in the hands of US Army soldiers. Auto-Ordnance makes a classic Roaring Twenties gangster-style 'violin case' for Thompsons, as well as a more staid FBI-style hard case; both provide space for extra clips and drum magazines, as well as handsome protection for your 'Tommygun.'

The Thompson .22 caliber 1927 A-3 semiautomatic has an optional 30-round 'banana' clip. The Thompson M-1 submachine gun is .45 caliber. The 1928 Full Auto is the classic 'Tommygun.' The A-1 Deluxe is yet another variation.

The Thompson 1927 A-1C Lightweight shaves 20 percent from the carbine's weight with no loss in performance or handling characteristics, has such Deluxe model features as traditional finger-grooved vertical foregrip, adjustable rear sight and compensator, blue-burnish finish and handsome walnut stock and grips. The Thompson A-1 in automatic mode is in an unusual configuration—without a muzzle blast compensator, which usually is needed to keep the .45 Tommygun's muzzle from 'climbing' when firing. Particular A-1s can be or-

Auto-Ordnance 1911 A1 Government Model Pistol

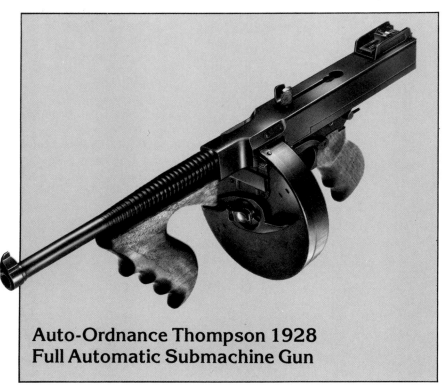

Auto-Ordnance Thompson 1928 Full Automatic Submachine Gun

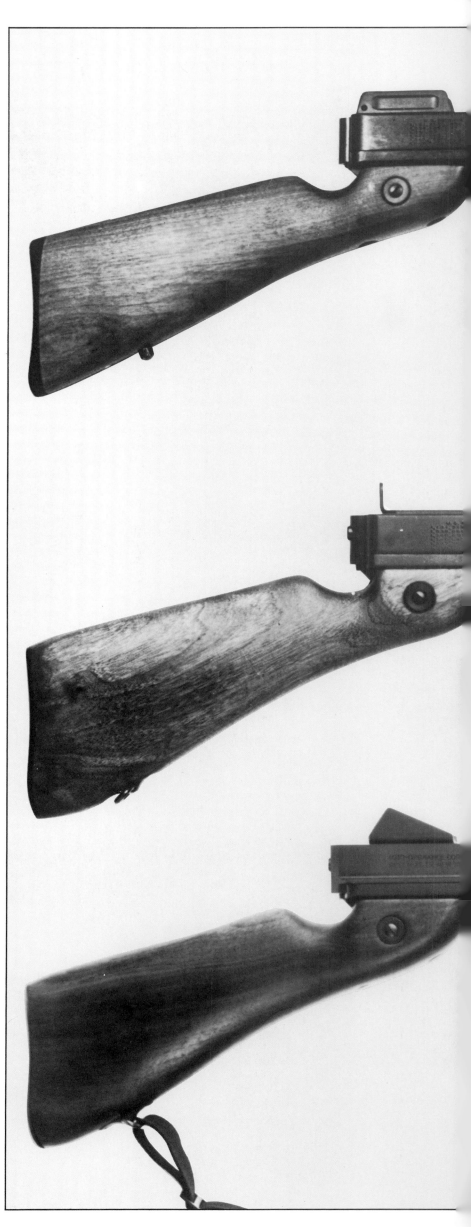

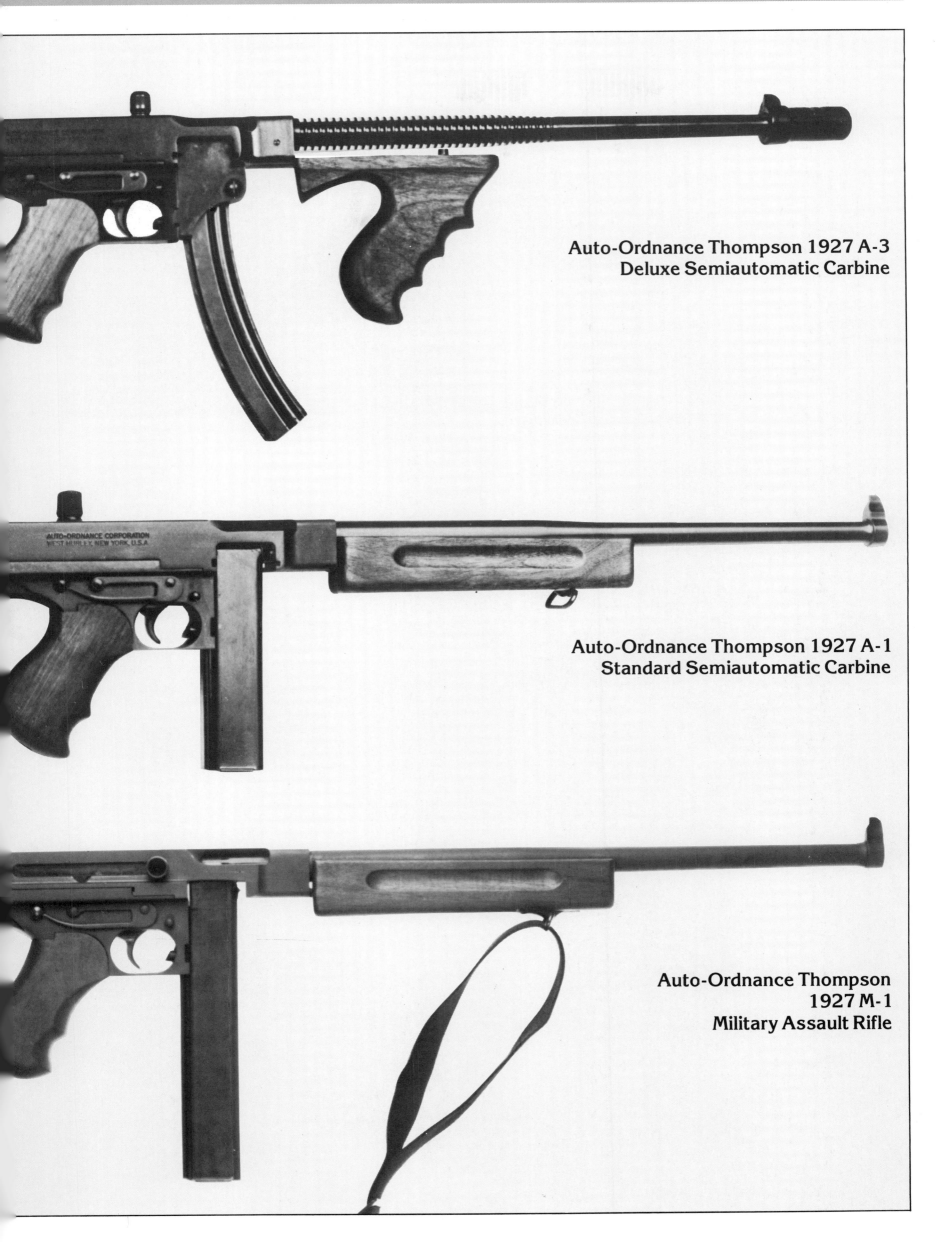

**Auto-Ordnance Thompson 1927 A-3
Deluxe Semiautomatic Carbine**

**Auto-Ordnance Thompson 1927 A-1
Standard Semiautomatic Carbine**

**Auto-Ordnance Thompson
1927 M-1
Military Assault Rifle**

dered personalized with 'pistol' styling (no butt stock), and with the Thompson drum magazine—the new models of which hold 39 rounds; the vintage originals (hard to get these days) hold 50 rounds.

Bushmaster's Combination Weapons System—a quick change choice of receivers and stocks for the Bushmaster Assault Rifle.

A-Square's .500 Hannibal Magnum is a big-game sporter with P-17 Enfield action; open, receiver or telescopic sights; heavy, well-bedded stock; and other features to ensure hunting success and shooting comfort.

The **Champlin** Bolt Action Rifle features a very strong and fast bolt action, fully adjustable trigger, choice of right or left handed action and a standard tapered octagonal or round barrel.

The **Chipmunk Manufacturing, Inc** Single Shot Rifle features two stock treatments—camouflage and natural walnut finish. This manually-cocked rifle is the perfect 'plinker.' The Chipmunk Silhouette Pistol comes equipped with a walnut stock.

The **Colt Industries** one-of-a-kind 150th Anniversary Exhibition Gun is fittingly based on Colt's most famous firearm—the Single Action Army Revolver, aka the 'Peacemaker' of the Wild West—and is chambered for .45 caliber, one of Colt's most famous calibers. Starting with the grips, engravings feature the young seaman Sam Colt whittling the prototype from which the modern revolver would evolve; a head portrait of Samuel Colt on the receiver flange; the Colt firearms' 'rampant colt' logo on the cylinder; and on the Buntline-length barrel, a portrait of Colt's Python Ultimate revolver, one of Colt's most recent designs, and a portrait of Colt's Officers ACP, a

Champlin Custom Crown Rifle

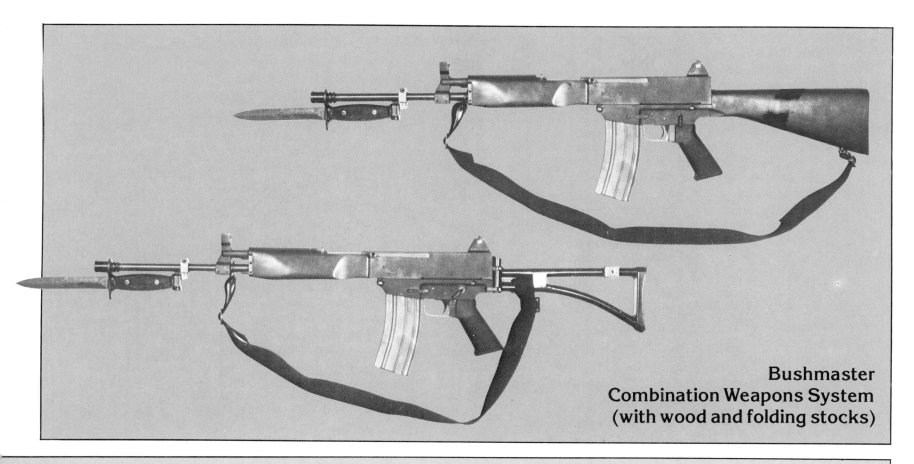

**Bushmaster
Combination Weapons System
(with wood and folding stocks)**

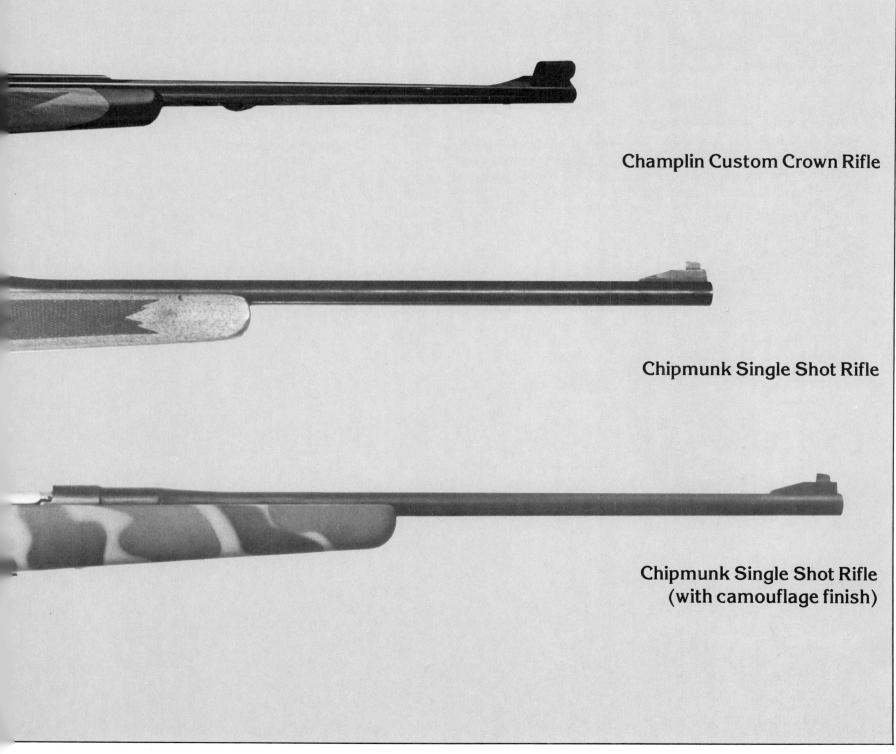

Champlin Custom Crown Rifle

Chipmunk Single Shot Rifle

**Chipmunk Single Shot Rifle
(with camouflage finish)**

contemporary version of the famed 1911 Government model. The Colt single action would just let you pull that trigger until doomsday, without firing a shot—it had to be cocked by hand, first. The single action eventually did give way to the hammer-cocking trigger mechanism of the double action, and they made films of the good old days.

Two highly polished stainless steel pistols were offered in a matched set, each bearing the logo 'Double Diamond' to commemorate Colt's 150th anniversary. The set is comprised of a six inch barrel .357 Magnum Colt Python Ultimate Revolver and a Colt Officers ACP, bearing matching serial numbers and cased with a 150th anniversary medallion in a custom-fitted case. Both pistols have rosewood grips. The Python is considered to be one of the world's finest production revolvers. Colt's Gold Cup National Match is based on the 1911 Government model, but is equipped with an Accurizor barrel, adjustable rear sight and adjustable trigger stop. The Colt Mark IV Series 80 Government model 1911A1 has an Accurizor barrel and is available in three calibers.

The Colt Peacekeeper is a medium frame .357 Magnum revolver with a non-glare matte blue combat finish, Colt 'gripper' combat grips and the choice of either four inch or six inch barrel length. The Colt Python .357 Magnum revolver is available in barrel lengths of 2.5 inches, four inches, six inches and eight inches. Colt's Mustang 380 is .5 inch shorter and .5 inch less in height than the standard 380 Government model, and can be tucked away 'as neatly as most .25 autos.' Limited edition Mustang 380s come with their own spec sheet. Spec sheets and Historical Letters on various Colt firearms are available from the company.

**Colt Agent
.38 Special Revolver**

Colt Python .357 Magnum 6" and 2.5" Revolvers

Colt Peacekeeper .357 Magnum Revolver

Colt MK IV Series 80 Government Model Pistol

Engravings, ivory grips and special finishes are provided by the Colt Custom Shop, which offers various products and services to customers who wish to personalize and adorn their firearms. The Colt Custom Shop has produced many custom historical and commemorative editions for both individual and institutional customers.

Colt's 150th Anniversary Engraving Sampler was available on any current blue or nickel finish gun only during Colt's 150th anniversary year, 1986. It featured custom ivory grips and the four most popular engraving styles in Colt's history—Henshaw, Nimschke, Helfricht and Colt Contemporary—blended tastefully, with each style devoted to a particular part of the gun.

Examples of the decorative art of the Colt Custom Shop include Colt's American-style Scroll engraving, and Oakleaf-style Scroll. The .357 Magnum Python revolver is available with, among other Colt engraving treatments, Colt's 'American-style.' Available to owners of both new and older Colt models is the Colt Historical Letter on the gun owners' Colt weapon's background as an individual firearm. The Colt stainless steel .357 Magnum revolver features barrel lengths of four inch or six inch, adjustable rear sight and moderate price tag. The Colt Detective Special with its three inch barrel has been a favorite for plainclothes policemen since 1927. Of the same design as the Detective Special, Colt's Agent model features an aluminum alloy frame and matte blue finish. The small frame of Colt's Diamondback fits most shooters' hands.

Colt's Model AR 15 rifle is available in a number of high velocity calibers. The AR 15A2 H-Bar and the AR 15A2 Sportster are both de-

**Colt Diamondback
.38 Special Revolver**

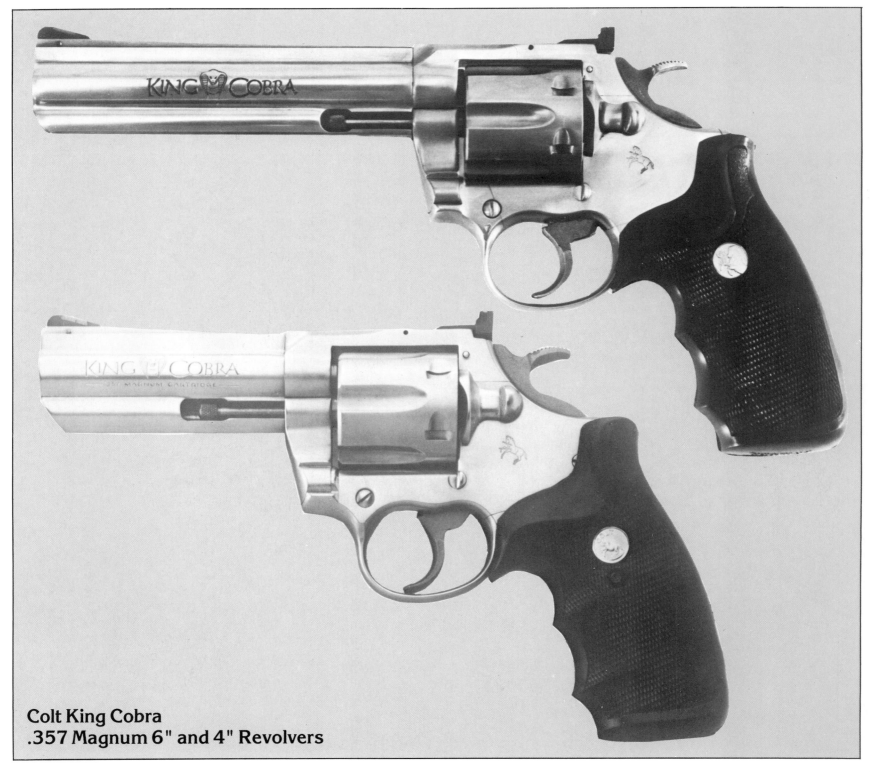

**Colt King Cobra
.357 Magnum 6" and 4" Revolvers**

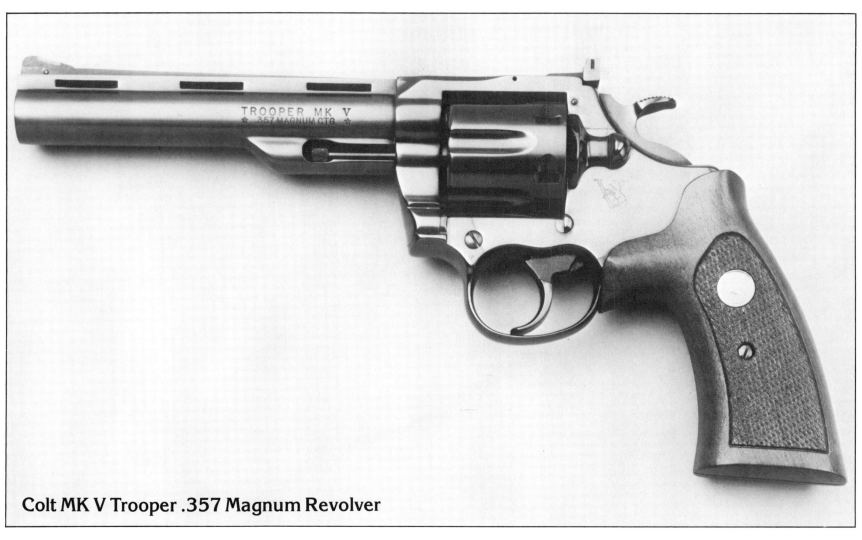

Colt MK V Trooper .357 Magnum Revolver

Colt MK V Lawman .357 Magnum Revolver

Colt M16A2 Assault Rifle

Colt Delta H-Bar Rifle

Colt M203 40mm Grenade Launching Rifle

rived from the M16, which, with target sights, heavy target barrel and case deflector for left handed shooters, makes a very good sporter.

The M16A1 has a seldom heard-of carbine version. The simplicity of design and construction which is at the heart of the M16A1 is responsible for its operating excellence. The M16A1s saw action in the Grenada invasion of 1983, the Beirut crisis and in Vietnam.

The Colt M16A1 Automatic Rifle was standard US Armed Forces issue for years, but was replaced by the M16A2 automatic three shot burst/semiautomatic model which is issued in the handy Commando Carbine configuration (with 16 inch barrel and folding stock) and also as an 'H-Bar' (heavy barrel) AR15 Sporter civilian model. The M16A2 Commando Carbine sees a lot of US military guard duty.

In their famous roles as the Lone Ranger and Tonto, Clayton Moore and Jay Silverheels brandished Colts. The Lone Ranger's metaphysically-inspired silver bullets and incognito guardianship of the unarmed and defenseless added medieval depth to the concept of 'Colt justice.' Colt enjoyed its sesquicentennial last year, with a corporate outpouring of special commemorative models. Part of Colt's long, 150-year groundbreaking history is the vast importance of Colt firearms in the pre-Civil War and post-Civil War settling of the US, in the Civil War itself, the Spanish-American War, World War I, World War II, Korea and in every phase of sport shooting since the early 1800s. American troops wielded Colt M16s during the Vietnam War, in Grenada and during training exercises in Europe.

Especially respected and feared by the Viet Cong during the Vietnam War were Long Range Patrol units armed with Colt M16s.

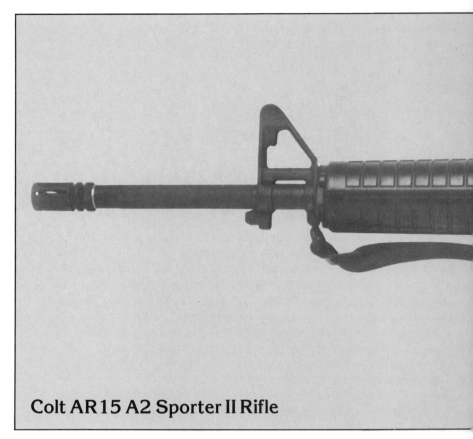

Colt AR15 A2 Sporter II Rifle

Colt 9mm Submachine Gun

Colt M231 Port Firing Weapon

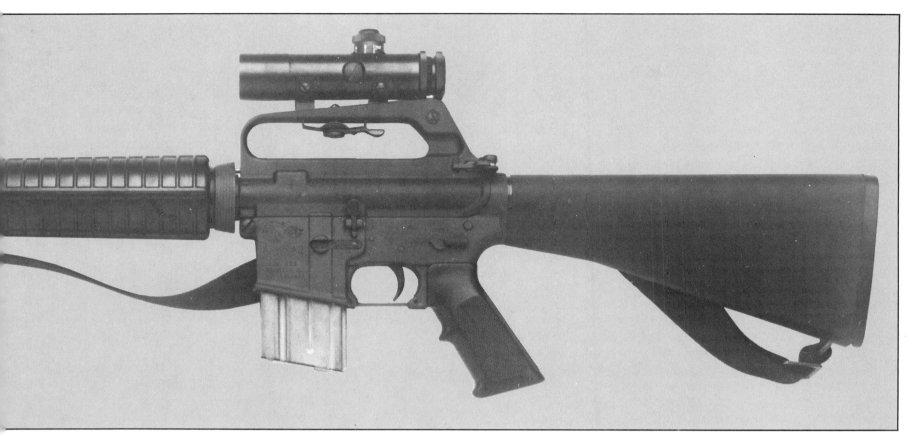

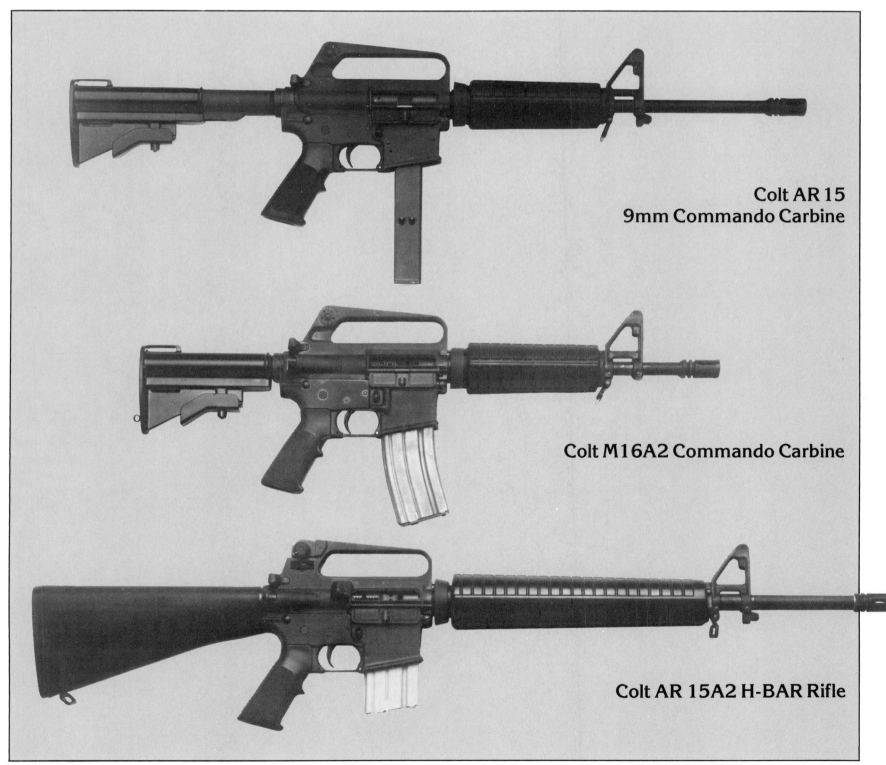

Colt AR 15
9mm Commando Carbine

Colt M16A2 Commando Carbine

Colt AR 15A2 H-BAR Rifle

Soldiers in US Army war games use, on occasion, the MILES (Multiple Integrated Laser Engagement System)-equipped M-16 to 'shoot' their enemies without harming them—quite an advance over squirt guns and ketchup. The M-16A2 seems likely to uphold the M-16 military tradition.

The **Coonan Arms** autoloader translates more of its .357 Magnum power to muzzle velocity than most other autos, due to its improved slide locking mechanism.

Dan Wesson's .357 Magnum revolver has quick-change auxiliary barrels and the Dan Wesson SuperMagnum has a compound barrel structure. Dan Wesson pistols feature the 'Pistol Pac' system of quickly interchangeable barrel lengths. The Dan Wesson .357/.375 Super-Magnum has ventilated barrel shroud, which greatly reduces the chance for heat distortion. Dan Wesson Arms also offers DW System set and accessories.

Detonics' Combat Master in .45 ACP is more compact than the standard 1911A1 model pistol, yet retains a good weight-to-recoil ratio. Detonics also offers a reloading kit.

The **FIE** Texas Ranger Revolver is available with special custom grips—the Texas Ranger comes with standard hand-rubbed walnut grips. The FIE D86 Derringer features an automatic internal transfer bar firing system for safety, and a built-in spare ammo compartment. Reproductions of the famous Colt single action six shooter, the FIE Texas Ranger and Little Ranger revolvers feature floating firing pins, hammer block safety mechanisms and manufacture to modern standards. They are available in .22 short, long or long rifle, and .22

**Detonics Combat Master
.45 Automatic Pistol**

Coonan Arms .357 Magnum Automatic Pistol

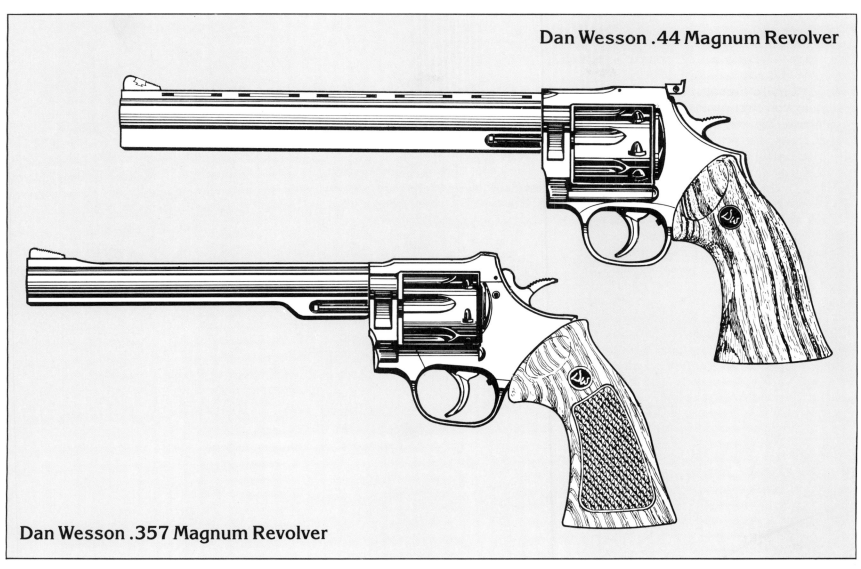

Dan Wesson .44 Magnum Revolver

Dan Wesson .357 Magnum Revolver

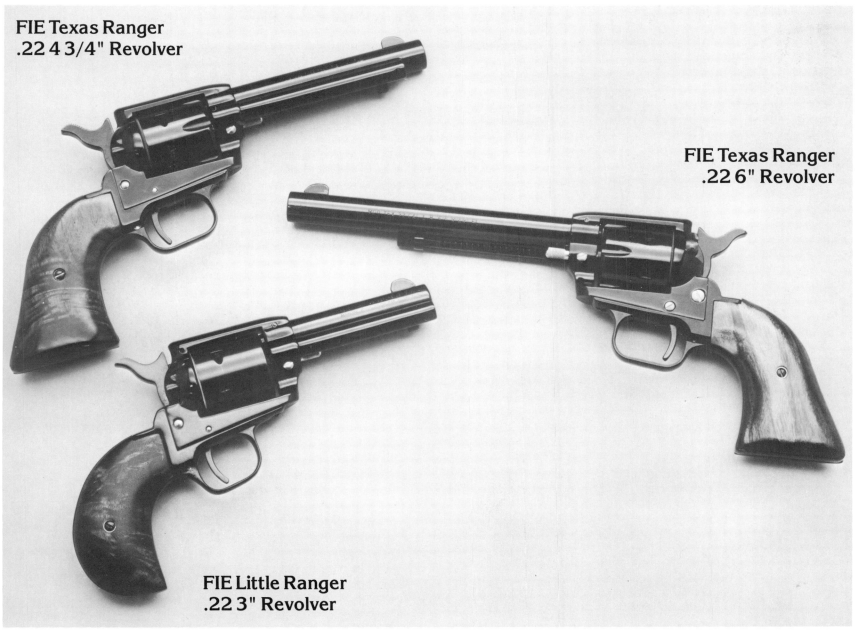

FIE Texas Ranger
.22 4 3/4" Revolver

FIE Texas Ranger
.22 6" Revolver

FIE Little Ranger
.22 3" Revolver

Magnum calibers. The Little Ranger has a 3.25 inch barrel, and the Texas Ranger has optional barrel lengths. The FIE Titan II is a compact, easy-to-take-down .22 long rifle autoloader with a 10 shot magazine capacity.

Dick Casull's **Freedom Arms** manufactures the .454 Casull (.45 Magnum) Revolver, which has supplanted the Smith & Wesson .44 Magnum as the world's most powerful handgun. Freedom Arms also manufactures the very compact Mini Revolver in .22 long rifle, Magnum and percussion models. Available from the manufacturer is a Mini Revolver concealing belt buckle holster and engraving for both the .454 Casull and the Mini Revolver. Freedom Arms offers, among other accessories, a tilt-top pistol holster .454 Casull Revolver.

Hopkins & Allen's elegant and classic percussion cap and flintlock rifles include the Buggy Rifle, a light, fast 'brush country' underhammer; the Deerstalker, a heavy bore underhammer; the Plainsman, with windage-adjustable sights and a solid brass rib barrel; the Schuetzen, a hand-crafted match grade target rifle; the Target Rifle, designed for use at a bench rest; and the Tryon Trailblazer, a reproduction of the George Tryon Plainsrifle of the 1820s. The finely designed Hopkins & Allen Double Barrel Percussion Shotgun features hook breach design. Hopkins & Allen have long been manufacturers of fine firearms.

Ithaca Gun Company's Model 37 Featherlight pump shotgun line includes the Field Grade Vent, the Deluxe Vent and the Model 37 Ultralight. Ithaca's LAPD model has an 18.5 inch barrel, and is a popular law enforcement weapon. The DSPS II and the M&P II both feature a five round magazine and a variety of chokes. Ithaca's Handgrip Shot-

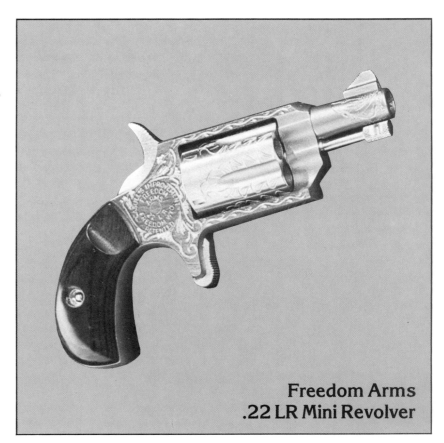

Freedom Arms
.22 LR Mini Revolver

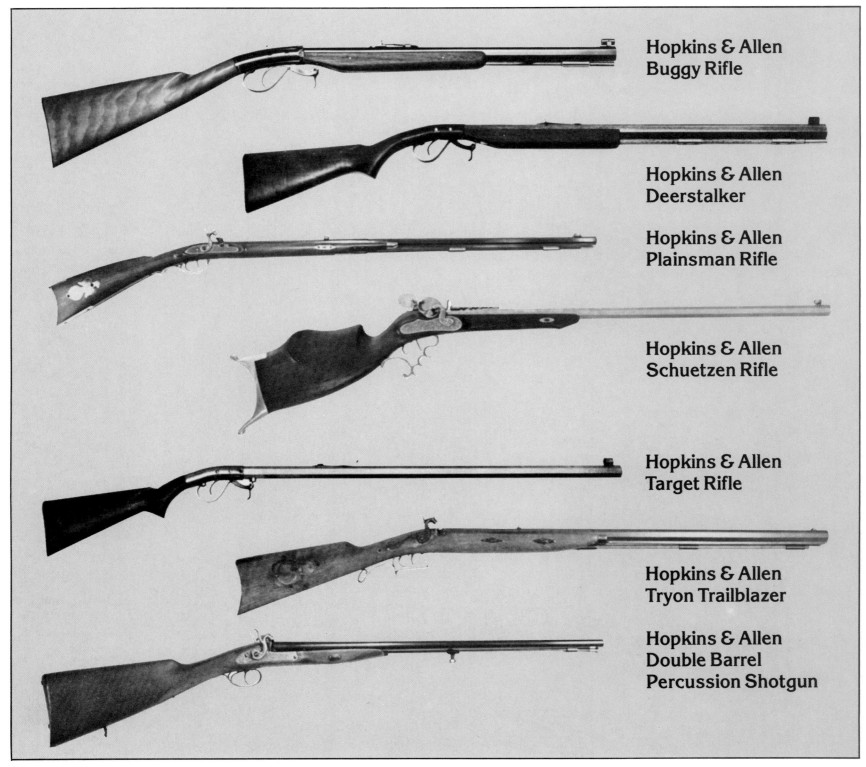

Hopkins & Allen
Buggy Rifle

Hopkins & Allen
Deerstalker

Hopkins & Allen
Plainsman Rifle

Hopkins & Allen
Schuetzen Rifle

Hopkins & Allen
Target Rifle

Hopkins & Allen
Tryon Trailblazer

Hopkins & Allen
Double Barrel
Percussion Shotgun

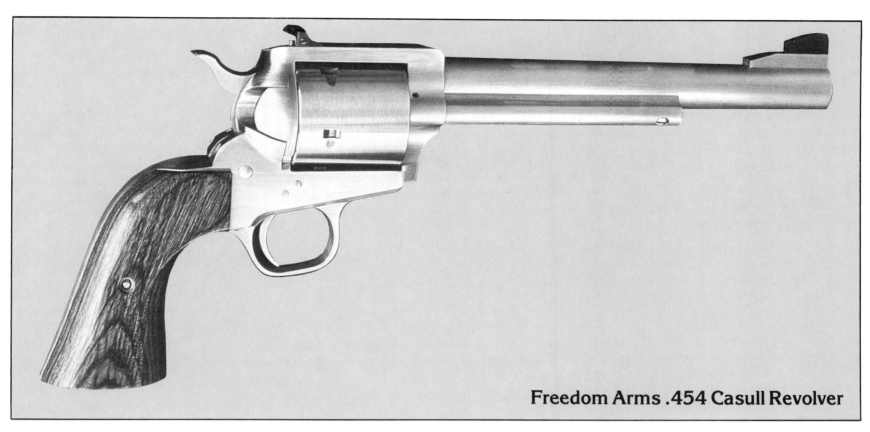

Freedom Arms .454 Casull Revolver

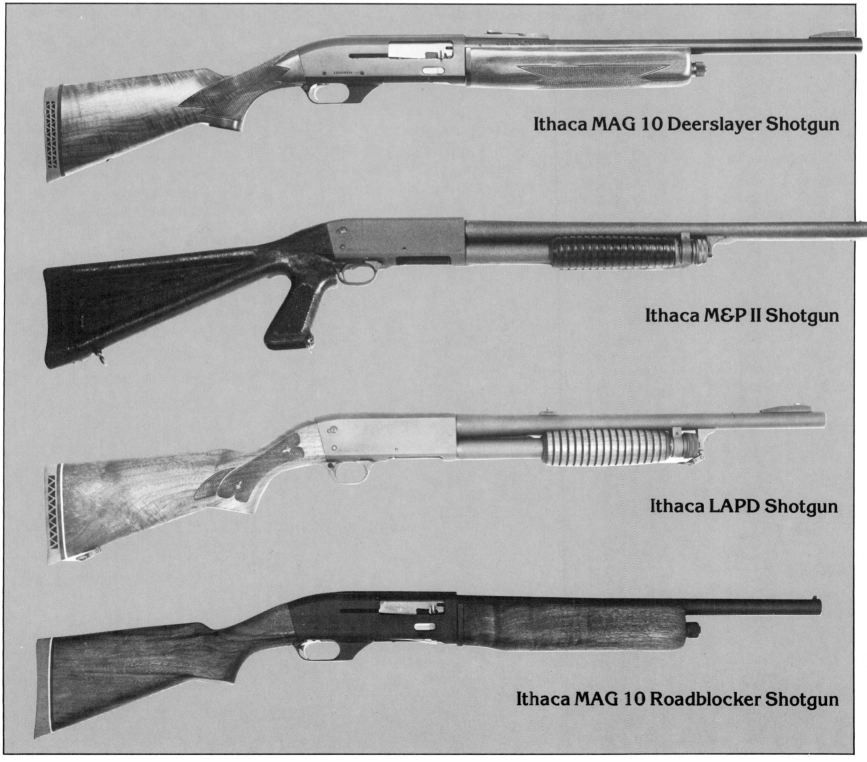

Ithaca MAG 10 Deerslayer Shotgun

Ithaca M&P II Shotgun

Ithaca LAPD Shotgun

Ithaca MAG 10 Roadblocker Shotgun

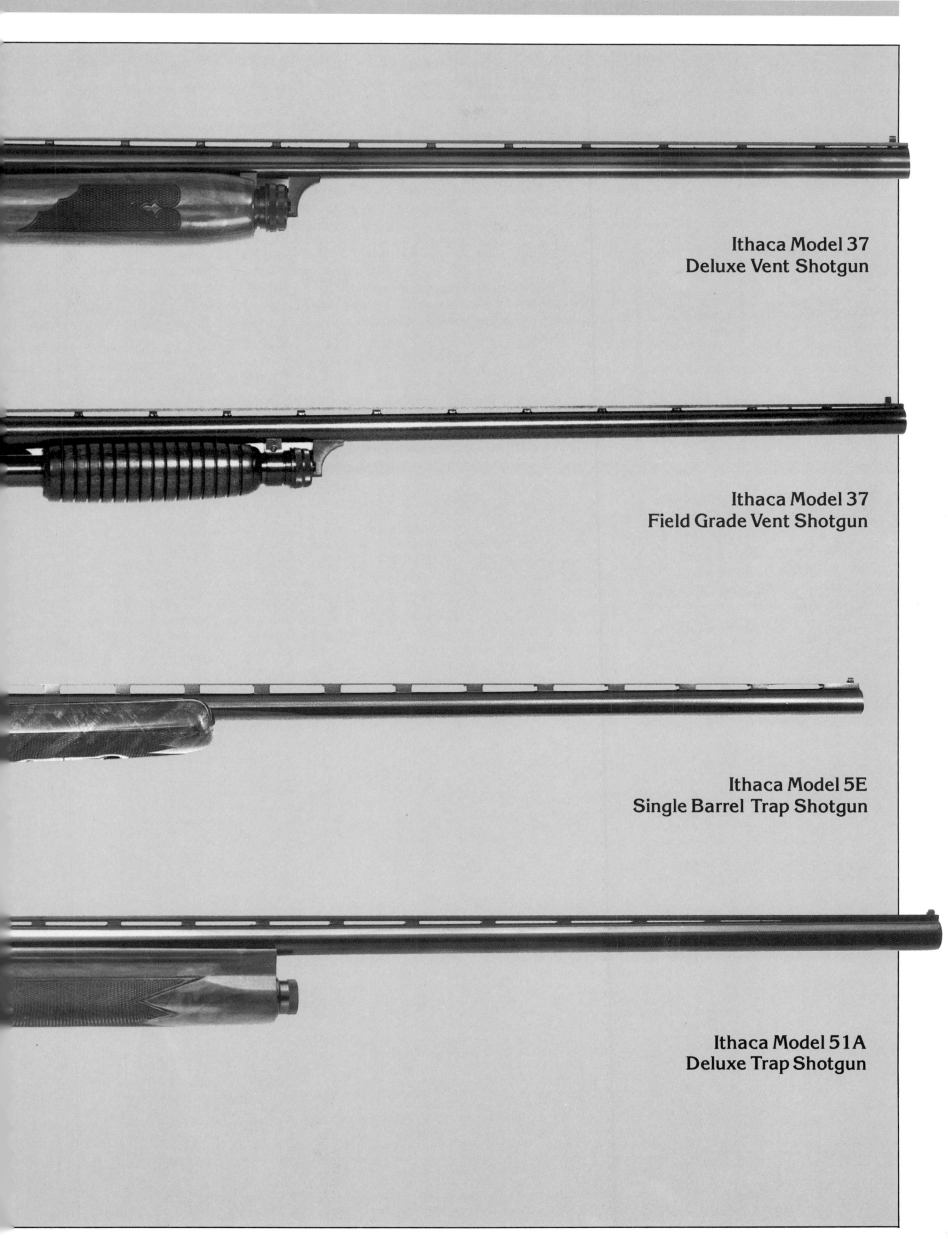

Ithaca Model 37
Deluxe Vent Shotgun

Ithaca Model 37
Field Grade Vent Shotgun

Ithaca Model 5E
Single Barrel Trap Shotgun

Ithaca Model 51A
Deluxe Trap Shotgun

gun carries five rounds in its magazine and features maneuverability and two optional barrel lengths.

Ithaca Model 51A semiautomatics include the Deluxe Trap and the Turkey Gun, both of which are 12 gauge and carry three rounds. Ithaca Mag 10 semiautomatics are loaded with three rounds of 10 gauge knockdown power; in a bore favored by the legendary 'Shotgun Gibbs' of Wild West fame, Ithaca's design reduces recoil and delivers all the 10 gauge wallop to the business end. The Mag 10 Standard Vent, the Standard Plain and the Deerslayer—equipped with adjustable rifle sights—are three of the Mag 10 models.

The Mag 10 Camo Vent and the Mag 10 Deluxe Vent are high grade sporting shotguns. The Mag 10 Supreme has a 32 inch barrel; the Mag 10 Roadblocker has a 22 inch barrel and holds three rounds; and the Ithaca 5E Grade Single Barrel Trap Shotgun is one of two specially crafted Ithaca collector's items, in 12 gauge, with full choke and barrel lengths of 32 inches or 34 inches.

Marlin makes, and has historically made, some of the sleekest, slickest and handiest rifles in the business. Three Marlins which are based on the famous Marlin side ejection, solid receiver lever action design are: the .45-70 Government 1895 SS, the .444 Marlin 444 SS and the .356 Winchester 336 ER. Marlin Semiautomatic Carbines include the New Model 45 in .45 ACP and the Model 9 in 9mm Luger. Marlin lever actions are available in .375 Winchester, as well as a number of other calibers. Other Marlins are the Marlin Model 990 .22 semiautomatic and the Marlin Golden 39A .22 lever action.

More Marlin models are the Model 782 seven shot .22 Magnum; the Model 783 12 shot .22 Magnum; the Model 25M seven shot .22 Rim-

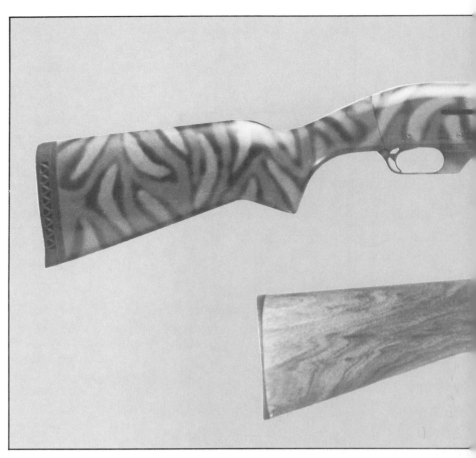

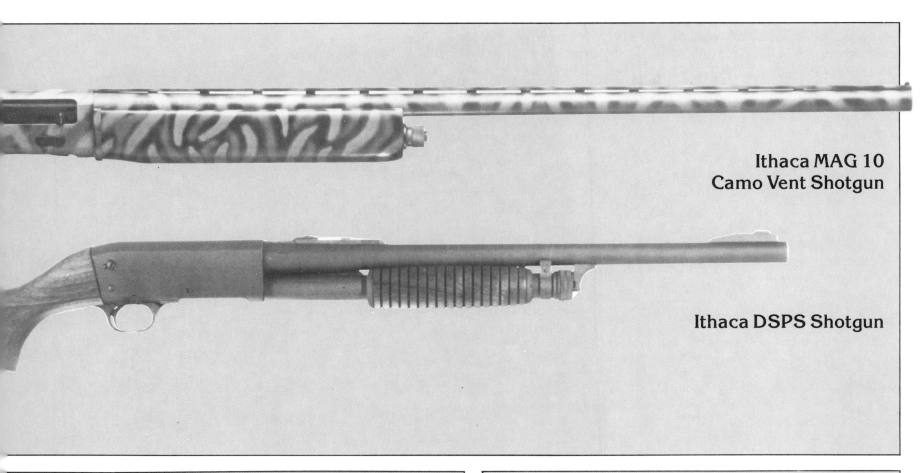

Ithaca MAG 10
Camo Vent Shotgun

Ithaca DSPS Shotgun

Marlin Model 336ER
Lever Action Rifle

Marlin Model 783
Bolt Action Rifle

Marlin Model 45
Semiautomatic Carbine

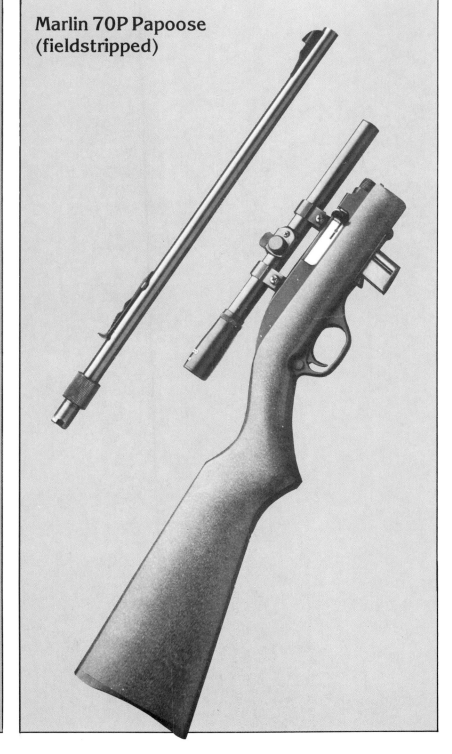

Marlin 70P Papoose
(fieldstripped)

fire; the Model 70P semiautomatic; the Model 70 semiautomatic; and the Model 995 semiautomatic. The Marlin 70P 'Papoose' breaks down easily for portability.

Mossberg & Sons, Inc's Law Enforcement/Security Model 500 shotguns feature six to nine round capacity, an anti-jam mechanism and three bore sizes. The Mossberg Persuader has optional short and long barrels. Mossberg's LE/SM Model 3000s also have the anti-jam feature.

Mossberg's Model 712 Accu II and 712 Slugster feature Mossberg's 'steel to steel' action; the Regal 712 and Regal 500 feature fine finish work; and the Model 1000 Super comes in 12 and 20 gauge.

Mowrey Muzzleloaders feature curly maple stocks—as their ancestors often did. Mowrey reproduces the glories of famous classic muzzleloader designs. Examples of Mowrey's fine craftsmanship and precision care include the Mowrey IN30 conical bullet rifle; the Plains Rifle, a repro of an Ethan Allen design; the Rocky Mountain Hunter with adjustable sights; and the handfitted, boxlock Squirrel Rifle. Mowrey's Muzzleloading Shotgun features fine craftsmanship and materials.

The **Navy Arms** Hawken Rifle is made for left handers; and the Navy Arms Morse Muzzleloader features precision rifling and a 'pre-straightened' barrel for accuracy. Navy Arms' Morse Muzzleloading Shotgun is a fine reprise.

The **Raven Arms** Model MP-25 Pistol features walnut or simulated ivory grips, nickel, blue or chrome finish, and individual testing on all pistols before their sale to the public.

Raven Arms MP-25 Pistol

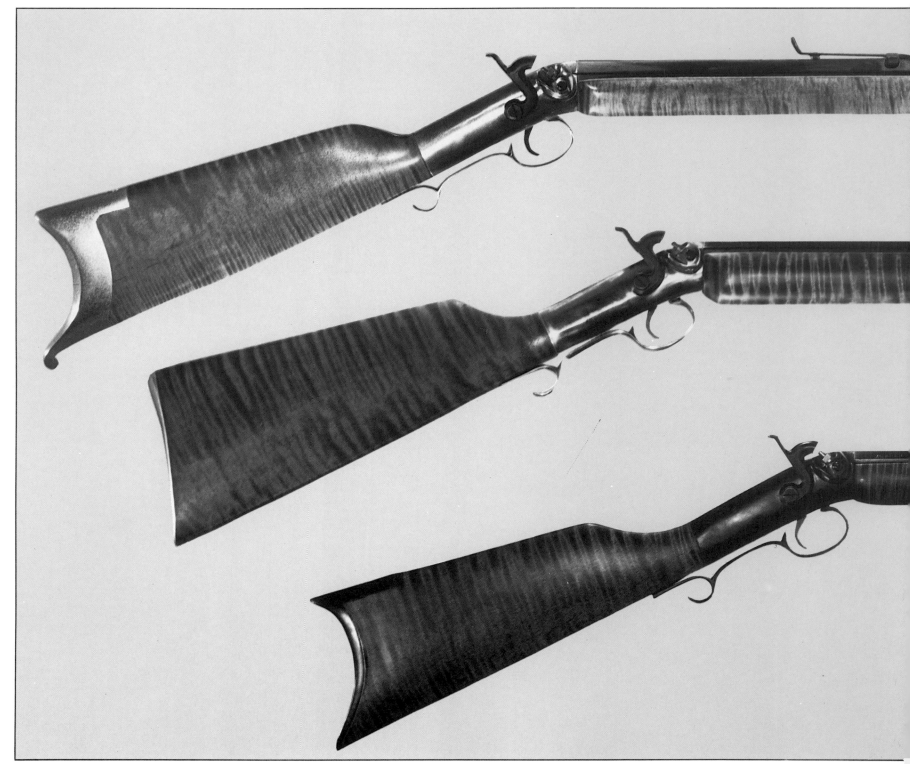

Mossberg Model 500 Shotgun

Mossberg Model 3000 Shotgun

Mossberg Model 1500 Shotgun

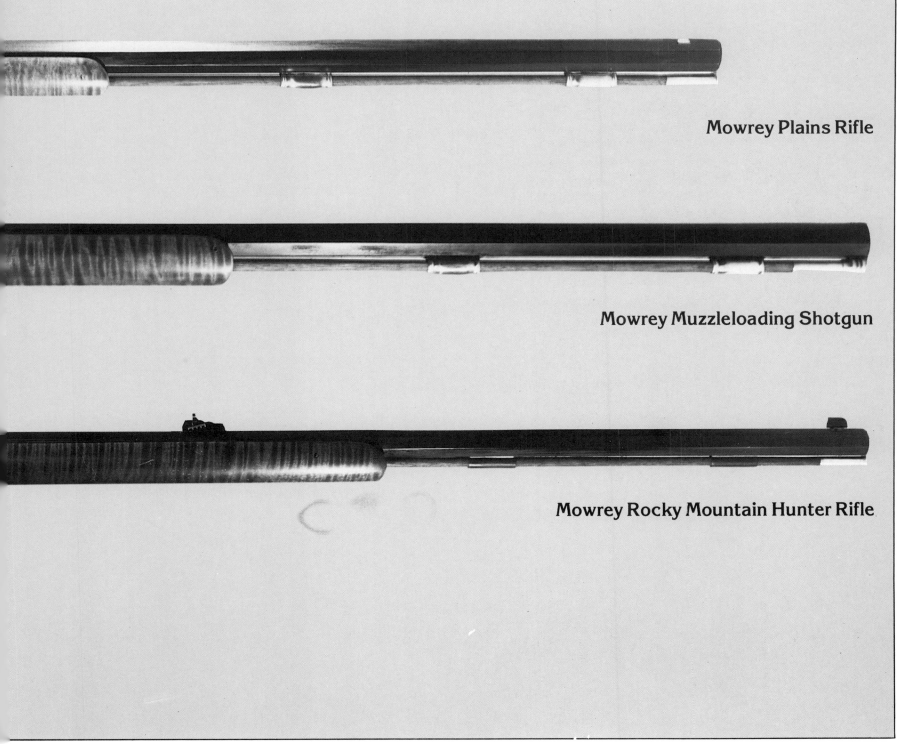

Mowrey Plains Rifle

Mowrey Muzzleloading Shotgun

Mowrey Rocky Mountain Hunter Rifle

One of the most prolific, popular and longest-lived US firearms manufacturers is the **Remington Arms Company.** Started at the beginning of the nineteenth century by Eliphalet Remington and continued by his son Eliphalet Jr, Remington began its history with the manufacture of parts and barrels for rifles, and eventually began to manufacture custom rifles for select customers. At the time of the Civil War, Remington was in full production, and, for a brief period, branched out into the manufacture of pistols. The proud Remington name continues, now associated with the illustrious firm of Du Pont.

The classic Remington Model 4 autoloading rifle is available with Monte Carlo stock. The legendary Remington 700 series Mountain Rifle is available in a wide variety of big game calibers, and has newly had its weight pared by way of a slenderer stock and tapered barrel. The Remington Model 7600 Pump Action Rifle features the slick, handsome Remington pump mechanism, and the Remington Model 4 Autoloader is another outstanding Remington sports rifle.

The .22 caliber, five shot Remington Sportsman 581 is an almost archetypal 'plinking' rifle, and has killed many a tin can. The Remington Sportsman 74 autoloader's gas metering system reduces recoil; the Sportsman 76 pump action is fast and smooth; the Sportsman 581S is chambered for .22 caliber. Remington Model 700 is a bolt action and Model 6 is a pump.

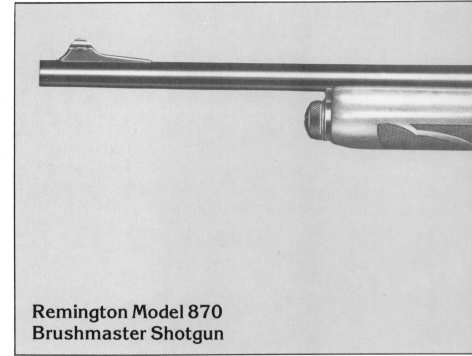

**Remington Model 870
Brushmaster Shotgun**

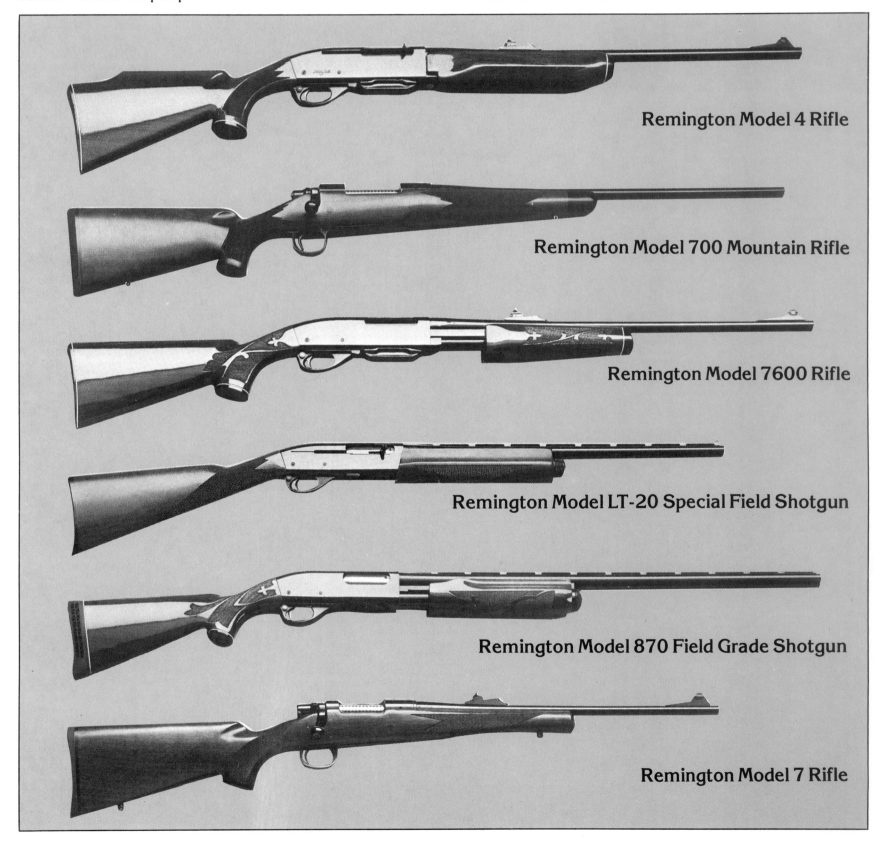

Remington Model 4 Rifle

Remington Model 700 Mountain Rifle

Remington Model 7600 Rifle

Remington Model LT-20 Special Field Shotgun

Remington Model 870 Field Grade Shotgun

Remington Model 7 Rifle

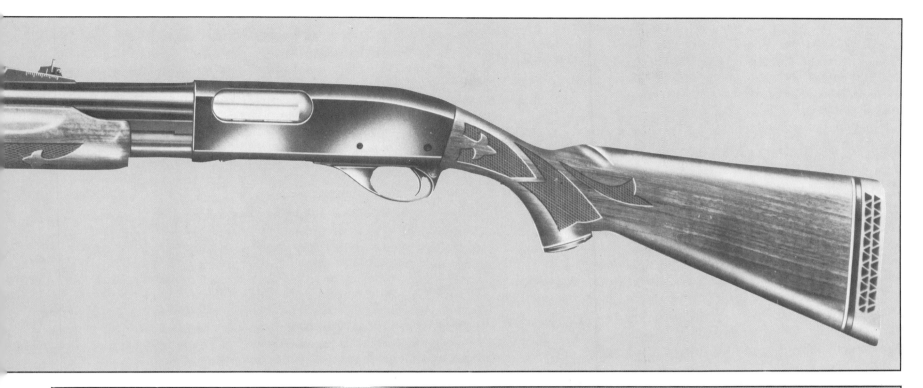

Remington Model 870 Wingmaster Shotgun

Remington Model 7400 Rifle

Remington Model 700 BDL Rifle

Remington Model 6 Rifle

Remington Model 1100 LT-20 Youth Shotgun

Remington Model 700 Varmint Special Rifle

Remington's Model 870 Pump Action Shotguns feature the famous 'Rem' interchangeable choke tubes, 'vibra-honed' parts for smooth operation, good looks and double action bars for quick repeating fire. Remington's Model 1100 automatics feature a recoil-reducing gas metering system, right-and left-handed versions, 7 styles and extraordinarily fine finish.

Durable, rugged and versatile, the Remington 870 series of automatics include the 870 Field Grade, the Wingmaster, the Special Field, the Brushmaster and the Youth Gun. Model 870 receivers are milled from solid blocks of ordnance-grade steel. The Remington 1100 TA Trap model with Monte Carlo stock, the Model 870 Competition Trap gun, the 1100 SA Skeet model in right- or lefthanded versions and the Model 870 Brushmaster Deer Gun with rifle sights are excellent, craftsmanly firearms.

The Remington Arms Company not only makes fine firearms, but also supplies shooters with a wide variety of ammunition.

Remington's interchangable 'Rem' Chokes give Remington Model 1100 and 870 shotguns added versatility; Remington's widely-known rimfire cartridges and Remington-Peters shot shells are available in an antique-style box and, among many Remington offerings for the care and maintenance of firearms, the company offers its Rem Oil lubricant and rust protector.

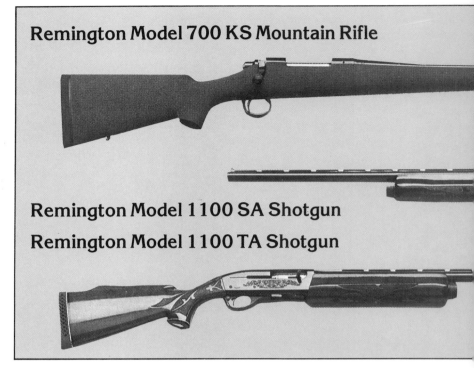

Remington Model 700 KS Mountain Rifle

Remington Model 1100 SA Shotgun
Remington Model 1100 TA Shotgun

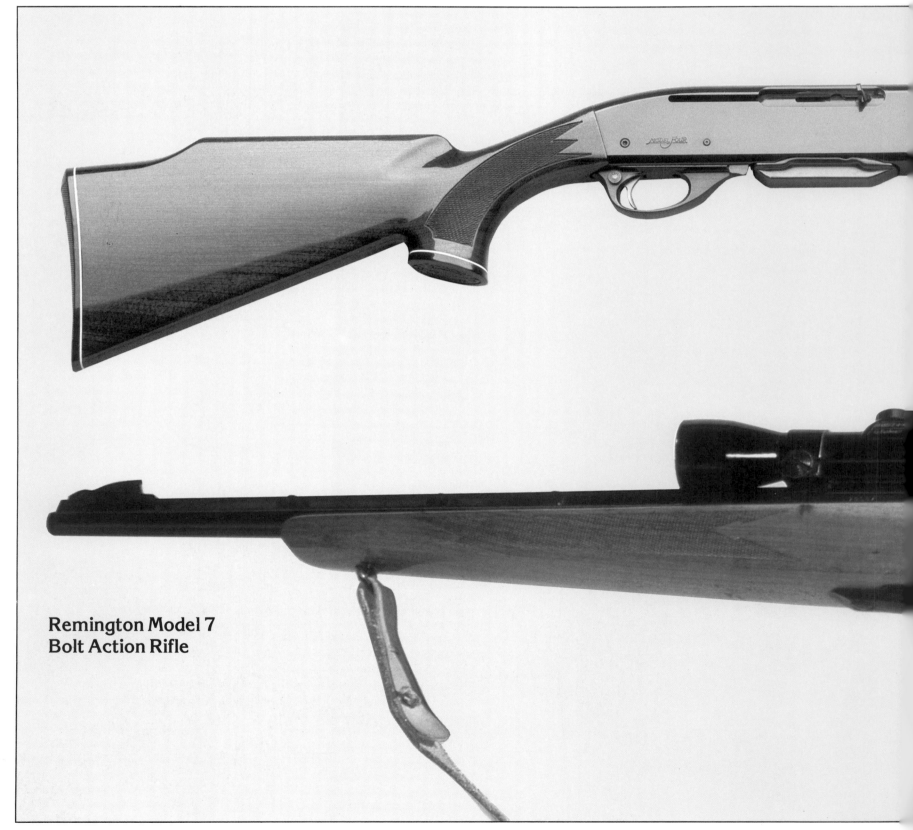

**Remington Model 7
Bolt Action Rifle**

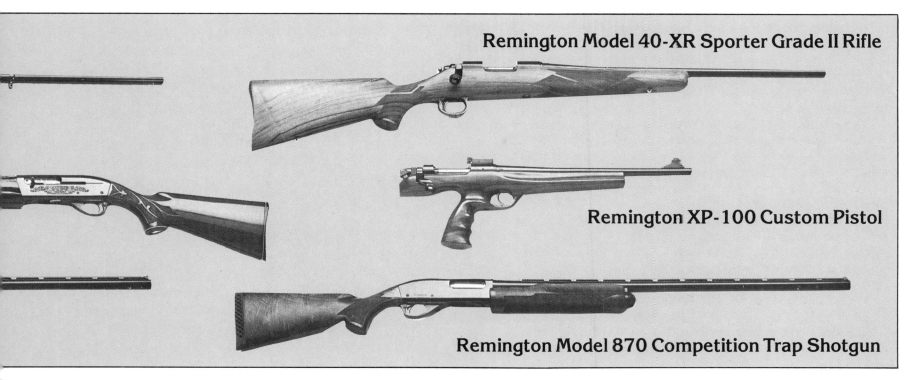

Remington Model 40-XR Sporter Grade II Rifle

Remington XP-100 Custom Pistol

Remington Model 870 Competition Trap Shotgun

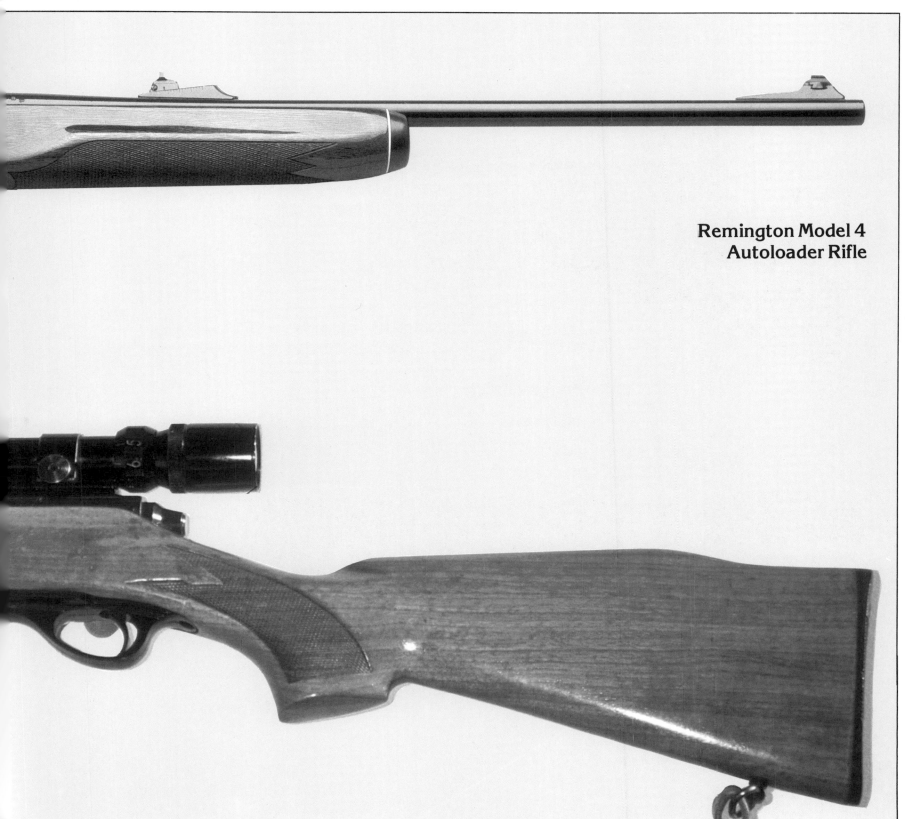

**Remington Model 4
Autoloader Rifle**

The **Ruger** GP-100 Double Action Revolver combines tried and tested Ruger design with various improvements to make this one of the best-handling Magnums available. Its full-length ejector shroud gives this firearm a muzzle-heavy balance, which helps to stabilize the .357 Magnum's muzzle-lifting recoil. The front sight is easily interchanged with alternate sights of various styles; the rear sight is adjustable for windage and elevation. The Ruger GP-100 handles all .357 Magnum loads, and is also available chambered for .38 Special. Also featured on this model are rubber or wood optional grip panels, anatomically designed for maximum comfort and durability.

The Ruger Super Blackhawk .44 Magnum can be set up for big game hunting, with telescopic sight, 7.5 inch barrel and 'brush country' sling swivels. The Mag-na-port company specializes in endowing various manufacturers' Magnum pistols with such features as two gas vents, or 'compensators,' which serve to keep the muzzle down by letting gas escape upward during recoil—for better accuracy; and they rid the bullet's path of the turbulence normally caused by excess gas buildup.

The Ruger GP-100, fieldstripped to show its components, reveals its cylinder assembly; main frame; trigger assembly with transfer bar, cylinder pawl and trigger spur; hammer assembly including spring arm; and grip. The GP-100 can be fieldstripped in seconds, without special tools.

The Ruger Bisley Single Action Revolver is patterned after the British 'flat top' target pistol. The Ruger Bisley is available in two frame sizes to handle many light and heavy calibers. Two variations of the

Ruger GP 100
.357 Magnum Double Action Revolver

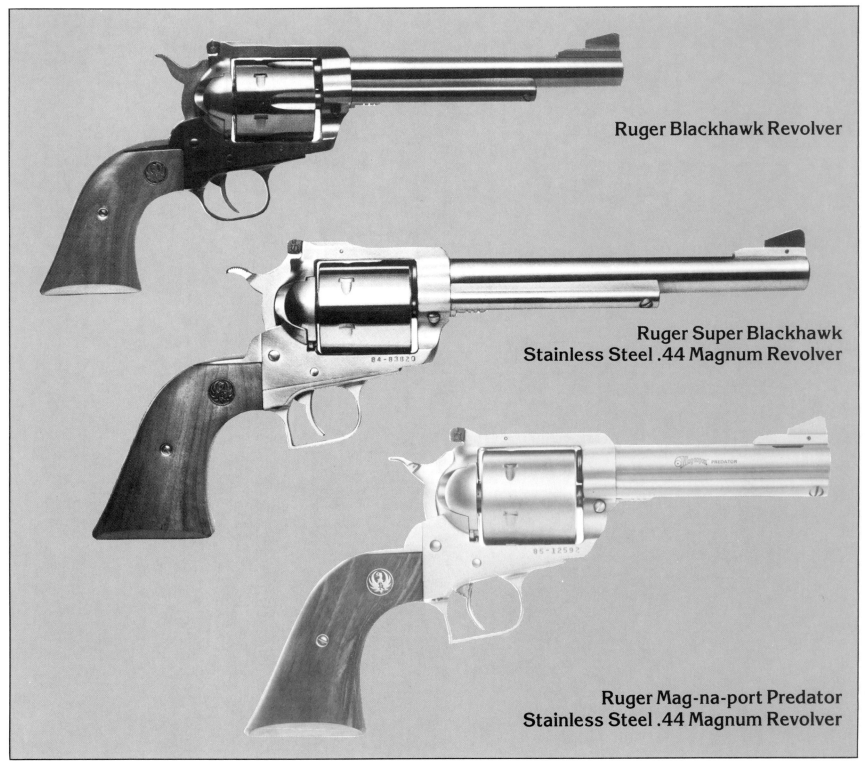

Ruger Blackhawk Revolver

Ruger Super Blackhawk
Stainless Steel .44 Magnum Revolver

Ruger Mag-na-port Predator
Stainless Steel .44 Magnum Revolver

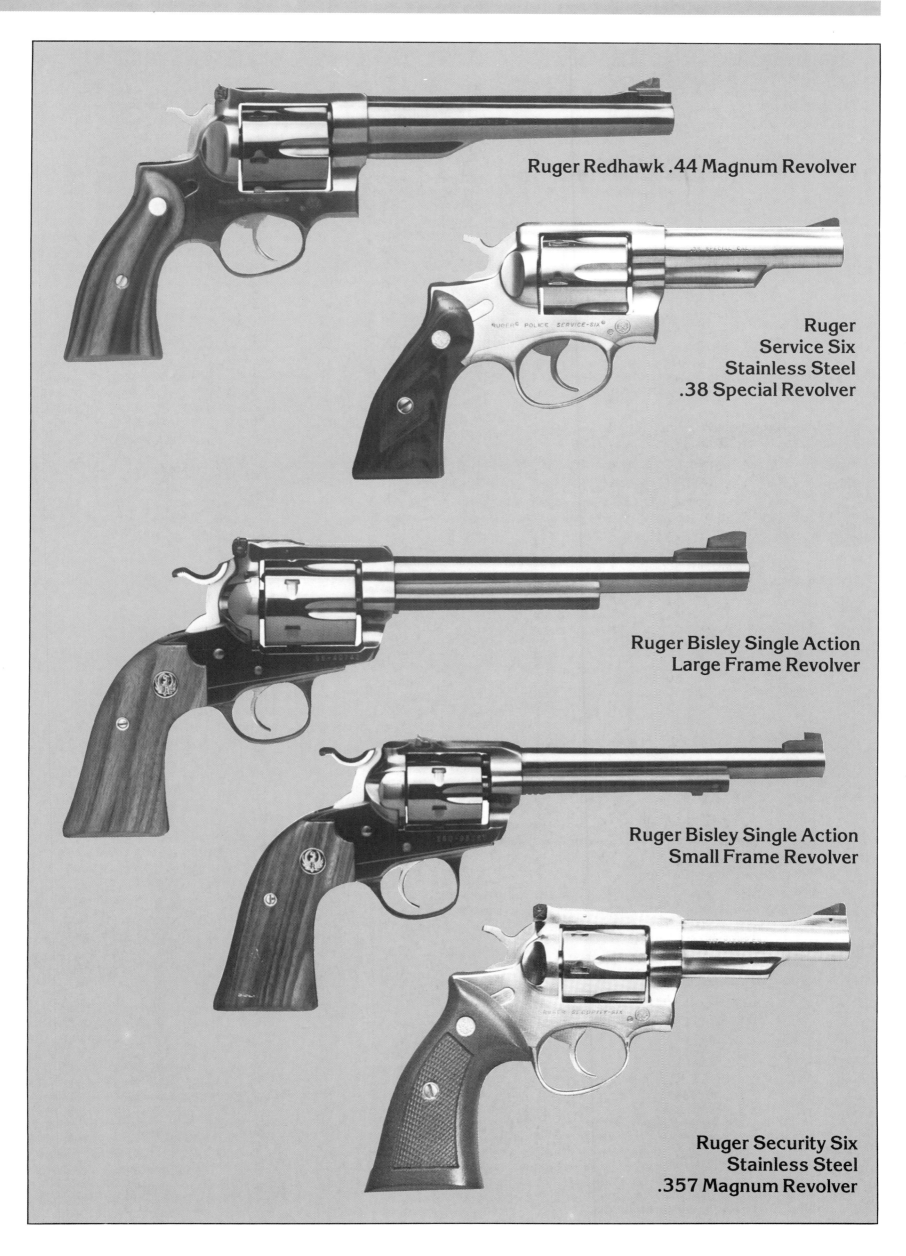

Ruger Redhawk .44 Magnum Revolver

Ruger
Service Six
Stainless Steel
.38 Special Revolver

Ruger Bisley Single Action
Large Frame Revolver

Ruger Bisley Single Action
Small Frame Revolver

Ruger Security Six
Stainless Steel
.357 Magnum Revolver

**Ruger Super Blackhawk .44 Magnum
Stainless Steel Revolver (with scope)**

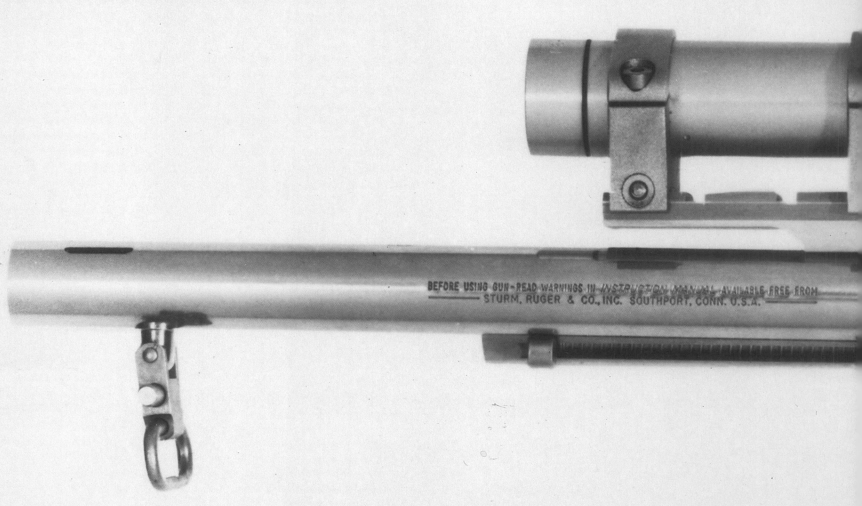

**Ruger Redhawk .44 Magnum
Stainless Steel Revolver (with scope)**

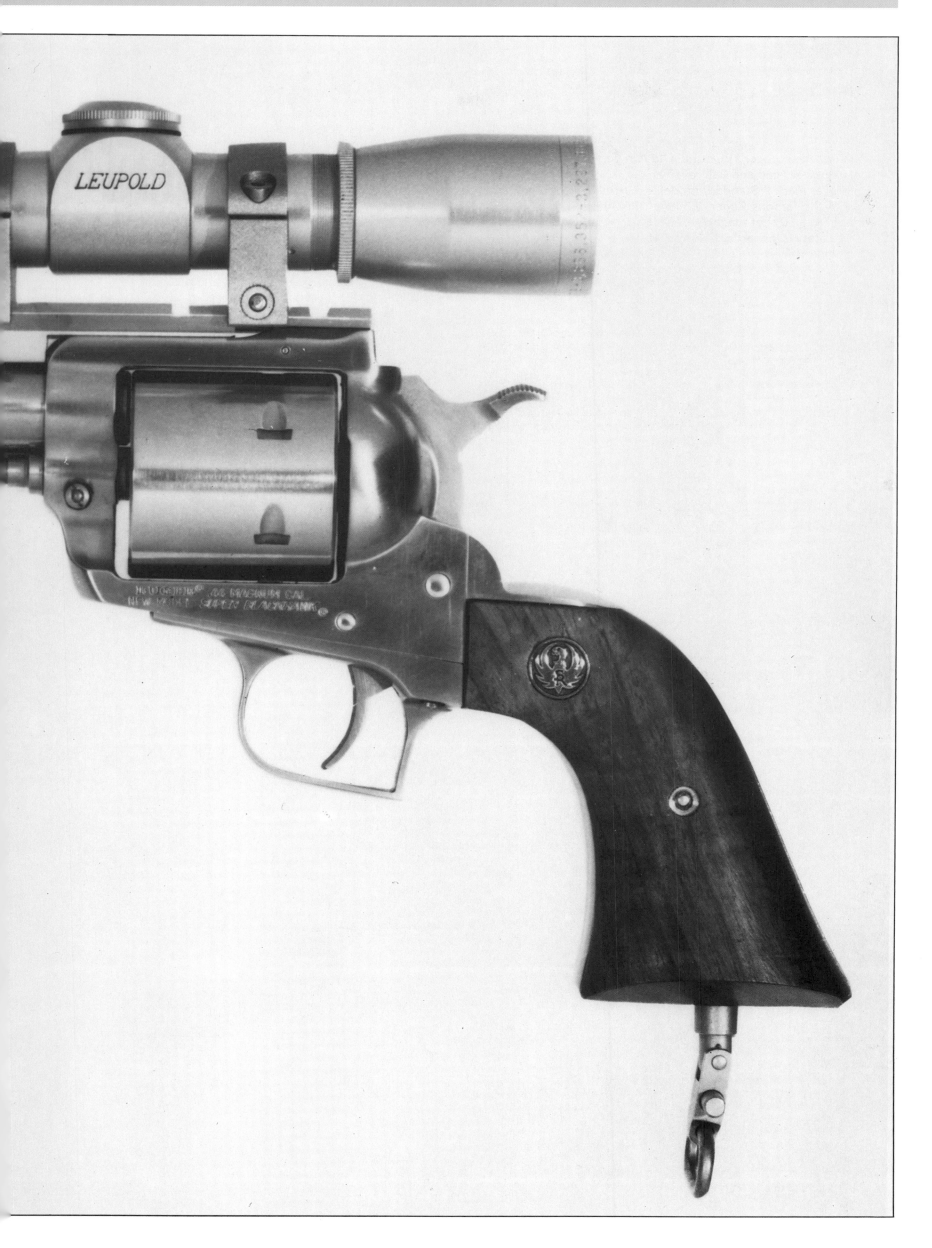

Ruger Mark II pistol include the 'Bull Barrel Model,' designed for shooters preferring muzzle-heavy balance, and the Mark II Target Model.

The Ruger New Model Super Blackhawk is offered with either a 7.5 inch or 10.5 inch barrel, and is designed specifically to chamber the .44 Magnum cartridge. The New Model Blackhawk features Ruger's patented transfer bar ignition mechanism for protection against accidental discharge. Ruger's beautiful Old Army model is a fine .44 caliber black powder cap and ball revolver.

The Ruger Mark II Standard model is a refined second generation version of the famous Ruger .22 long rifle autoloader. The Mark II Standard has a 10 shot magazine, a safety that permits bolt actuation while the safety is 'on' and a bolt stop which holds the bolt open when the pistol's last round has been fired. The Mark II Standard model's rear sight is a square notch type, dovetail mounted, is adjustable for windage and works well with Mark II's wide-blade Partridge style front sight. The Ruger Mark II Standard automatic pistol is available in stainless steel.

A side-section view would show Ruger's transfer bar safety mechanism in 'action.' The transfer bar literally blocks any hammer blow. New Model Single Six has transfer bar safety, a click adjustable rear sight, ramp front sight and walnut grips. Stainless steel versions of the .22 model—which is chambered for .22 short, long and long rifle—are also equipped with an extra cylinder for .22 Winchester Magnum rimfire cartridges. The New Model Single Six is also available in .32 H&R Magnum caliber which develops higher muzzle energy and velocity than the .38 Special cartridge.

Ruger Mark II Bull Barrel Model .22 Automatic Pistol

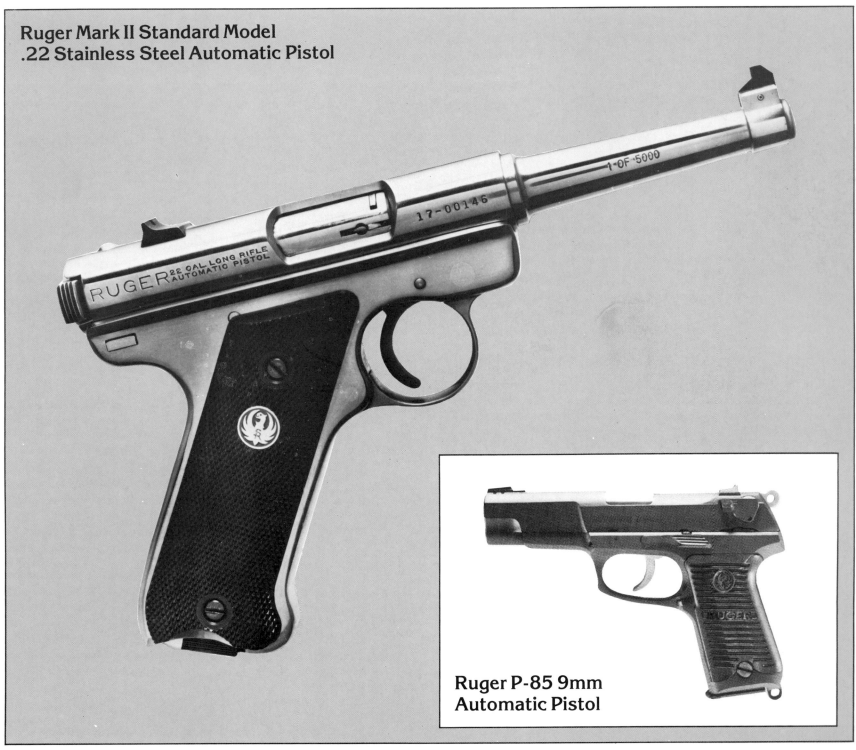

Ruger Mark II Standard Model .22 Stainless Steel Automatic Pistol

Ruger P-85 9mm Automatic Pistol

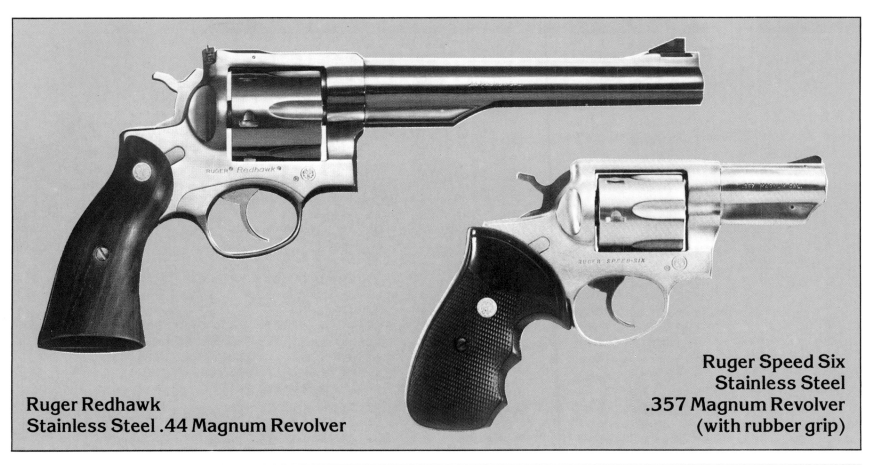

Ruger Redhawk
Stainless Steel .44 Magnum Revolver

Ruger Speed Six
Stainless Steel
.357 Magnum Revolver
(with rubber grip)

Ruger Model 77/22 Rifle

Ruger Model 10/22 Deluxe Sporter Carbine

Ruger Model 10/22 Standard Carbine

Ruger Bolt Action Rifle

Ruger International Bolt Action Rifle

Ruger Single Six Stainless Steel
Revolver (cutaway views)

Ruger Bisley Single Action
.45 Revolver (with engraved cylinder)

The Ruger Redhawk Double Action Revolver is available in .41 Magnum and .44 Magnum calibers. The Redhawk is also available with adjustable front and rear sights as well as the Ruger Redhawk integral scope mounting system. Ruger's Service Six Double Action Revolver features Ruger's transfer bar safety system, and is available chambered for .357 Magnum and .38 Special cartridges. Ruger's Speed Six is basically the same as the Service Six, but has a rounded butt style frame for compactness.

The very elegant Ruger 77/22 Rimfire Rifle features the patented Ruger 10 shot rotary magazine, has a solid component receiver and is made of heat-treated steel—a happy blend of Ruger M-77 model and Ruger 10/22 characteristics, including hand checkering on the stock's pistol grip. The 77/22 has no iron sights but is set up with Ruger scope rings—the scope is not included.

Each firearm being one of 21 special edition Ruger North Americans, Ruger No 1 Single Shot Rifles each bear a gold inlay, presentation-grade engraving of a North American game animal. Optional for many Ruger firearms is the Ruger Scope Mounting System. The Ruger M-77RL Ultra Light Bolt Action Rifle is a handy sporter; the M-77RS Tropical comes in .458 Winchester Magnum caliber; the M-77RSI International comes with, as one of several available lengths, an 18.5 inch barrel. The basic M-77 is offered with either a 'short stroke' or Magnum action; the Ruger No 1 Light Sporter is a great single shot rifle; the No 1 International with a selection of barrel lengths; as does the No 1 Special Varminter, also with optional heavy barrel; the No 1 Standard Rifle is available in calibers rang-

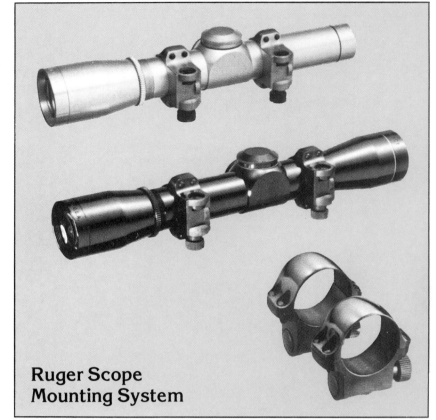

Ruger Scope Mounting System

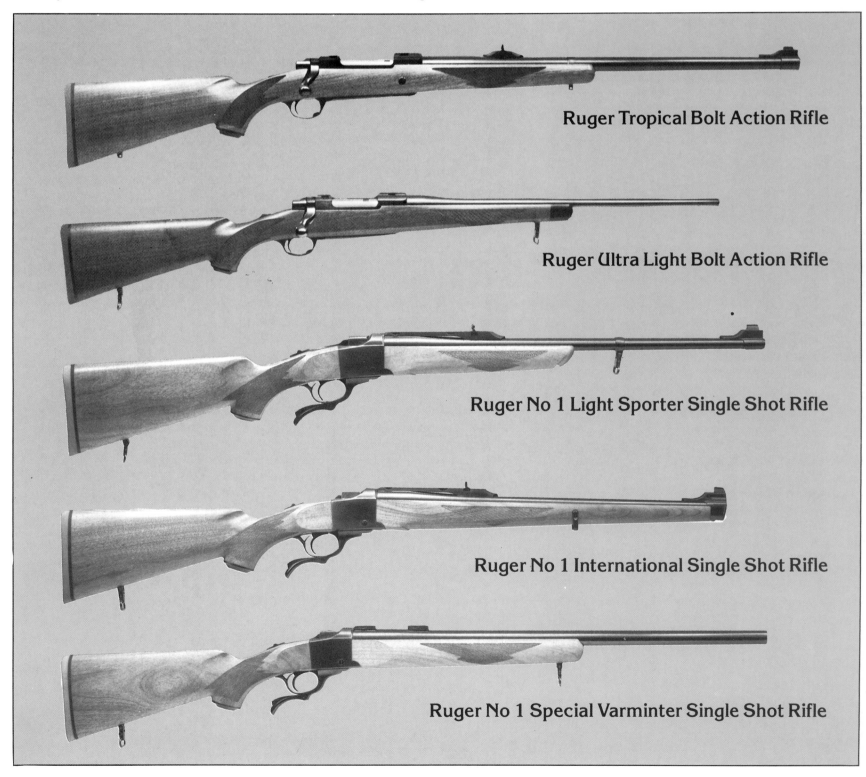

Ruger Tropical Bolt Action Rifle

Ruger Ultra Light Bolt Action Rifle

Ruger No 1 Light Sporter Single Shot Rifle

Ruger No 1 International Single Shot Rifle

Ruger No 1 Special Varminter Single Shot Rifle

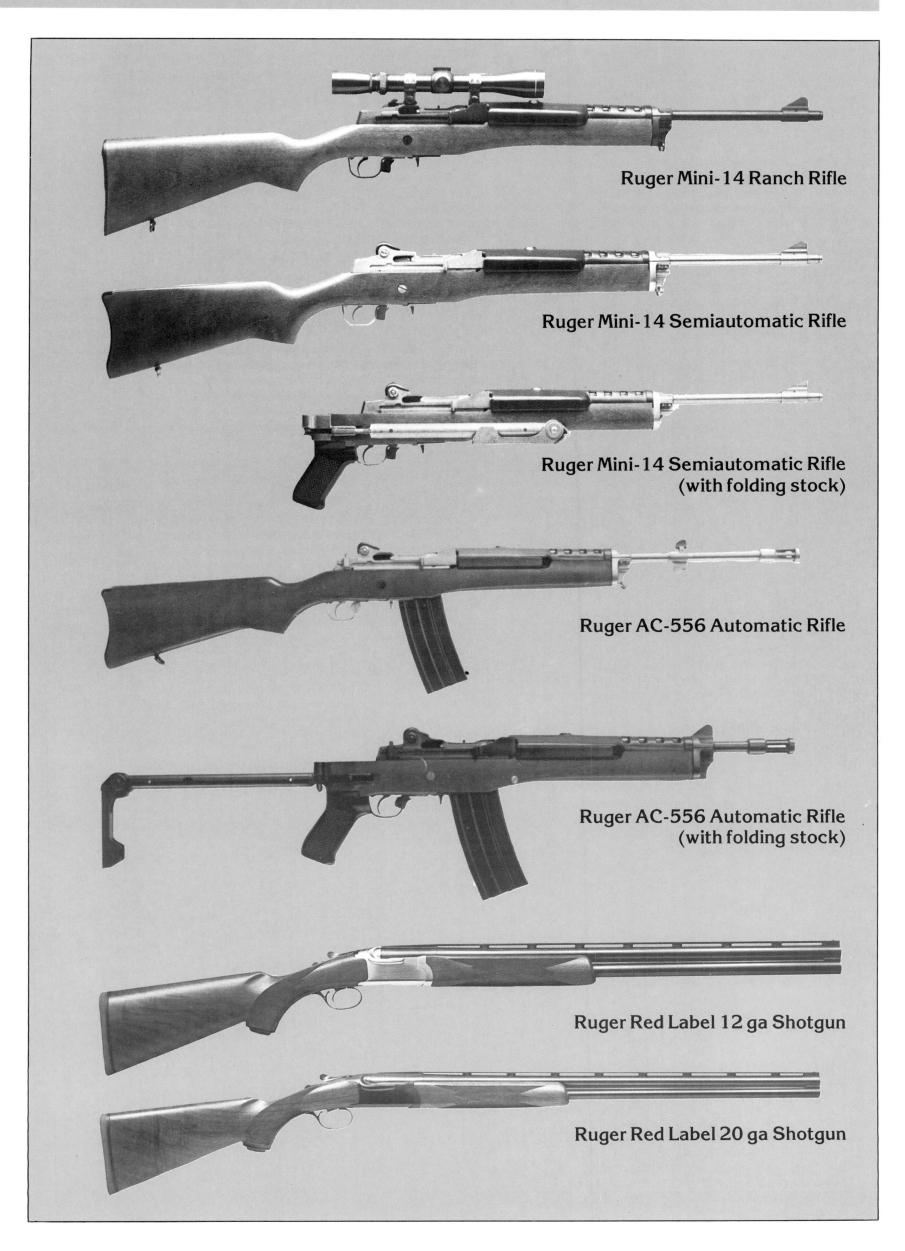

Ruger Mini-14 Ranch Rifle

Ruger Mini-14 Semiautomatic Rifle

Ruger Mini-14 Semiautomatic Rifle
(with folding stock)

Ruger AC-556 Automatic Rifle

Ruger AC-556 Automatic Rifle
(with folding stock)

Ruger Red Label 12 ga Shotgun

Ruger Red Label 20 ga Shotgun

ing from .22-250 to .338 Winchester Magnum; and the Ruger 77/22 Rimfire Rifle is a nifty little bolt action.

The Ruger .223 caliber Mini-14 Ranch Rifle comes with solid stock and in several variations such as the K-Mini-14 in stainless steel. The Ruger Model 10/22 Autoloading Carbines are available in both Deluxe Sporter and Standard models.

The Ruger AC-556 Automatic Rifle is capable of semiautomatic, three shot burst and full automatic (750rpm) operation. The Ruger AC-556F has a folding stock. The Ruger XGI autoloader has an improved Garand-type rotating bolt mechanism. The Ruger K-Mini-14/5RF Ranch Rifle in stainless steel has a folding stock and (like all Ruger Ranch Rifles) a patented recoil shock buffer system for telescopic sights.

Sturm Ruger & Company, Inc's Red Label Over & Under Shotguns are available, with variations, in 12 gauge and stainless steel; and in 20 gauge with blued finish. The Ruger over-and-under breech features advanced-design locking lugs and ejectors. The Ruger Red Label 20 gauge and the Red Label 12 gauge are excellent examples of US gunsmithing. Sturm Ruger & Company Inc's dramatic avian trademark is much in evidence at Ruger's high precision Pine Tree investment castings plant. Ruger sponsors a double action pistol training school and supplies each graduate with a certificate and lapel or shoulder patch.

The **Saco Defense, Inc** M60E3 is a lighter weight variant of a US Armed Forces standby for the past 25 years, the M60 Machine Gun. The M60E3 features an ambidextrous safety, accurized sights and

Ruger Mini-14 Ranch Rifle (with folding stock)

Ruger North American Single Shot Rifle

Saco Defense MK Mod 3.50 Machine Gun

Ruger North American Rifle
(in custom case)

other improvements. M60 series machine guns have a 500-650rpm cyclic rate of fire. The Saco Defense M60 machine gun has been US military infantry unit standard issue for over 25 years. Saco Defense began manufacturing military firearms during World War II.

The **Savage** Model 99C lever action is available in .243 or .308 Winchester calibers and its clip magazine is designed to permit easy chambering of these cartridges. The extremely simple Savage Industries' Stevens Model 72 Crackshot falling block rifle in .22 caliber is ideal for beginners. The Savage Model 110-V Varmint Rifle has an internal box magazine, a heavy target barrel and is tapped for scope mounting. The Model 110 also is available in a silhouette shooting variation. The Savage Model 24C over-and-under 'Camper's Companion' is designed with a .22 long rifle barrel over a 20 gauge shotgun barrel. The Model 24-V is available with a .223 Remington, .243 or .270 Winchester barrel over a 20 gauge shotgun barrel.

Savage Industries, Inc produces the Stevens Model shotguns, in honor of the fine small arms firm which Savage bought in 1920. Stevens Models include such variations as the 311-R Double Barrel Shotgun with law enforcement 18.5 inch barrel; the Stevens Model 67 Pump with top tang safety; the 67-VR with ventilated rib barrel; the 67 Slug with rifle sights; and the Savage Model 69-RXL law enforcement riot gun.

Famous and historic **C Sharps Arms'** fine heavy caliber black powder rifles include the Number 3 Standard Sporter with tang sight; the Deluxe Sporter, a cartridge rifle featuring a traditional cheek rest buttstock; and the very handy Saddle Rifle. The C Sharps Long Range

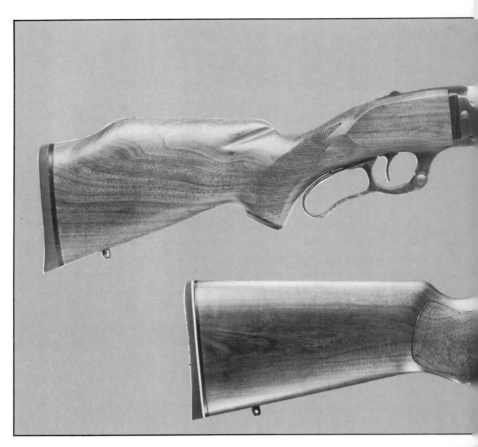

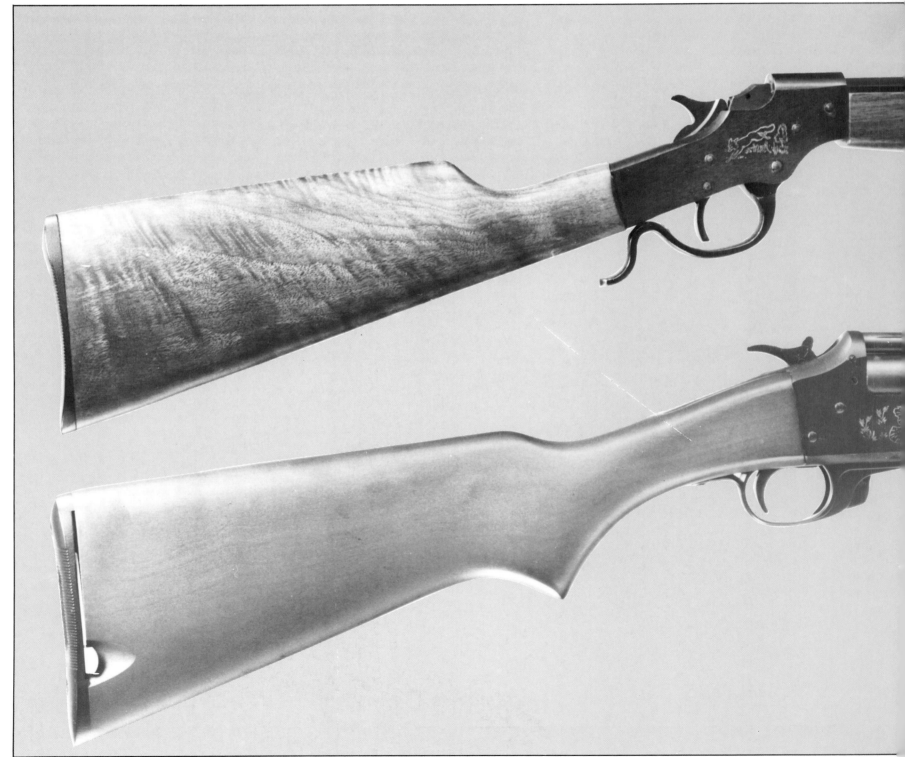

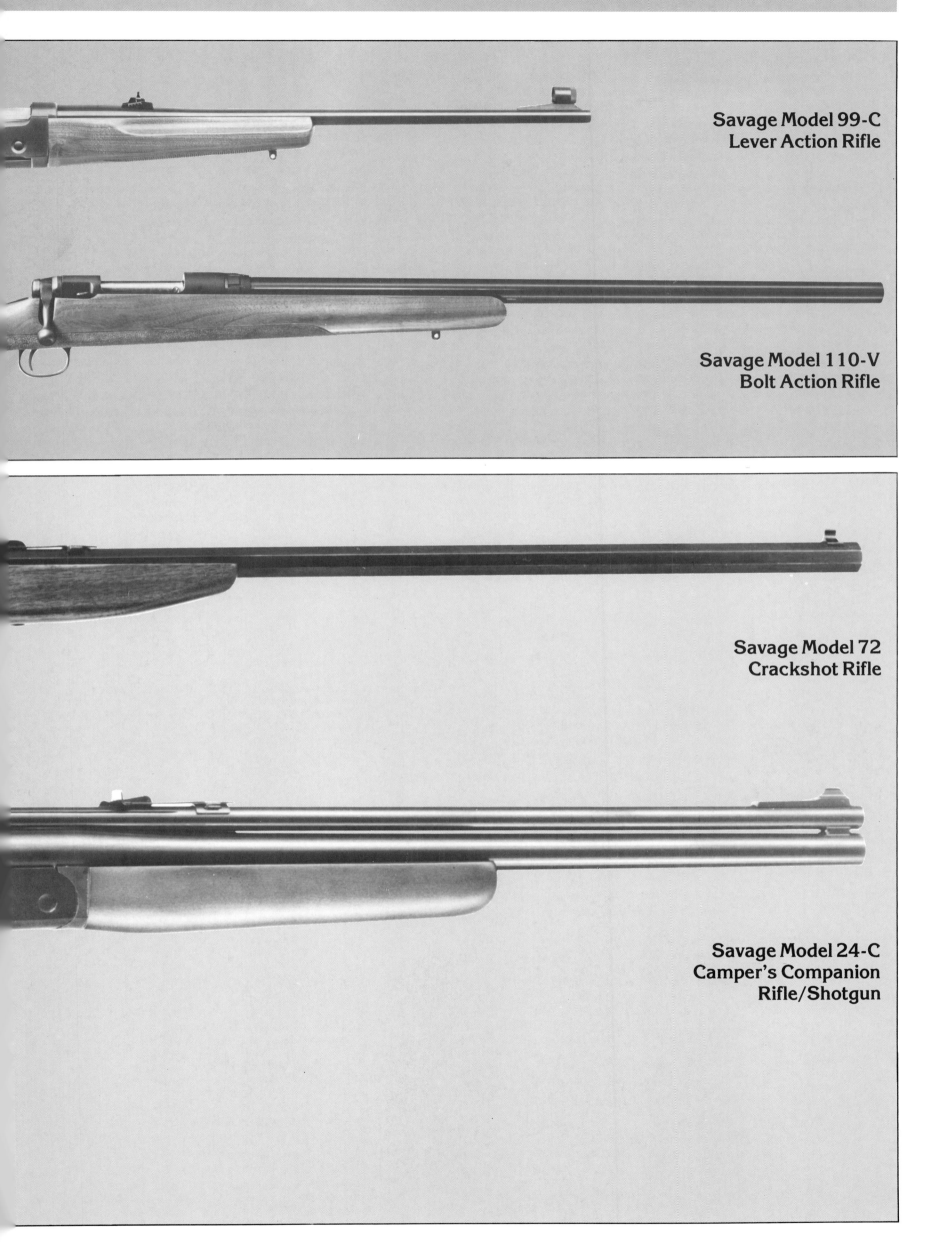

Savage Model 99-C
Lever Action Rifle

Savage Model 110-V
Bolt Action Rifle

Savage Model 72
Crackshot Rifle

Savage Model 24-C
Camper's Companion
Rifle/Shotgun

Saco Defense M60E3 Machine Gun

Saco Defense MK 19 Mod 3 Machine Gun

Express Rifle is based on a model of truly legendary long range accuracy: the New Model 1875 Carbine sports a 'newfangled' round barrel; and the New Model 1875 Saddle Rifle has a tapered octagonal barrel and buckhorn rear sight. C Sharps Arms has long been known for the long-range accuracy of its heavy caliber hunting rifles— hence, Sharps' 'The Scout & The Tenderfoot' logo, with Sharps rifles in evidence—the Tenderfoot having a rifle rest composed of two rods in an 'X'—de rigueur for the genteel, as well as the very serious, shooter of the 1870s. Scouts, hunters and lovers of heavy-caliber accuracy in general utilized the Sharps rifles.

Smith & Wesson's Model 686 Distinguished Combat Magnum has excellent balance for reduced recoil and better sighting. A law enforcer's favorite is the very accurate Smith & Wesson Model 459 9mm Semiautomatic Pistol. The Model 669 9mm Semiautomatic Pistol comes with two 12 round magazines, and a 20 round magazine is available from the company. Most S&W automatics incorporate trigger pull cocking double action, including the .45 ACP Model 645 Semiautomatic.

The Smith & Wesson Model 19 .357 Combat Magnum, made of carbon steel, has optional four inch and six inch barrels. The 2.5 inch barrel version has rounded backstrap and rounded grips—the longer barrel versions have square grips for balance and handling. The Model 66 .357 Combat Magnum shares design specs with the Model 19, but the Model 66 is constructed of stainless steel. S&W has recently pioneered the first four-position fully adjustable front sight ever offered on a production revolver for its Models 29, 586 and 686. Most Smith &

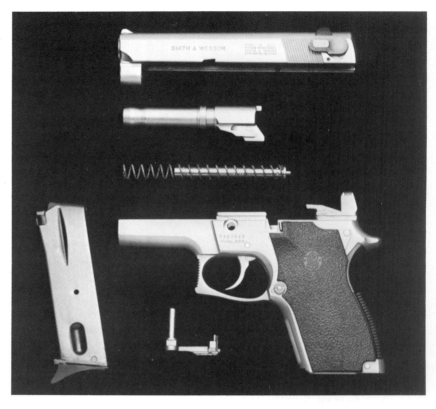

S&W Model 669 (stripped)

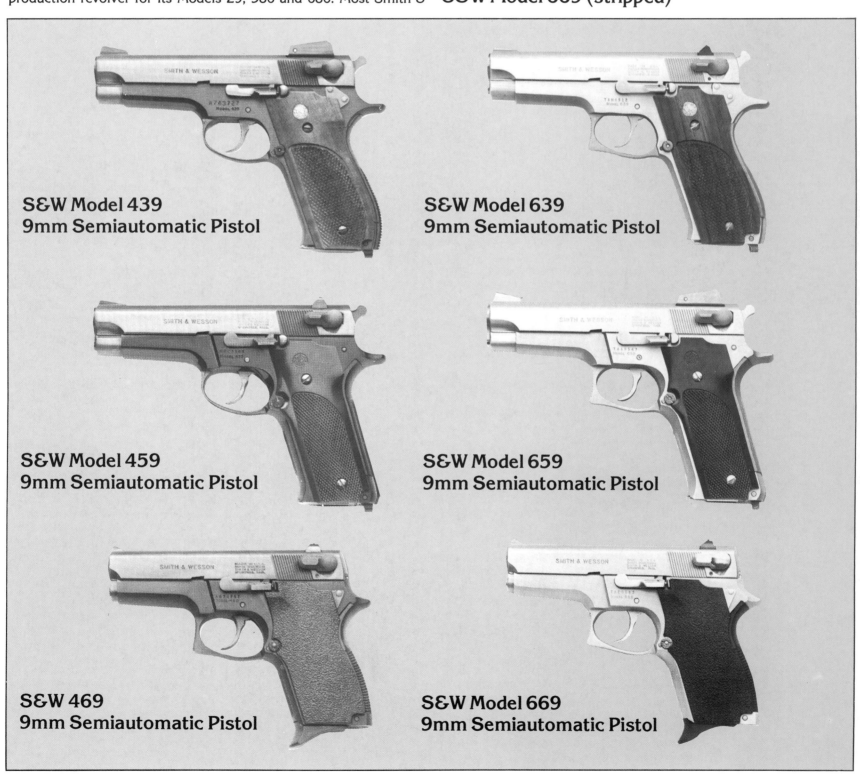

S&W Model 439
9mm Semiautomatic Pistol

S&W Model 639
9mm Semiautomatic Pistol

S&W Model 459
9mm Semiautomatic Pistol

S&W Model 659
9mm Semiautomatic Pistol

S&W 469
9mm Semiautomatic Pistol

S&W Model 669
9mm Semiautomatic Pistol

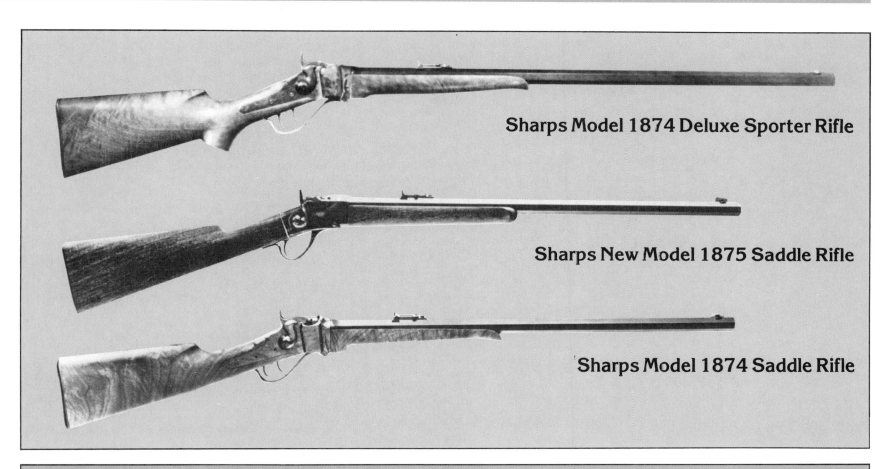

Sharps Model 1874 Deluxe Sporter Rifle

Sharps New Model 1875 Saddle Rifle

Sharps Model 1874 Saddle Rifle

S&W Model 645
.45 Semiautomatic Pistol

Wesson revolvers still bear a proud resemblance to the early Military & Police Model, brought out in the closing years of the 19th century— a pistol used very effectively by police and military personnel throughout the world, including the Royal Canadian Mounted Police.

The Model 586 Distinguished Combat Revolver from Smith & Wesson is available in .357 Magnum and .38 S&W Special, and has optional adjustable front and rear sights. The Smith & Wesson Model 629 .44 Magnum Revolver is made of stainless steel. S&W pioneered the first production Magnum pistols—the .357, .41 and .44 Magnums. The Model 639 9mm Semiautomatic Pistol in stainless steel features an ambidextrous safety.

Smith & Wesson's Model 34 1953 Kit Gun has a small frame and a micrometer click rear sight, making it a good target gun for beginners. The Model 624 in .44 Smith & Wesson Special features a variety of hammer and trigger styles, which are matched to the barrel length chosen for the pistol. The aluminum alloy Model 469 Semiautomatic fires 9mm ammunition and features compactness and good balance. Its 'twin' is the Model 669, manufactured of stainless steel. Smith & Wesson's Model 57 .41 Magnum Revolver is made of carbon steel and its stainless steel counterpart is the Model 657. Mag-na-port, a firearms customizing firm, modifies the Smith & Wesson Model 629s, as well as other Magnum pistols. The word 'Mag-na-port' refers to the gas ports which the firm cuts into the dorsal surfaces of these Magnum caliber pistols' muzzles. Such ports function as muzzle breaks, which are helpful with such as the Magnum load's high muzzle energy.

Among customized versions of Smith & Wesson pistols, the ASP conversion of a Smith & Wesson 'hammerless' model includes modifi-

S&W Model 10
.38 Revolver

S&W Model 31
.32 Revolver

S&W Model 34
.22 Revolver

S&W Model 36
.38 Revolver

S&W Model 37
.38 Revolver

S&W Model 65
.357 Revolver

S&W Model 64
.38 Revolver

S&W Model 63
.22 Revolver

S&W Model 66
.357 Revolver

S&W Model 67
.38 Revolver

Model 649
.38 Revolver

S&W Model 12
.38 Revolver

S&W Model 13
.357 Revolver

S&W Model 15
.38 Revolver

S&W Model 19
.357 Revolver

S&W Model 17
.22 Revolver

S&W Model 38
.38 Revolver

S&W Model 48
.22 Revolver

S&W Model 60
.22 Revolver

S&W Model 49
.38 Revolver

S&W Model 650
.22 Revolver

S&W Model 651
.22 Revolver

cations made for utility and convenience—such as 'see-through magazine' pistol grips, cowl sights atop the receiver and some obvious streamlining. Boasting 'the broadest handgun line in the world,' Smith & Wesson has contributed many models to the genre of autoloading pistols. The Smith & Wesson Model 52 .38 Master Semiautomatic Pistol is chambered for .38 Smith & Wesson Special mid-range wadcutter bullets, and is single action, which facilitates the target shooter's concentration as he systematically cocks and fires his pistol, setting up the 'semiautomatic' action which follows the initial cock-and-fire. The Smith & Wesson Model 52 comes with two five round magazines, micrometer click rear sight and partridge ramp front sight. The Smith & Wesson Model 645 Semiautomatic Pistol fires the .45 ACP, a cartridge which for years was ubiquitous in the world of semiautomatic pistols. Equipped with ramp front and fixed rear sights, made of stainless steel and featuring the high level of craftsmanship with which Smith & Wesson manufactures its firearms, the Model 645 is any shooter's 'safe bet.' Smith & Wesson also offers high-quality custom engraving.

Smith & Wesson's Model 41 Single Action Semiautomatic Target Pistol is a single action pistol, built extra heavy for sighting stability. The receiver 'overhangs' the shooter's thumb, both to aid balancing the 5.5 inch heavy barrel or seven inch barrel, and to promote the pistol's fitting snugly to the shooter's hand. Its .22 long rifle cartridges develop sufficient velocity to provide moderate-range target shooting accuracy, and lack the unsettling recoil that many high velocity cartridges produce. At 41 to 44 ounces, depending on barrel length, and

S&W Model 39 Semiautomatic Pistol

S&W Mag-na-port .44 Magnum Revolver

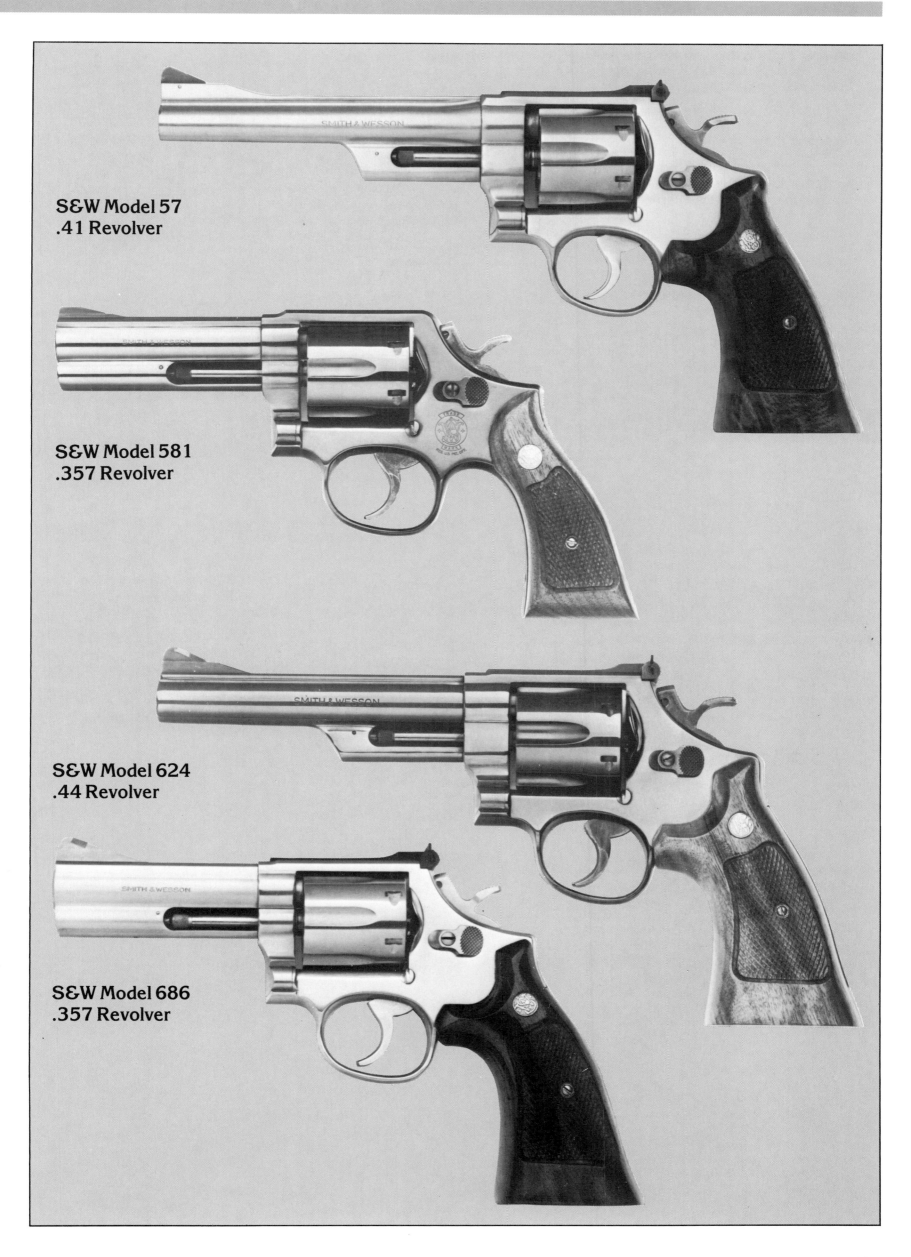

S&W Model 57
.41 Revolver

S&W Model 581
.357 Revolver

S&W Model 624
.44 Revolver

S&W Model 686
.357 Revolver

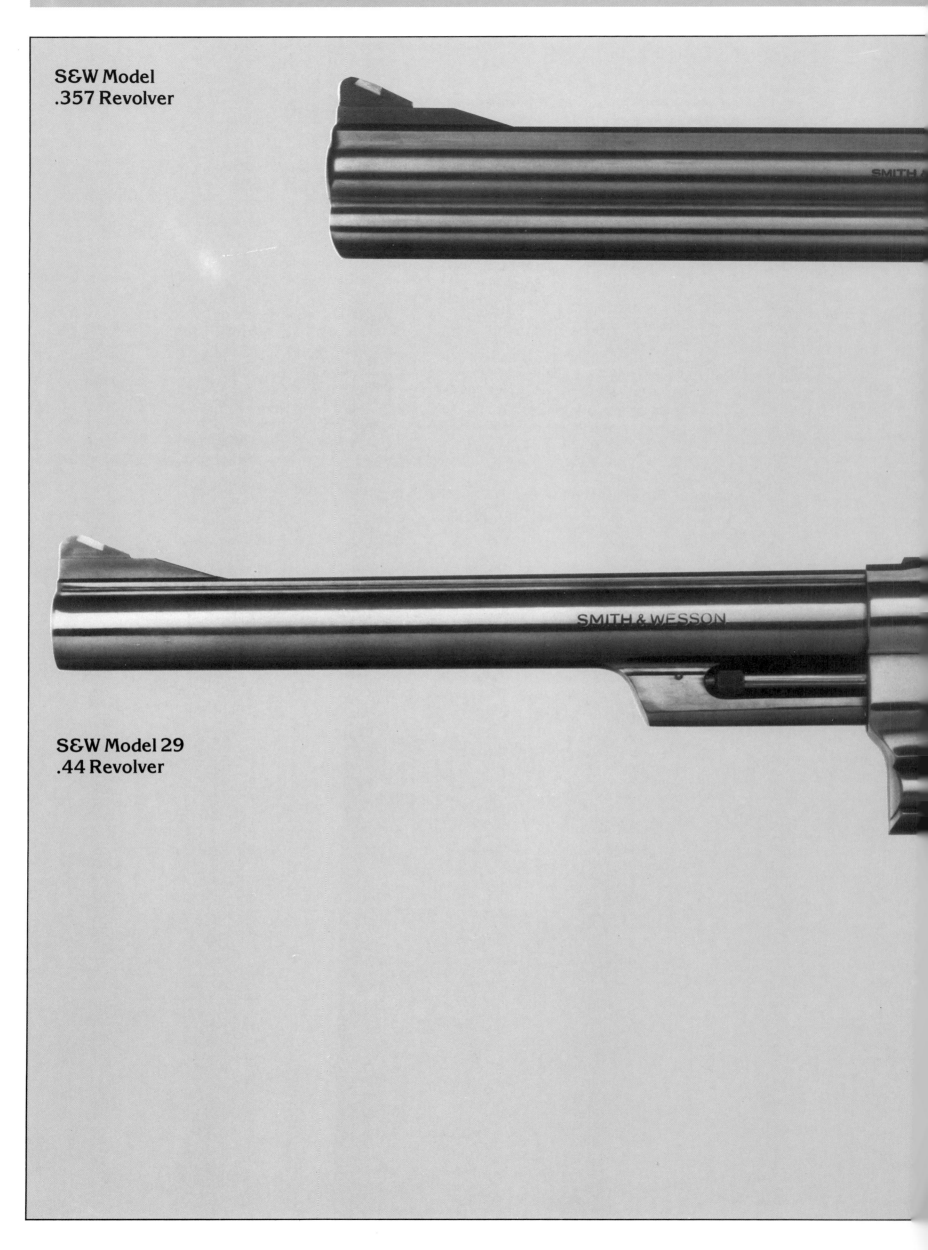

**S&W Model
.357 Revolver**

**S&W Model 29
.44 Revolver**

with a windage and elevation adjustable micrometer click rear sight, the Smith & Wesson Model 41 promises to be a very comfortable and accurate target pistol. Its grips are made of walnut, with checkering and modified right or left handed adaptable thumb rest.

The Smith & Wesson Combat Masterpiece is a six shot revolver chambered for .38 Smith & Wesson Special—a cartridge which has seen much service with police departments throughout the United States. The thumb toggle just below the hammer is the cylinder catch—one push of this release and the pistol's cylinder hinges down and outward for speedy reloading. Just snap the cylinder into place again and the pistol is ready for more shooting. The Combat Masterpiece is available with a number of barrel lengths—8.38 inch, six inch, four inch and two inch.

A Smith & Wesson Model 28 revolver was recently used as the control weapon in British pistol tests. Highway patrolmen often wear the Smith & Wesson Model 681 and/or the Smith & Wesson Model 669. Beautiful and precision-machined '1 of 10' Smith & Wesson custom models feature Smith & Wesson's fine engraving, available in three grades of coverage. These special quality firearms can be ordered as commemorative arms; for a recent Smith & Wesson '1 of 10' series pistol celebrates the great state of Alaska's Silver Anniversary (1959-1984). Standard, machine or custom engraving is available. Law enforcement officers, including many of the officers who guard the White House, tend to prefer Smith & Wesson revolvers.

The **Springfield Armory** has a long history as armorers to the US military. From the 18th century forward, Springfield has consistently

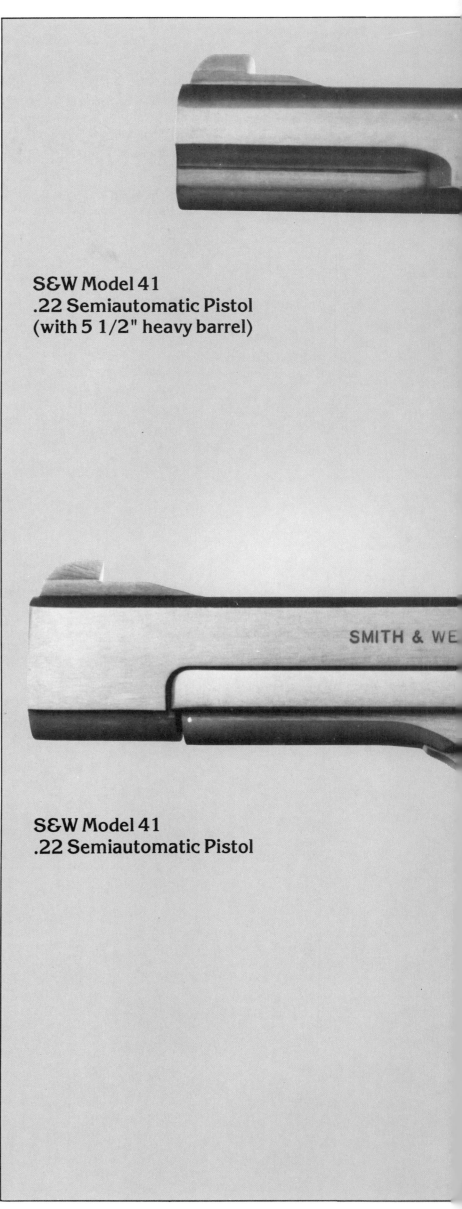

S&W Model 41
.22 Semiautomatic Pistol
(with 5 1/2" heavy barrel)

S&W Model 41
.22 Semiautomatic Pistol

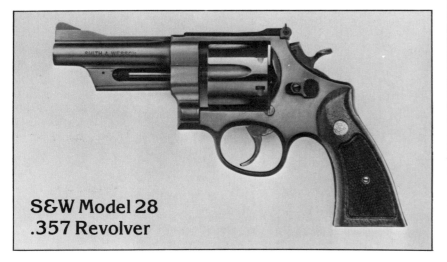

S&W Model 28
.357 Revolver

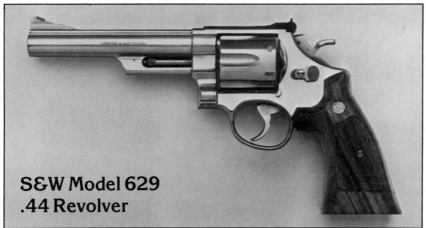

S&W Model 629
.44 Revolver

S&W Model 52
.38 Semiautomatic Pistol

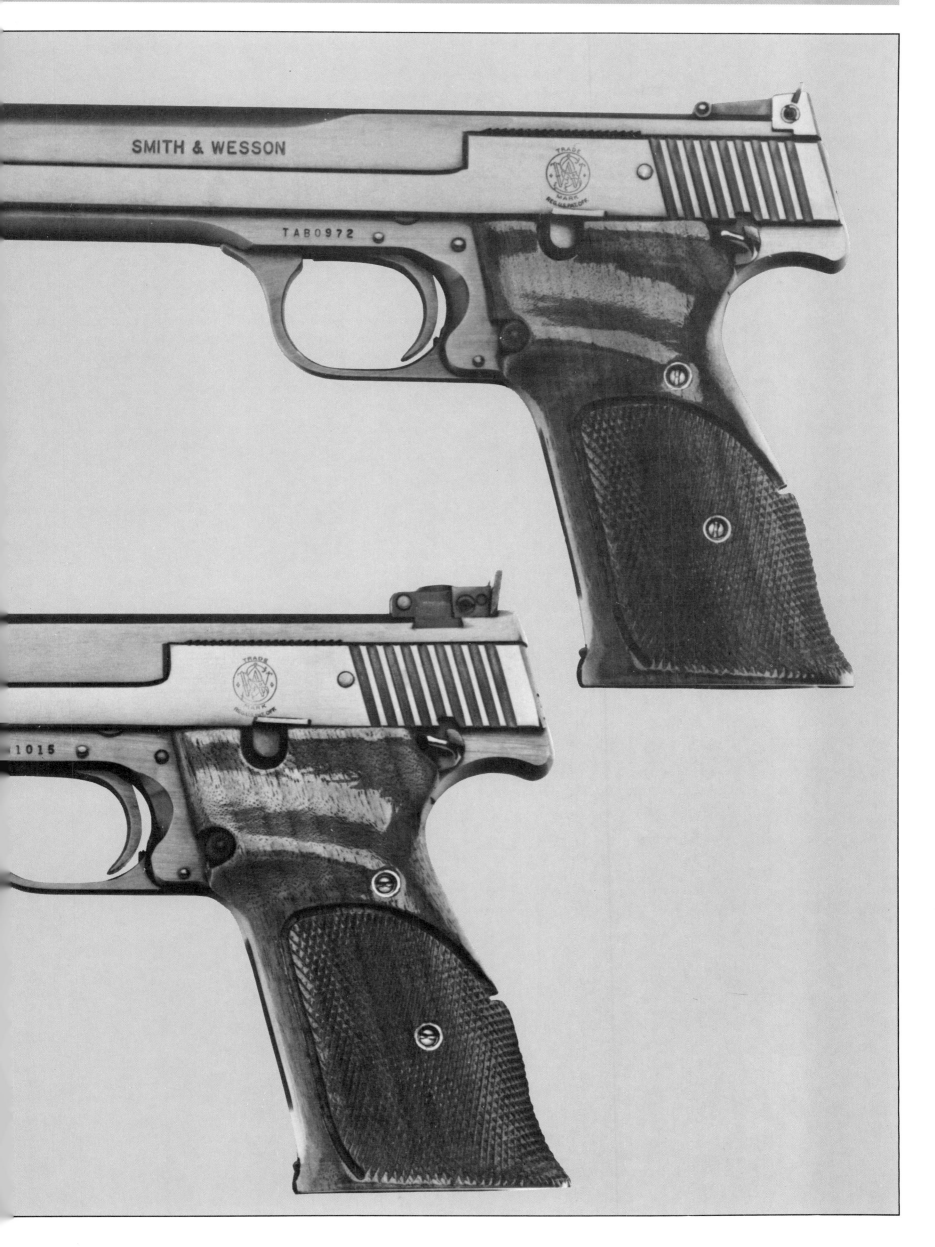

produced some of our finest military arms. The nearly apocryphal 1911-A1 semiautomatic pistol, chambered for the .45 ACP cartridge, is a weapon that is not exactly meant for target shooting, but is truly a combat arm—it has plenty of knockdown power, and can empty its clip in a hurry. Springfield makes its 1911-A1 in two calibers—.45 ACP or 9mm Parabellum, and in three versions—any one of which is parts-interchangeable with the Standard 1911-A1 model; also, Springfield's Custom model can be built to individual specs using the Standard 1911-A1 as a base.

Springfield Model 1873 rifles, which were Army standard issue from 1872-94, fired the 45-70 cartridge. Springfield Armory duplicates the famous M-1 Garand in various configurations, such as M-1 Standard model with a commercial scope and the M1-D Sniper Rifle. It's M-1 Garand comes complete with various historic and accurizing accessories. The M-1 was US military standard issue in World War II and Korea. The Springfield M6 Scout is a single shot .22/.410 over-and-under which can store 15 .22s and four .410s in its detachable stock. The Springfield M1A is the civilian version of the M14, has a maximum range of 4103 yards and has a wide range of accessories for optimum stylization.

The gas operated semiautomatic Springfield M1A 7.62mm/.308 Caliber Rifle in its Super Match configuration is hand-assembled with National Match sights, main spring guide, flash suppressor, gas canister and air-gauged heavy barrel—all improvements to an already highly accurate and reliable design. Available with the rifle is an optional burly walnut stock, 3 × 9 scope and leather sling.

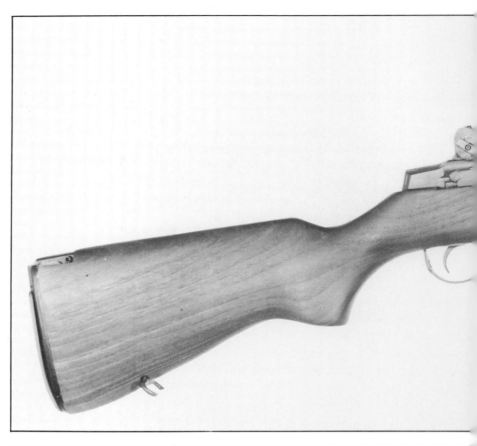

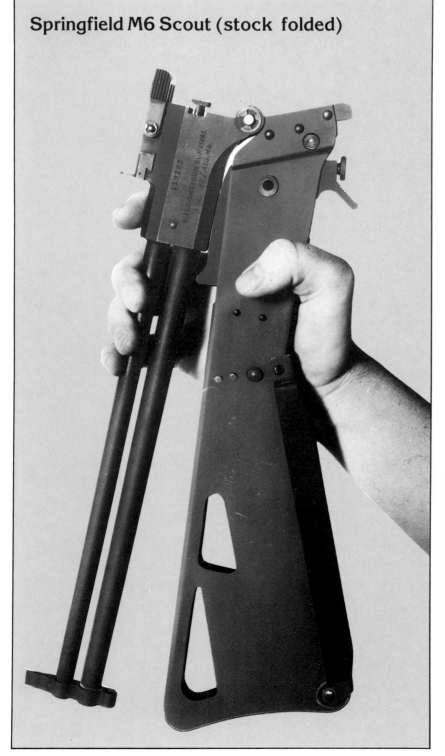

Springfield M6 Scout (stock folded)

Springfield M1A Super Match Rifle

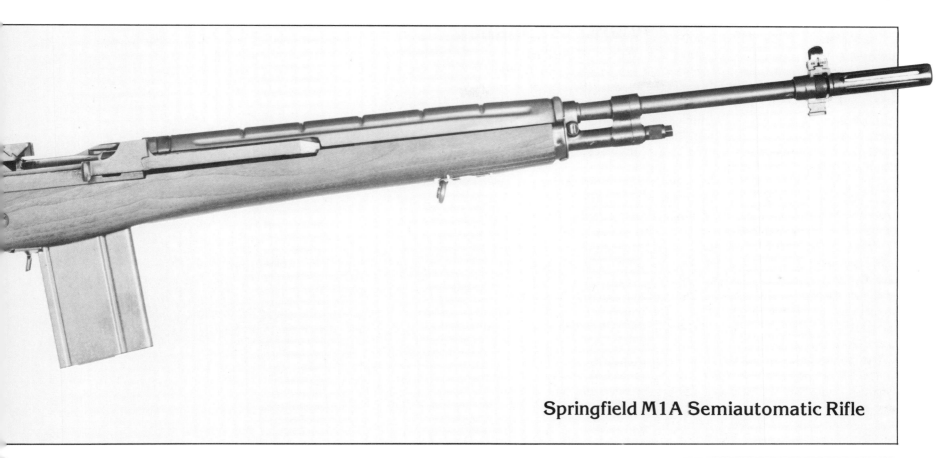

Springfield M1A Semiautomatic Rifle

Both sides in the US Civil War used Springfields 'fixed' with the three-sided, barrel-collar bayonets of the time.

In the pre-1870 early days of railroading, workers were wide open to Indian and bandit attack—that's why they stacked their arms military fashion in a central location—when they met each other at the rifle stack, they were reminded of who was on their side, and knew, more or less, where each other was—'which shadows to shoot at'—because considerable dust would be kicked up in the noise and confusion, and the black powder used then created, literally, clouds of smoke. The weapons they and their military guards used seem mostly to have been Springfield, Sharps and Remington breechloaders.

In several Frederick Remington paintings, cavalrymen wear new web belts—to carry .45-70 ammo for their newly issued Springfield carbines. Sidearms for these folks were probably Colts and a few old Remingtons—a mix of cartridge and cartridge-conversion (from cap and ball) revolvers. World War I 'Yanks' depended upon their Springfield 30-06s. Springfield was the chief armorer for the American forces during the War of 1812.

Steel City Arms' Double Deuce in .22 caliber is produced in a high-tech assembly shop to exacting specifications. It features rosewood grips, fixed sights and an ambidextrous thumb-release safety.

The **SWD, Inc** Cobray M-11 9mm Submachine Gun has a magazine capacity of 32 rounds, is 11.25 inches long, fires at a rate of 900rpm and weighs just 3.75 pounds.

**SWD Cobray M-11
9mm Submachine Gun**

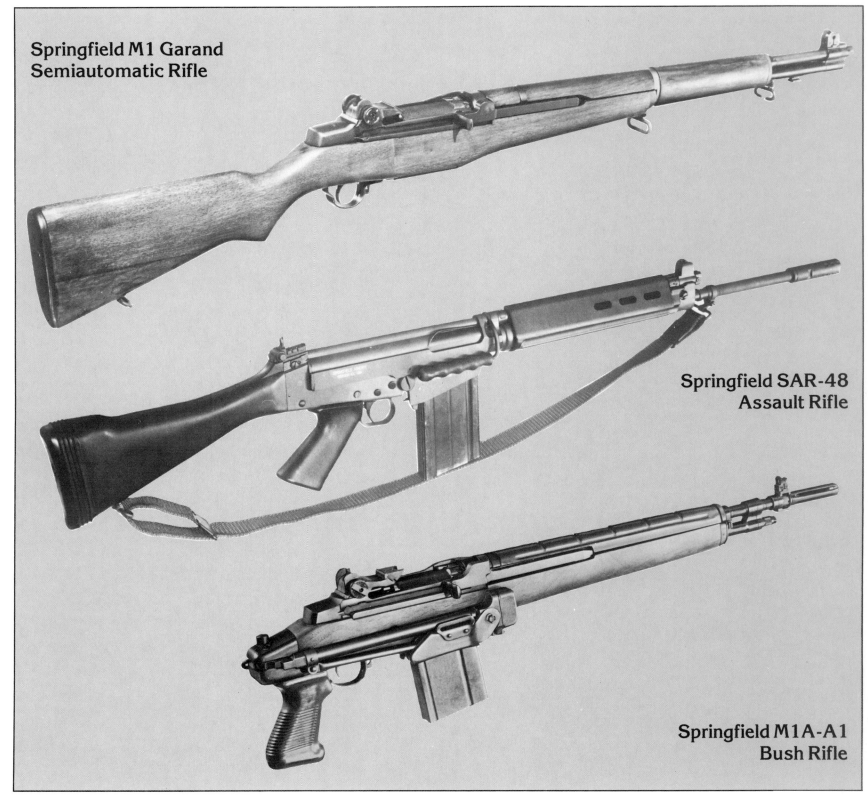

**Springfield M1 Garand
Semiautomatic Rifle**

**Springfield SAR-48
Assault Rifle**

**Springfield M1A-A1
Bush Rifle**

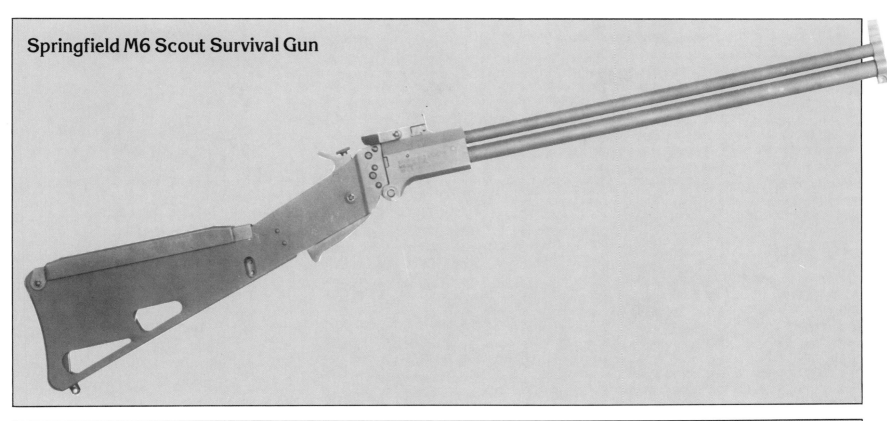

Springfield M6 Scout Survival Gun

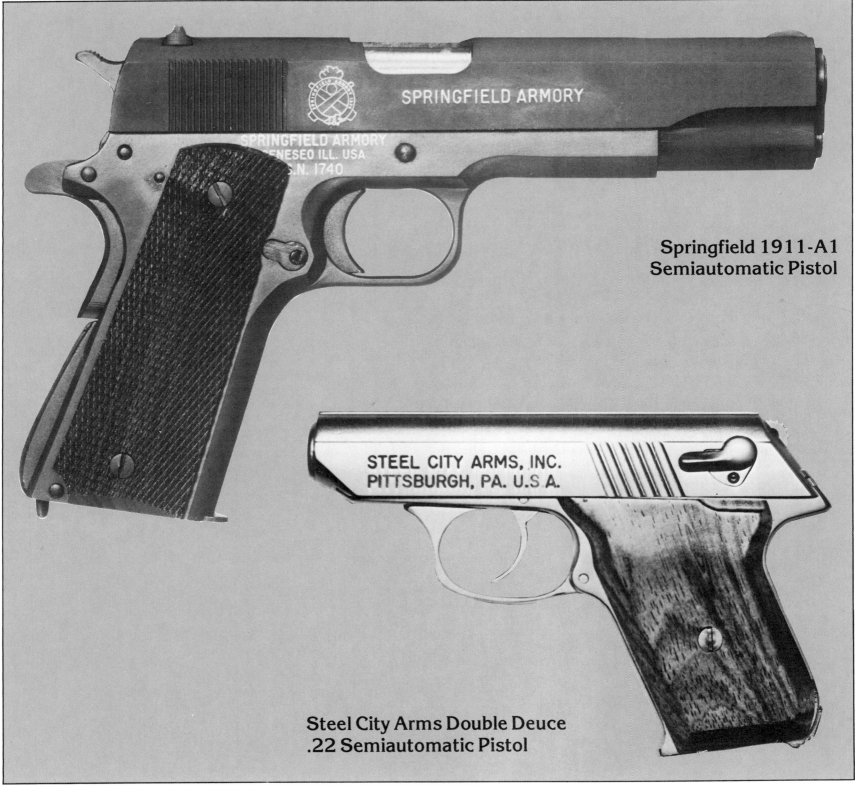

Springfield 1911-A1
Semiautomatic Pistol

Steel City Arms Double Deuce
.22 Semiautomatic Pistol

141

Thompson/Center Arms' Contender Single Shot Pistols are available in several models, based on barrel type, including the Contender Bull Barrel with a heavy 10 inch barrel—available in 18 different calibers—and the Contender Vent Rib/Internal Choke model—available in .45 Colt/.410 caliber. Thompson/Center Arms Contender models all include an automatic safety and an interlock safety.

Thompson/Center's Patriot Percussion Pistol was developed with the thought in mind that the single shot percussion pistol had reached a pinnacle of perfection in the 19th century that deserved at least an encore. Thus, Thompson/Center Arms discreetly combines modern, improved materials with the elegant refinements of the past to present the Patriot in .36 or .45 caliber with adjustable Partridge style target sights, target- and dueling-style set triggers, solid brass trim, investment-cast steel barrel and frame, and the weight and balance of the finest target pistols of the cap and ball era.

The Thompson/Center Arms Cherokee Percussion Sporting Rifle has interchangeable accessory barrels in .32 and .45 calibers to provide a wide range of hunting possibilities, and its sights are windage and elevation-adjustable. Thompson/Center's Contender Carbine is an elegant, strong and accurate single shot, available in eight rifle calibers as well as .410 (three inch shotshells). The Contender has adjustable iron sights, and its 21 inch barrel is tapped and drilled for scope mounts. Thompson/Center Arms' big bore Hawken Muzzle-loading Sporting Rifle is available in .45, .50 and .54 calibers and has

**Thompson/Center Arms
Patriot Percussion Pistol**

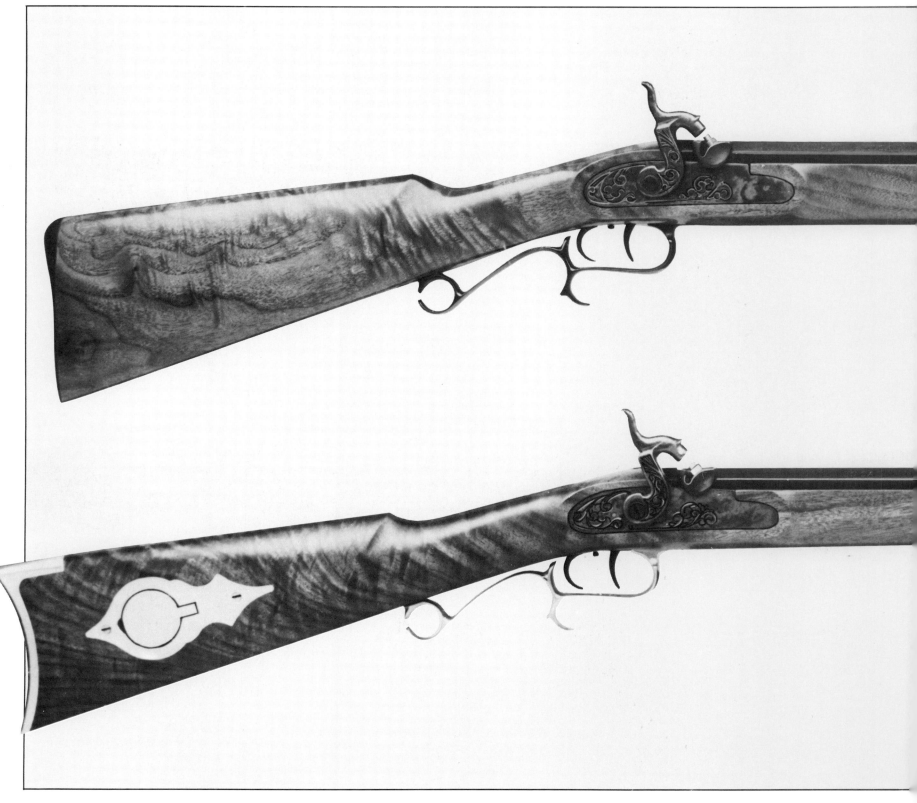

Thompson/Center Arms Contender Single Shot Pistols

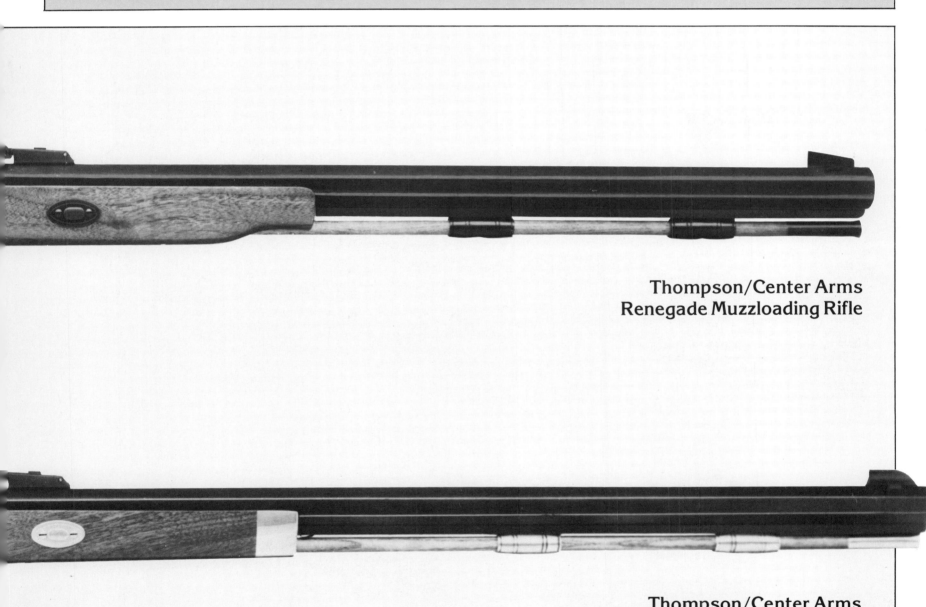

**Thompson/Center Arms
Renegade Muzzloading Rifle**

**Thompson/Center Arms
Hawken Muzzleloading Rifle**

adjustable hunting sights. TCR's Renegade muzzleloader is made of modern steel, has 'workhorse reliability' and a lifetime guarantee.

Thompson/Center Arms' Seneca is patterned after an early New England hunting rifle and has fully adjustable triggers and sights. Among TCR's cartridge-firing Single Shot Rifles, the Hunter Field model features an adjustable trigger and interchangeable barrels for firing a variety of cartridges.

Thompson/Center Arms, Inc's Contender Pistol and its fellow Thompson/Center Arms production are available with such accessories as T/C accessory case; T/C Numbers 8305, 8306 and 8307 Recoil Proof Handgun Scopes; T/C Patriot Pistol Kit; and T/C Frontier Rifle Cover.

Ultra Light Arms, Inc melds aerospace technology with sound gunsmithing to produce high-quality firearms of amazing lightness. Their Models 20 and 28 are available in right or left handed configurations.

The **US Repeating Arms Company** manufactures the following Winchester Model 70 Bolt Action Centerfire Rifles: the XTR Sporter is available in both Standard and Magnum models; the Super Express comes in .375 H&H Magnum or .458 Winchester Magnum; the Lightweight Carbine weighs six pounds, and has a 20 inch barrel; the Ranger comes in .270 Winchester and .30-06 Springfield, and has an adjustable rear sight; and the Ranger Youth model weighs just 5.75 pounds and is scaled down to smaller shooter's bodies. The Winchester Model 94 Carbine is a long-time standard.

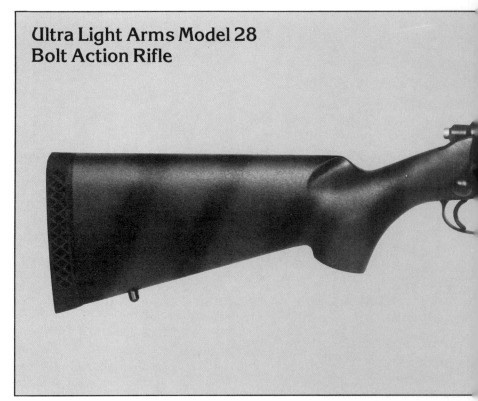

Ultra Light Arms Model 28 Bolt Action Rifle

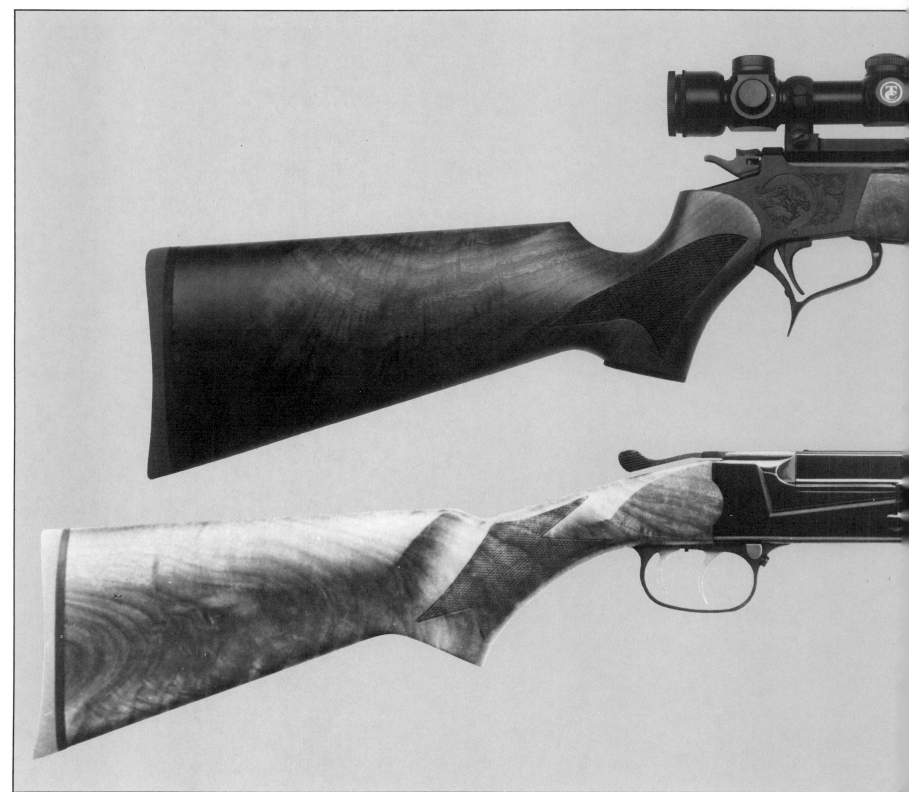

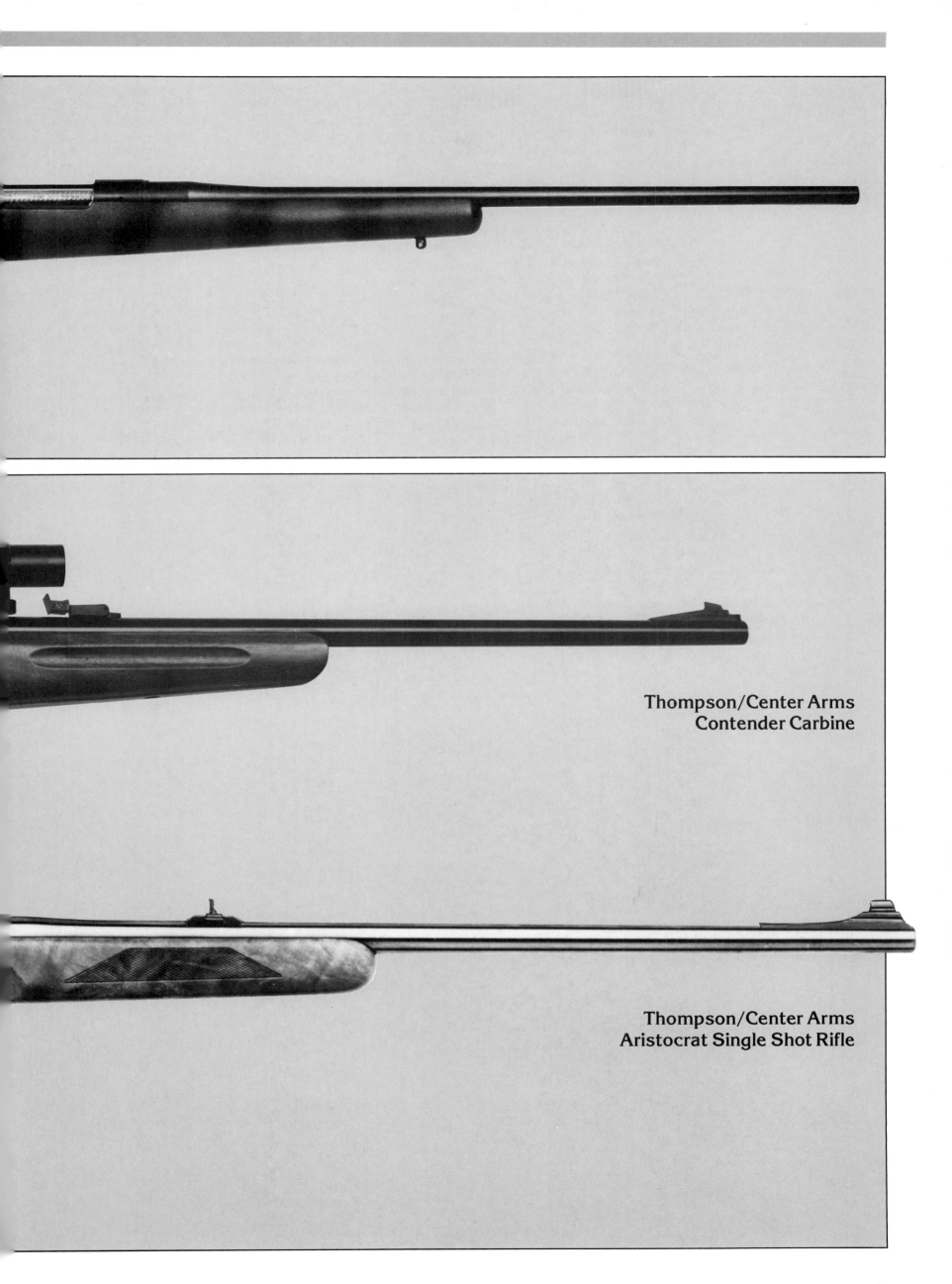

**Thompson/Center Arms
Contender Carbine**

**Thompson/Center Arms
Aristocrat Single Shot Rifle**

Winchester's legendary Model 94 Carbine versions include the .30-30 caliber XTR; the 7-30 Waters XTR; the 94 Standard; the 16 inch barrel, big bore Trapper; and the Ranger, in .30-06 Springfield. John Wayne posed with many an antique Winchester carbine in his movies—for Old West authenticity. The Chief Crazy Horse Model 94 Winchester celebrates the great Sioux chief and his people, is beautifully and symbolically engraved and is chambered for the classic 38-55 Winchester cartridge. The Annie Oakley Commemorative Model 9422 Rifle is also a highly decorative .22 caliber lever action. The beautifully and informatively engraved Winchester/Colt Commemorative set combines two legends of the Wild West. Oliver Winchester's likeness is engraved and inlaid on the rifle's receiver.

US Repeating Arms' Winchester Commemorative Models are all limited edition firearms, featuring handsome Winchester engraving, which, in commemorative models, is designed around historical images and tastefully calligraphic lettering. Insofar as the Annie Oakley is the first US firearm to commemorate an historic woman, the Boy Scout Commemorative Model 9422—which comes complete with commemorative .22 long ammunition— may well claim to be the first such honor for that organization. The Winchester Model 9422 Standard is available in several barrel lengths; has ramp bead front and semi-buckhorn rear sights; and adjustable thumb-hammer extension for right or left handed shooting. US Repeating Arms' Winchester

The Winchester Colt Commemorative Set

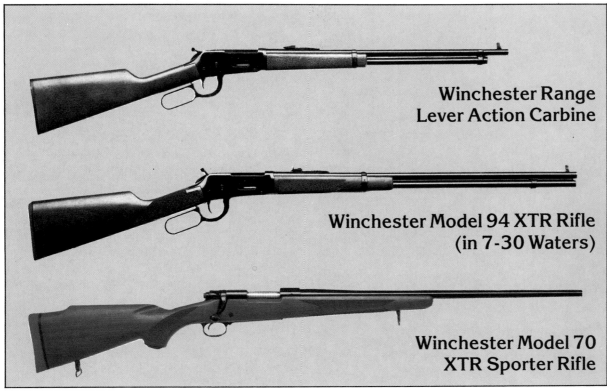

Winchester Range Lever Action Carbine

Winchester Model 94 XTR Rifle (in 7-30 Waters)

Winchester Model 70 XTR Sporter Rifle

Winchester Model 70 Rifle

Winchester Chief Crazy Horse Commemorative Model 94 Lever Action Rifle

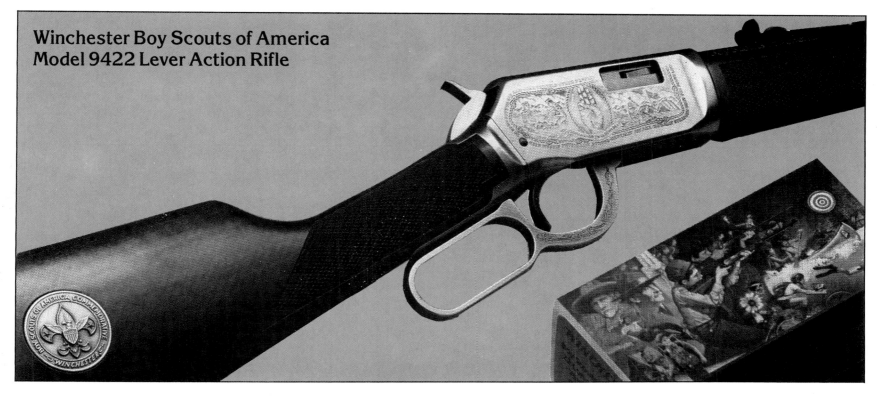

Winchester Boy Scouts of America Model 9422 Lever Action Rifle

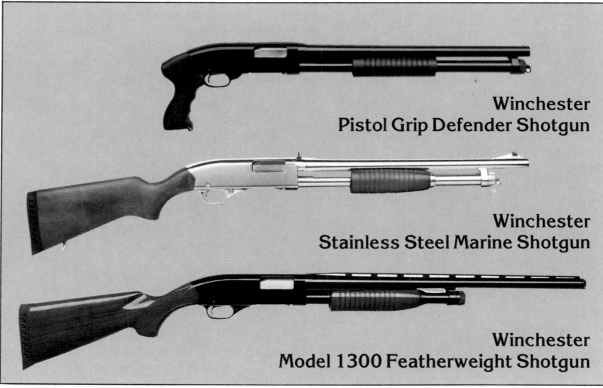

Winchester
Pistol Grip Defender Shotgun

Winchester
Stainless Steel Marine Shotgun

Winchester
Model 1300 Featherweight Shotgun

Winchester
Model 94 Carbine

Winchester
Model 1300 Shotgun

Winchester
Annie Oakley Commemorative
Model 9422 Lever Action Rifle

Model 1300 pumps include the Featherweight, the Turkey gun and the Magnum.

The Winchester Defender slide action shotgun is designed for security and police work, with a recoil-assisted slide action, short overall length and five 2.75 inch shotshell capacity. The Winchester Ranger Semiautomatic Shotgun with a 28 inch Winchoke barrel; the Ranger Semiautomatic Deer Gun with rifle sights; the 28.63 inch overall Pistol Grip Defender; the standard Defender with metal bead sight; the Stainless Marine model with rifle sights; and the ordnance steel barrel Stainless Police. US gunsmithing is alive and well—perhaps symbolic of its progress are these newer chapters from the Winchester story. The supremely handy Model 70 bolt action carbine; the updated, classy Model 94 XTR lever action rifle and the sleek and sturdy Model 1300 slide action shotgun.

Weaver Arms, Ltd's Nighthawk semiautomatic carbine combines nylon, aluminum and steel in a rugged, high-quality 9mm firearm.

Wilkinson Arms's 9mm Luger caliber 'Linda' Pistol comes equipped with a bolt safety and magazine catch, 31 round magazine, and wind-blocked Williams adjustable sights. The Linda autoloader also has a dovetail scope mount built into its receiver. Wilkinson Arms' 'Sherry' Pistol features a cross bolt safety and is chambered for .22 long rifle, is 9.25 ounces light, and is 4.38 inches long.

Wilkinson Arms
Sherry .22 Pistol

Weaver Arms 9mm Semiautomatic Carbine

Wilkinson Arms 9mm Semiautomatic Pistol

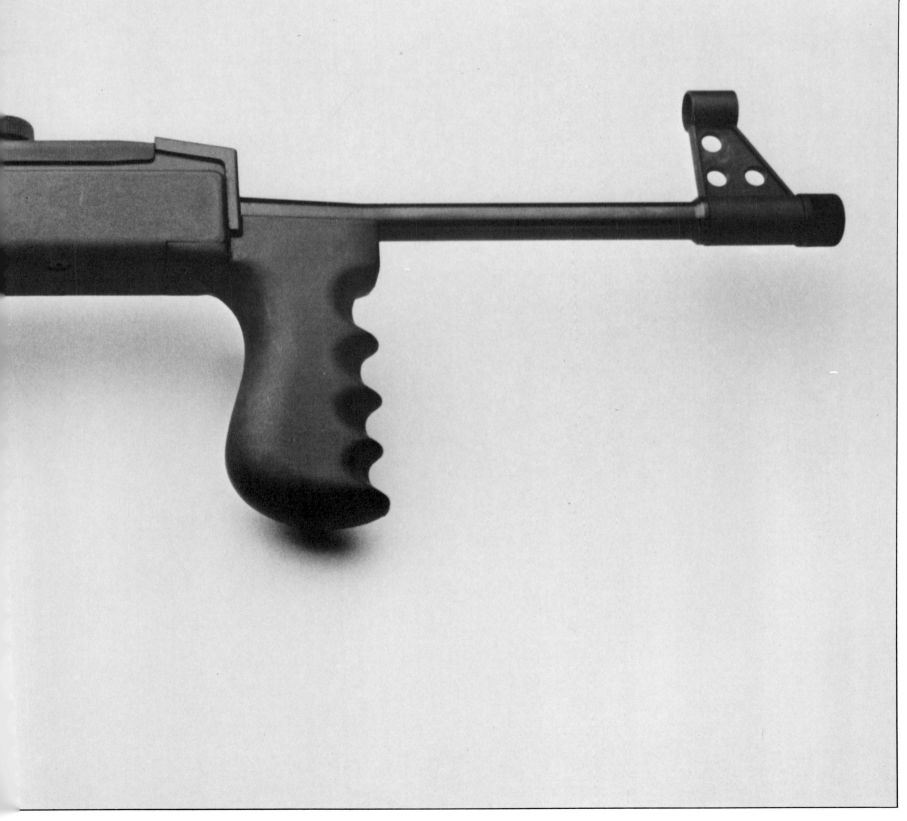

WEST GERMANY

Walther has recently celebrated its 100th anniversary (1886-1986), and is currently celebrating the 50th anniversary of its phenomenal P38 pistol (1938-1988); therefore, this section contains a wealth of historical—as well as technical—information.

All Walther pistol models can be delivered as special designs bearing either oak leaf or scroll work pattern engraving, satin blue finish, grey finish, chromium plated, nickel plated, silver plated, or gold plated. Pistols made to specifications are available upon request.

The Walther P88 automatic pistol in 9mm Parabellum was developed according to the latest knowledge for military and police purposes as well as for self-defense. Its features are immediate first shot potential, optimal safety level, easy handling for both right hand and left hand, appropriate shape, robust construction, safe function, rapid aiming and large magazine capacity.

The P88 is a locked-breech recoil loader with double action trigger lockwork, automatic firing pin, safety and ambidextrous one-lever operation. Immediate first shot potential with optimal dependability are provided by the combined trigger, decocking and striking system.

The four built-in safety features are downward retention of the firing pin; recess in the striking face of the hammer; hammer safety notch; and locking safety (disconnector). The hammer can only strike the firing pin when the slide is in the locked-breech mode and the trigger is pulled completely through.

Hence, the P88 is safeguarded against impact, dropping, or inadvertent hammer tripping when thumb-cocking the weapon. All safeties remain fully effective when the operation lever is thumbed to decock the system. The double action pattern provides immediate first shot potential when the weapon is loaded and decocked. The ambidextrous one-lever operation provides clear manipulation and eliminates handling errors even in stress situations. Its 15 shot capacity reduces, for policemen, the potential problem of having to reload in a stress situation. For sportsmen, the additional capacity is a matter of yet one more of Walther's craftsmanly courtesies to its customers.

The Walther P38 design benefits from Walther's more than 50 years in the production of innovative, groundbreaking automatic pistols and is the most well known Walther production pistol.

Walther P88 9mm Semiautomatic Pistol

Walther Model 1
6.35mm Semiautomatic Pistol

Walther Signal Pistol

Walther P38 9mm Semiautomatic Pistol

The prototypal period of development for the P38 was roughly from 1935-37. Ground for this famous pistol was broken with the development—way back in 1929—of Walther's PP autoloading pistol. This design was truly a groundbreaking design, and it made way for the advent of the double action P38 design with the droplever safety mechanism. In 9mm Parabellum caliber, this pistol had (and has) knockdown power, but not nearly the extreme recoil and instability of .45 caliber designs then (and now) extant.

Prototypes in the factory museum of Zella-Mehlis gave testimony about the Walther brothers' interests in trying out new solutions to technical problems. Nobody outside the factory knew about it until the American troops occupied Zella-Mehlis in 1945. The Americans dissolved the museum and brought the pistols to the United States for souvenirs. Not long ago, a Walther pistol in prewar finish appeared in the USA; this might have been meant as a replacement model of the service pistol Pi08, as the pistol in question is in 9mm Parabellum caliber, and has a toggle action and a magazine capacity of 16(!) rounds.

The P38 in its current configuration arose out of the pre-models 'Armeepistole,' 'Heerespistole' and 'Militärpistole.' The Armeepistole Model AP had a magazine capacity of eight rounds of 9mm Parabellum ammo. The overall length was 8.5 inches, the length of barrel 4.8 inches. The barrel had six grooves right hand twist. The pistol weighed, unloaded, 28.2 ounces. The AP—as this precursor to the P38 was factory designated—had the double action system of the PP and PPK but stronger; the hammer was fully covered by slide and frame. This pistol had a small production run, because the

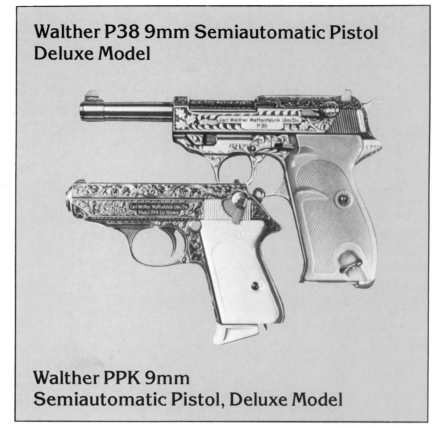

Walther P38 9mm Semiautomatic Pistol Deluxe Model

Walther PPK 9mm Semiautomatic Pistol, Deluxe Model

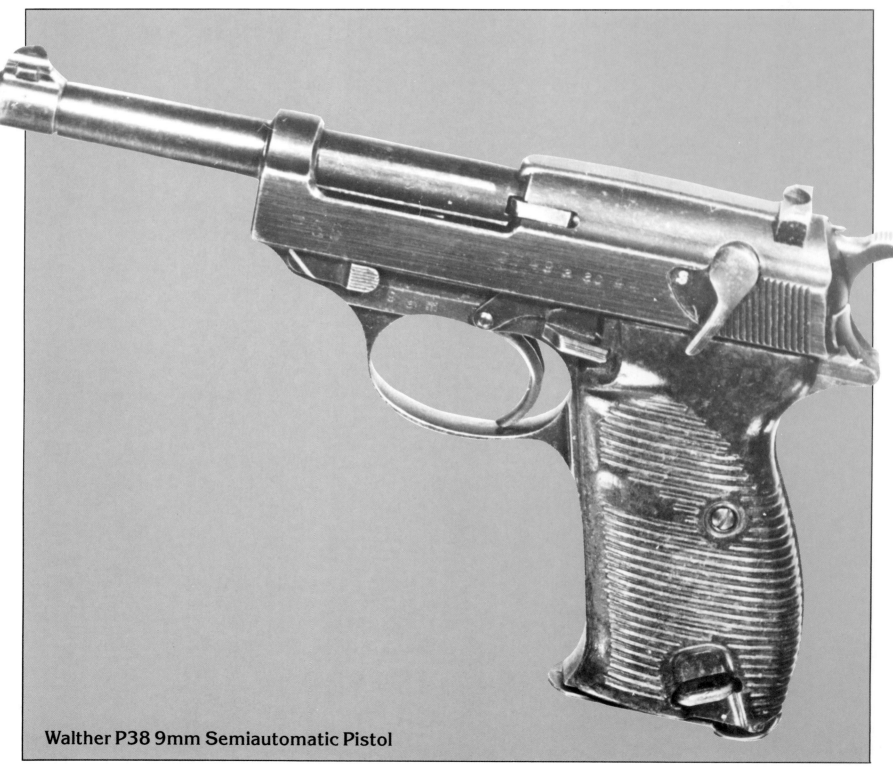

Walther P38 9mm Semiautomatic Pistol

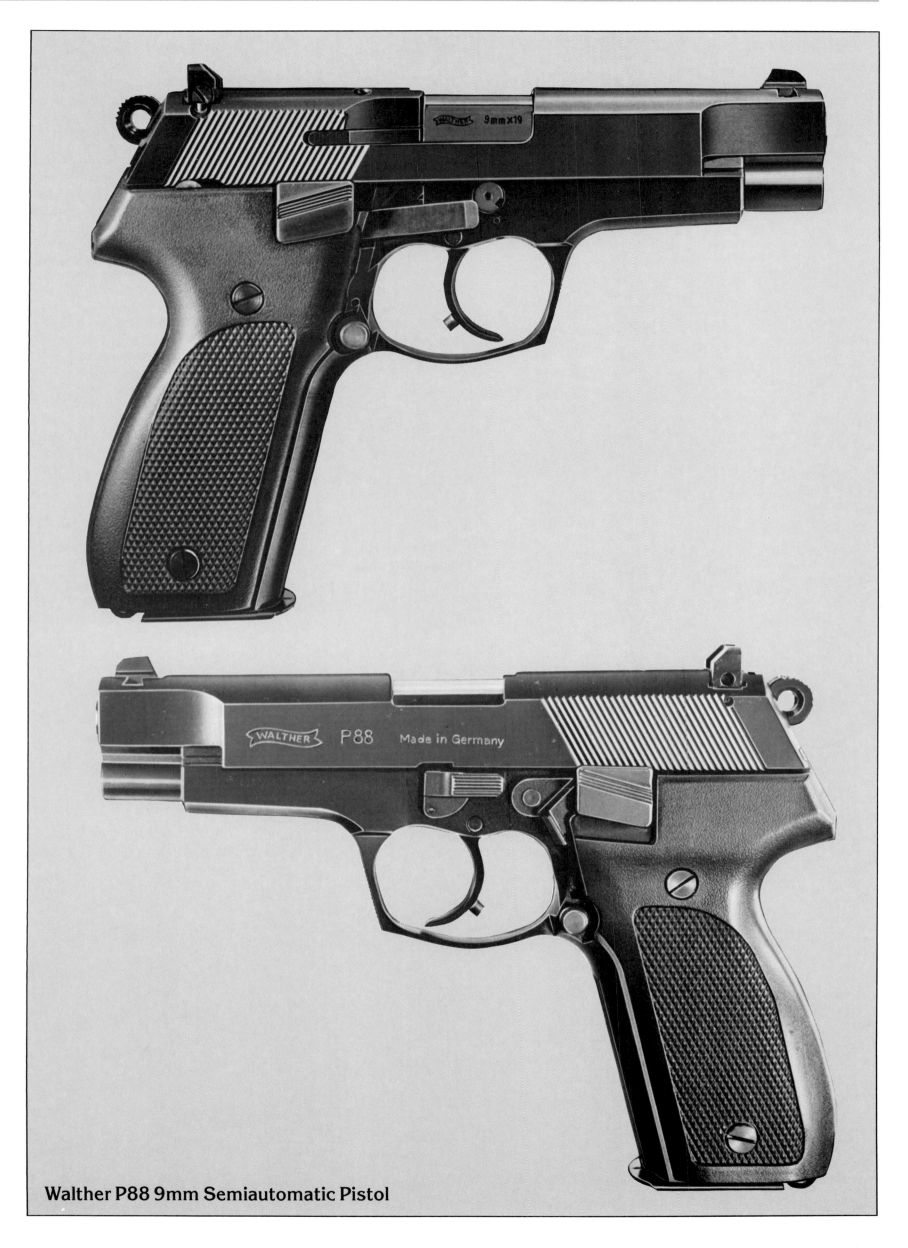

Walther P88 9mm Semiautomatic Pistol

Walther P38 9mm Semiautomatic Pistol

Waffenfabrik Ulm/Do.
P 38

F

project was abandoned in view to the HP. The Heerespistole HP was the real foremodel of the P38 because it shows the slight differences in the action.

The Militärpistole MP was just a PP brought up to caliber 9mm Parabellum; at the beginning nobody conceded great chances to it because the MP did not have a locked breech.

The designation 'P38' was given to the pistol in accordance with its year of adoption by the German Army in 1938. In Sweden it was named 'P39.'

Until 1940–41 the P38 was manufactured to prewar specifications. It also was offered—named HP—for civilian purposes or export. During the HP's prewar production, the Walther factory could comply with the special wishes of its various customers, so we still find prewar custom-built P38s with collectors. While the war was on, the need for pistols grew steadily. To fulfill these demands, Walther had to cooperate with other weapons manufacturers and contractors of small parts. When the production of the Pi08 was stopped, firms engaged in this business then produced the P38.

Sales to civilians were totally stopped. The demands of war—fabrication of more pistols in shorter time—forced Walther to cut some fabrication steps, such as those involved in giving the pistol its prewar excellent finish. For example, blued parts were not truly blued, but received phosphateimpregnation, and instead of molded grips the pistols had grips made of sheet metal. All these restrictions of course had no negative impact on the function or reliability of the weapon.

Eventually, the American troops left Zella-Mehlis, Russian troops came in and dismounted all facilities and tools; and the Walther fac-

Walther Commemorative Model P5
9mm Semiautomatic Pistol

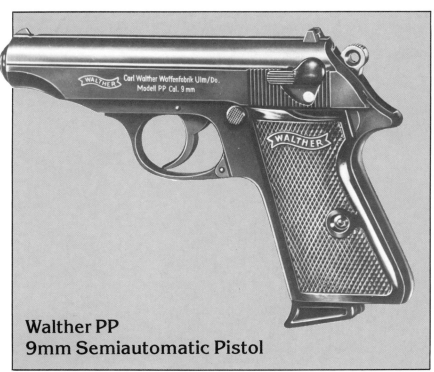

Walther PP
9mm Semiautomatic Pistol

Walther PPK/S
9mm Semiautomatic Pistol

tory was blown up. At the same time—just with short interruption—the production of firearms was still going on under French supervision at the Mauser-Werke at Oberndorf. Within this French program P38s were built, too. It speaks for the quality of this pistol that it was chosen by the Bundeswehr to become its main regulation pistol after the war, when Germany again had an army.

But not only the Bundeswehr was interested in this famous pistol; many other nations use it for service with military or police units. Portugal bought large numbers; Pakistan equipped its airforce with it; Ghana has it in service with the Ghanian army; and military units of Venezuela, Colombia, Argentina and Uruguay trust on the proven and substantiated reliability of the P38. Because of the modern and advanced design of the Walther P5, the sales of the P38 naturally have decreased, but in South America and in Asia the P38 still has an unrivalled reputation.

Proceeding from the fact that the first patent for the construction of the P38 was established in February 1936, the Walther company can say' '100 years Walther; 50 years P38.' This big bore pistol has been produced in an almost unchanged way for 50 years. More than one million pistols of this model have established the P38's world wide reputation for reliabilty and operational safety.

For collectors Walther has earmarked a limited quantity of 500 units. The inscription inlayed with gold, the gold plated hammer trigger and extractor, as well as the wooden grip plates with oakleaf carvings recall the preceding commemorative models PP, PPK and P5.

Standard equipment for these limited edition firearms also includes an identically numbered walnut case with oakleaf carvings as decorative protection for this elegant firearm. Each commemorative P38 is

provided with a deed showing the serial number and original signature from Walther's Managing Director.

In the early 1970s, officials of the Federal Republic of Germany began searching for the optimal standard police pistol. Although the Walther PP and PPK had already proven themselves, something a bit more modern was desired. The new pistol had to fire 10,000 rounds without mechanical, material or structural failure, and had to have four built-in safeties, comprising the following qualities: downward retention of the firing pin; a recess in the striking face of the hammer; a hammer safety intercept notch; and a locking safety (disconnector).

The Walther company came up with a design to fulfill the above—and other stringent requirements—and the first deliveries of this pistol were made in 1978 to the Bundesländer (land governments) of Baden-Würtemberg and Rheinland-Pfalz for the equipage of their police forces.

One year later the Rijkspolitie of the Netherlands, too, ordered more than 35,000 models P5, and meanwhile also the 'Bereitschaftpolizeien' (special police forces of the Bundesländer) of Baden-Würtemberg and Rheinland-Pfalz ordered, under agreement with the minister of the interior of the Federal Republic of Germany, the Walther P5.

Excellent lining, sturdiness and perfect workmanship have made the P5 a most accepted police pistol with an extremely high degree of safety.

The hammer cannot strike the firing pin unless the slide is fully in battery and the trigger is pulled completely through—therefore, the P5 is safeguarded against impact, dropping or inadvertent hammer tripping when thumb-cocking the weapon.

All safeties remain fully effective when the decocking lever is

Walther PP 9mm Semiautomatic Pistol

Walther PPK 9mm Semiautomatic Pistol

**Walther Commemorative P38
9mm Semiautomatic Pistol
(with custom case)**

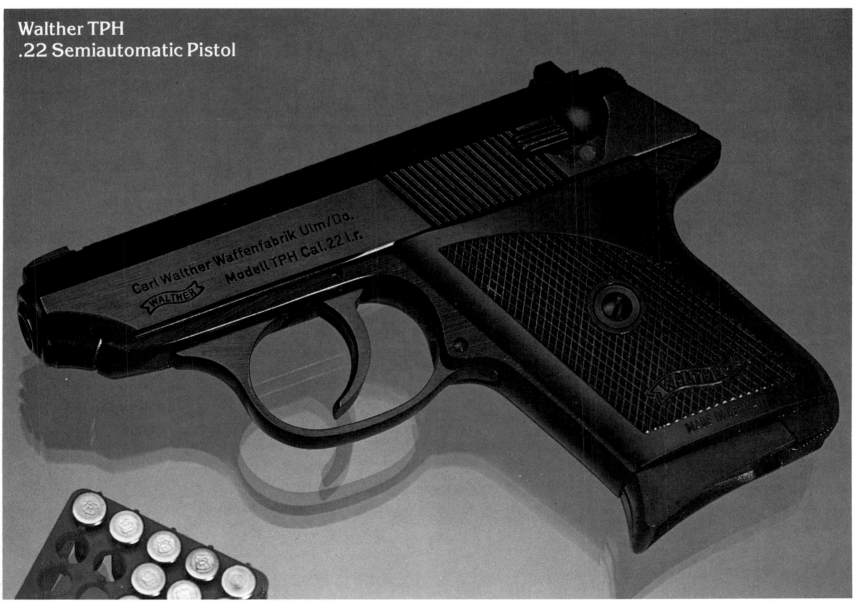

**Walther TPH
.22 Semiautomatic Pistol**

thumbed to decock the action. The double action pattern provides immediate first shot potential when the weapon is loaded and decocked.

Altogether, the salient characteristics of the Walther P5 are: a modern pistol design for law enforcement and self-defense purposes, incorporating a new handling and safety system with four independent safety functions; double action trigger pattern and elimination of manual safeties, which provides rapid reaction times; automatic firing pin retention, which guarantees optimal safety level, even if the weapon is dropped (a shot can only be discharged if the trigger is pulled completely through); the P5 can be carried safely in the loaded condition because the firing pin is automatically retained; the decocking lever permits the cocked hammer to be lowered into the safety intercept notch without risk; rapid target acquisition with high-contrast sight elements and white pickup markings; slide is held in the open position following the last shot; simple takedown into four main assemblies without using tools; outstanding evaluation results from international firearms specialists; two magazines, each with eight rounds in 9mm × 19 Parabellum (Luger) or 7.65 Parabellum caliber: low weight factor thanks to the special grade light alloy receiver; proverbial Walther quality, firmly established for decades by Walther's internationally renowned PP, PPK and P38 models; extended service life and absolute dependability; compact appearance and sleek lines; drawn barrel to typical Walther quality standards; and closed design concept largely eliminates ingress of sand and dirt.

In addition to these features and qualifications, an optional conversion barrel for the P5 is available—this barrel is made for 8.2mm

Walther P5 9mm
Semiautomatic Pistol

Walther TPH Deluxe Model Pistol

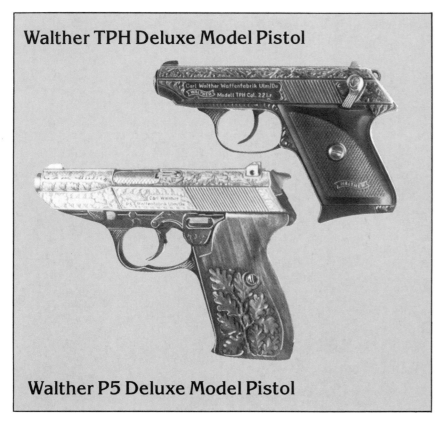

Walther P5 Deluxe Model Pistol

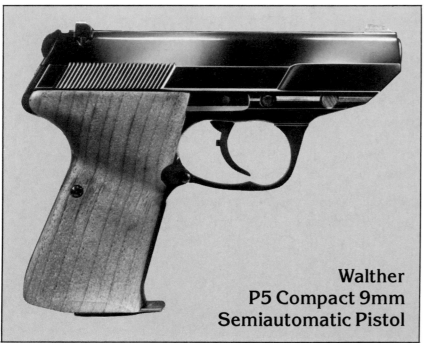

Walther
P5 Compact 9mm
Semiautomatic Pistol

plastic bullets. Overall dimensions for the P5 are: 7.1 inches by 5.1 inches by 1.3 inches, with an empty weight of approximately 28 ounces.

A smaller and handier version of the Walther P5 is the P5 Compact which is also in 9mm Parabellum caliber. The main features of the Walther P5 Compact, in comparison with the standard Walther P5, are as follows: it is seven mm shorter and weighs less; the shape and size of its grips are ideal for small hands, too; its laterally mounted magazine catch is easy to operate with the thumb; its favorable exterior shape and rounded-off hammer are designed for the hidden portability of the weapon; and its polished finish and wooden grip plates provide the weapon with a truly handsome appearance.

The Walther P5 Compact has overall dimensions of 6.7 inches by five inches by 1.3 inches. This locked-breech automatic has an unloaded weight of 27.9 ounces. It has a low weight factor thanks to the special grade light alloy frame, simple takedown into four main assemblies without using tools, and a modern pistol design for self-defense purposes incorporating a new handling and safety system with four independent safety functions. The P5 Compact's small and efficient appearance and sleek lines combine with its other excellent features to give the shooter more than his money's worth.

The P5 can be carried safely in the loaded condition because the firing pin is automatically retained. The P5 Compact's decocking lever permits the cocked hammer to be lowered into the safety intercept notch without risk. Its double action trigger pattern and elimination of manual safeties provide rapid reaction times. Automatic firing pin retention guarantees optimal safety level, even if the weapon is drop-

ped. A shot can only be discharged when the trigger is pulled completely through. Two magazines, each with eight rounds in 9mm Parabellum (9mm × 19) caliber provide adequate firepower.

Built into the P5 Compact is the proverbial Walther quality, firmly established for decades by Walther's internationally renowned PP, PPK and P38 models. Extended service life and absolute dependability are expected of, and delivered by, this model. It has a drawn barrel to typical Walther quality standards; its closed design concept largely eliminates ingress of sand and dirt; rapid target acquisition with high-contrast sight elements and white pickup markings is yet one more feature of this firearm; and its slide is held in the open position following the last shot. All in all, the Walther P5 Compact is a fine pistol, in the tradition of Walther gunsmithing.

Walther pistol models PP and PPK belong to the history of firearms. The British pistols expert and author of several books on firearms, Ian V Hogg, is quoted in the Walther promotional material as saying: 'The introduction of this model in 1929 rendered every other selfloading pistol obsolete overnight, so advanced was its design. For the first time a selfloader was produced with a workable and reliabe double action mechanism, a device which had tempted designers and eluded inventors since the beginning of the century. Several other minor innovations were married together in this pistol. . .'

In 1929, nobody could recognize that the Walther PP and PPK would be among the most successful pistols ever made and that they would carry the name of Walther into the farthest corners of the world. Now, both models have been on the market for nearly half a century.

**Walther P5 Compact
9mm Semiautomatic Pistol**

Walther P5 (stripped)

Their popularity is based on reliability, accuracy of fire and classic styling.

With the construction of the PP, Walther entered a fully new field. For the first time all demands of police and customs service as well as forestry and hunting purposes were matched in one pistol design. This pistol combines the superiorities of a selfloading pistol with the safety of a revolver; it can be carried loaded and safe and therefore it is ready for action at all times.

The PP was—and still is—made in .22 long rifle, 7.65mm and 9mm short calibers. The dimensions of these blowback operated pistols are nearly identical. The barrel lengths are 3.9 inches for the .22 long rifle and 3.3 inches for 7.65 and 9mm short. Calibers .22 long rifle and 7.65mm have a magazine capacity of eight rounds, and the nine mm magazine holds seven rounds.

Of course all the different models are operated in the same way. The Walther PP turned out well wherever it was in action. Because the pistol had an overall length of 6.7 inches, some people thought it too long for carrying concealed or without a holster. Walther solved this problem by constructing the PPK with an overall length of 6.1 inches.

The PPK was launched in 1931 and was the 'little sister' of the PP. Its construction, technology and handling entirely corresponds to the Walther PP, and it is manufactured in the same calibers. A slight alteration is found at the grip: the back of the PP grip is fixed by the frame, and in the PPK it is fixed by the molded grip. Another difference is that the magazine of the PPK holds one round less.

Like the PP, the barrel of the PPK also features six grooves with right hand twist. The PPK weighs less, too— 20 ounces for the .22 long rifle version and 21 ounces for the 9mm short.

While 'PP' stands for 'Polizei-Pistole,' ('Police Pistol') PPK can stand for 'Polizei-Pistole-Kriminal,' ('Police Pistol—Criminal') although it can stand for 'Polizei-Pistole kurz,' ('Police Pistol, short)—written PPk. Both model groups gained world wide success. They have been produced and sold in large numbers. In Germany all police units of the Bundesländer were at one time equipped. In the United States the PPK was so successful that in autumn 1968 the US government issued the Gun Control Act which led to the creation of the model PPK/S: the frame was that of a PP, the slide that of a PPK. The PPK/S has been manufactured in the US for several years.

Elegance in shape, excellent finish and immaculate quality of the parts are among the attributes of Walther PP and Walther PPK, and older PPKs and PPs are now desirable collector's items and have reached an astonishing increase of value. For instance, prewar Walther PPs in 6.35mm caliber have appreciated in value up to 1250 US dollars, and prewar PPs in 7.65mm or .22 long rifle cost between 450 and 500 US dollars. Pistols of World War II manufacture, lacking the peacetime Walther polish and fine finishing touches, are worth more than 350 US dollars. PP and PPk pistols still have their place to-day within the Walther program and there is no reason to abandon their production—now as before, they are reliable, easy to handle and have a high target accuracy.

The hand-size Walther TPH, in .22 long rifle and 6.35mm caliber, is an extremely wieldable small semiautomatic pistol. This smallest, safest and fastest pocket pistol that Walther has ever made is a weapon endowed with both an excellent performance and all the other advantages of Walther's larger pistol models. This small but handy weapon, when empty, weighs only about 11.6 ounces.

Walther PPK
9mm Semiautomatic Pistol

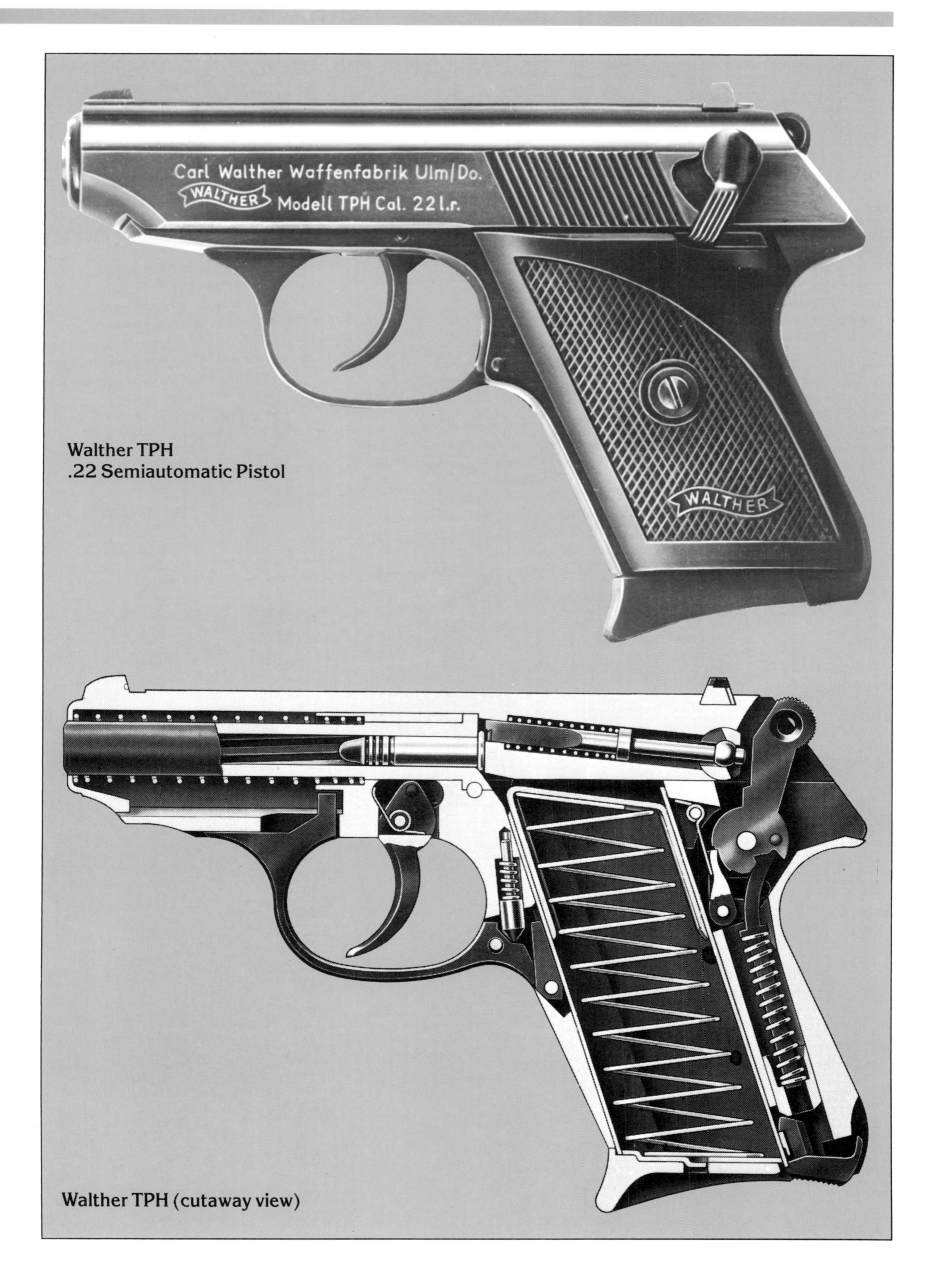

Walther TPH
.22 Semiautomatic Pistol

Walther TPH (cutaway view)

Carl Walther Waffenfabrik Ulm/Do.
WALTHER Modell TPH Cal. 22 l.r.

The rapid-fire pistol model OSP and the target pistol model GSP are top grade weapons with a long series of eminent international successes (Olympic winner, world record, world champion, national champion et alteral).

All models have the same frame in common so that three conversion units in the calibers .22 short, .22 long rifle and .32 S&W can be optionally fitted. The trigger units are interchangeable; trigger functions and finger positions are individually adjustable. The rear sights are vertically and laterally adjustable; front sights and rear sight blades are exchangeable.

The weapons are delivered with wooden grip plates featuring shelves for right and left hand shooters and, on request, without grip plates. Blanks for making custom-shaped grip plates and dry practice trigger units are also available.

Barrel, slide casing and frame of the GSP-MV .22 long rifle caliber are nickel satin finished. The conversion unit in .32 S&W caliber is made to match with this model. The barrel for the GSP Junior .22 long rifle caliber is approximately 3.2 ounces lighter than with the standard weapon, and the grip plates are designed for small hands. The pistols are supplied complete with a well-designed lockable carrying case, in which there is adequate additional space for a second OSP/GSP pistol, conversion units, trigger units, magazines and accessories.

The Walther OSP Match automatic pistol in .22 short caliber is among the most advanced rapid-fire pistols in the world. Its design enhances excellent wielding, firing stability and high target shooting efficiency. The OSP's grips have large, fully adjustable hand shelves,

Walther GSP .32 Target Pistol

1 trigger	6 hammer	11 slide locking lever
2 trigger level	7 firing pin	12 trigger unit
3 trigger bar	8 spring cocking lever	13 recoil spring
4 trigger pawl	9 slide	14 firing spring
5 sear	10 locking pin	15 magazine catch

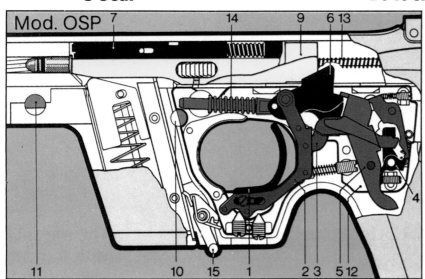

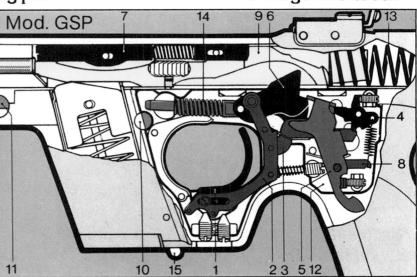

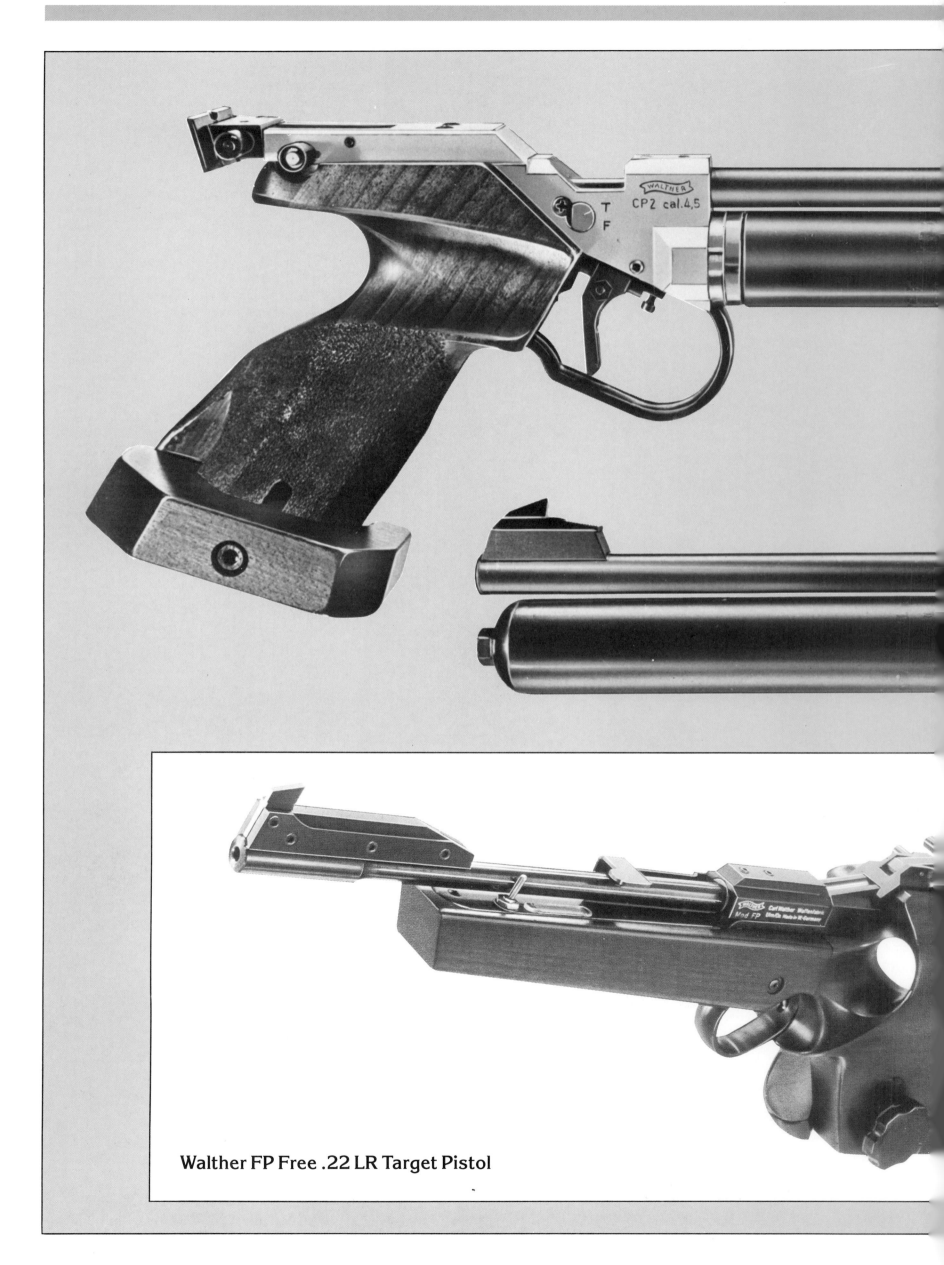

Walther FP Free .22 LR Target Pistol

Walther CP2 4.5mm Target Pistol

to provide a 'custom fit' for the shooter's hand. Especially taken into consideration in the designing of these adjustable grips is the crucial area between the thumb and the index finger. The short barrel offers more frame design possibilities without exceeding the maximum length. The compact concept of the weapon and the light slide promote the extremely stable firing 'feel' of the pistol. The OSP Match is delivered with a 40 gram barrel weight as standard equipment, making possible the optimum balance. A 100 gram barrel weight is offered optionally. When using ammunition with low gas pressure it is possible to close the rearmost gas equalizer hole with the pushing bar so that the weapon can compensate for the low-pressure ammo.

In 1934 Germany began to form its team for the Olympic Games in Berlin in 1936. The German competitors originally only had the Walther model 25 and some examples of the Colt Woodsman. Firing German ammunition caused difficulties because of the weakness of the copper cases, which Germany in the thick of its crushing depression, then used. Lack of foreign currency made it impossible to buy foreign ammunition, so Walther constructed a new sporting pistol which was given to the German team at the end of 1934; it was called 'Olympia Pistol.'

The Olympia Pistol had an exposed hammer and at the rear a spur that laid over the wrist. On top of the spur a sight holder could be attached so the sighting line was lengthened by some centimeters. Unfortunately this device did not work in practice as the rear sight and foresight were not well coordinated. From this model—'Olympia Model, Vormodell'—just few pistols were manufactured. Based on ex-

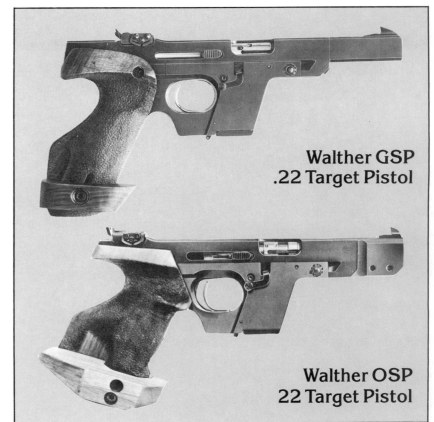

Walther GSP
.22 Target Pistol

Walther OSP
22 Target Pistol

Walther GSP .22 Target Pistol

Walther OSP .22 Match Pistol

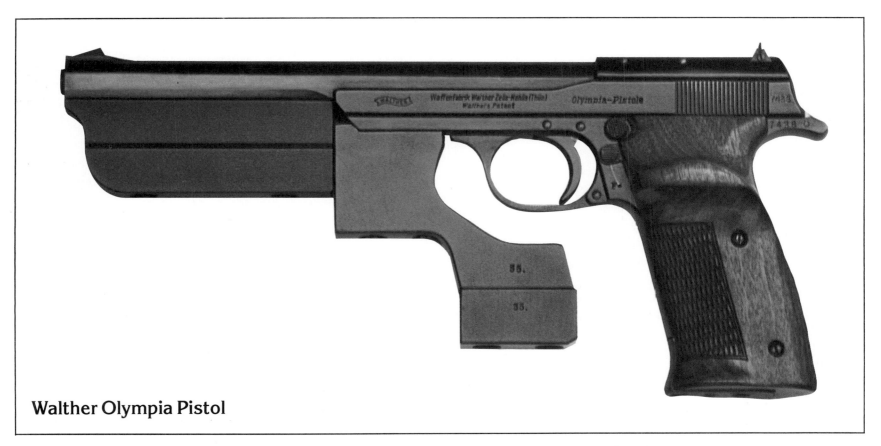

Walther Olympia Pistol

**Walther CP2
4.5mm Target Pistol**

periences with this model Walther reworked this pistol and gave it, now with an enclosed hammer, to the team selected for the Olympic games.

The Walther Model FP free pistol is an advanced high performance weapon embodying all the desirable features of a modern weapon for successful target shooting. The precision adjustable, electronic trigger design provides non-contacting, proximity discharge faster than any conventional pattern. The power source is a 9 V dry battery.

It features a low axis, free floating barrel made of top grade material, giving outstanding accuracy, and also features: Martini-type breech locking action; sight adjustment for windage and elevation; interchangeable rear notch and front blade; infinitely variable sight radius from 13.7 to 17.9 inches; and optimal hand position thanks to the anatomically compatible grip with adjustable palm rest: the back of the shooter's hand is firmly enclosed by the grip and the palm rest.

In spite of all demands in the production of pistols there was a great engagement at Walther in the development of smallbore sporting rifles. As an extension of beginnings that went back to the 1920s, they built a Sportbüchse (sporting rifle), a Meisterbüche (masters or match rifle), an Olympia Model and an Olympia-Sonderausfuhrung, a smallbore rifle for competition shooting.

There always was some competition with the firm of JG Anschütz, also coming from Zella-Mehlis and now also settled at Ulm. In this particular relation the often somewhat thoughtless slogan 'Competition is good for business' has its weight: Both firms are proud of the fact that about 98 percent of international top shooters use a smallbore rifle from Ulm.

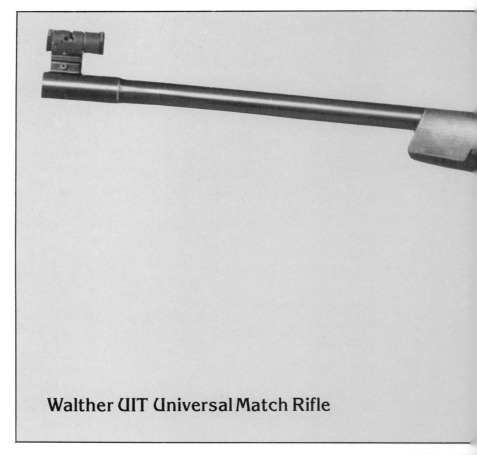

Walther UIT Universal Match Rifle

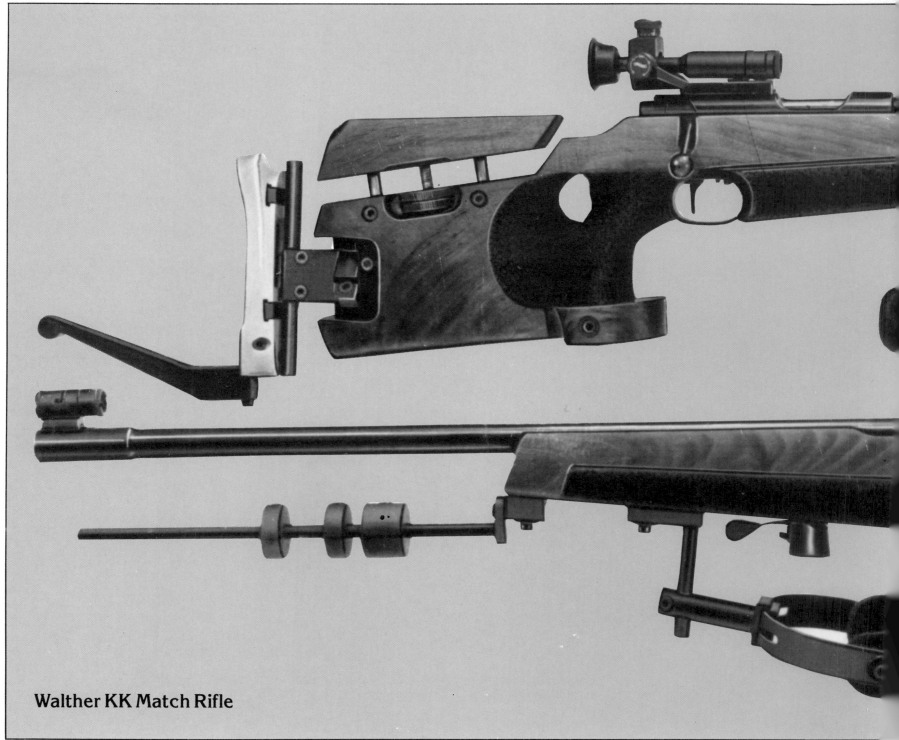

Walther KK Match Rifle

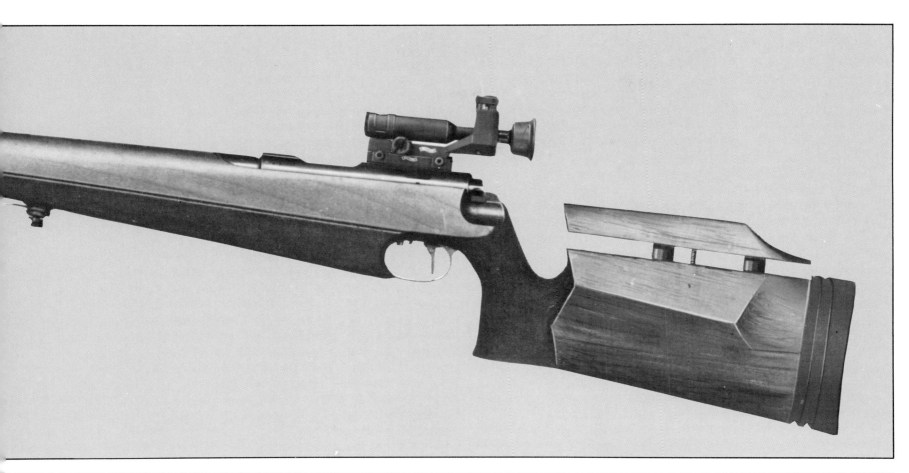

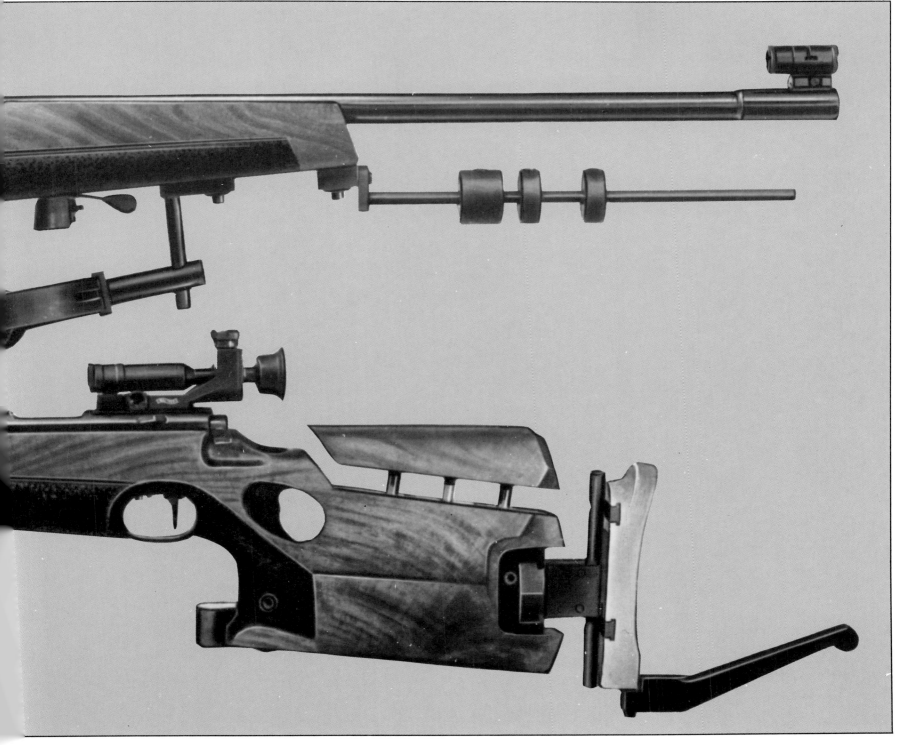

For Walther, international success started in 1976 when US marksman Lanny Bassham won the gold medal at the Olympic Games of Montreal in the competition smallbore rifle three positions—40 shots prone, 40 shots standing and 40 shots kneeling; he used a Walther KK Match in .22 long rifle caliber. Before this, Lanny Bassham had already won a number of American and international championships with his Walther.

In 1968 the Austrian Wolfram Waibel shot with his Walther a world record with 400 of 400 points in Olympic smallbore rifle prone position (at that time the program required 40 shots, now we have 60).

Englishman Malcolm Cooper scored with his KK Match at the 1984 Olympic Games in Los Angeles, under very tiring weather changes, 1173 points in smallbore rifle three positions. Therefore he gained Olympic gold and a special honoring by Her Majesty, the Queen. He shot a fantastic 392 points in the prone position and equalled the world record in the three-position event. At the International Match Week in Zurich, Cooper scored one point more; with a result of 1174 points he showed his great skill and proved the quality of the Walther KK Match. In August 1985 Cooper again eclipsed his marks with a score of 1185 in the smallbore three-position event.

Such a result has never been scored at international competitions. Cooper reached prone 398 points, standing 394 and kneeling 393—and this under bad weather conditions, strong wind and changing light. With this result of 1185 of 1200 points he overthrew the world record—held by him and the Russians Wlassow and Lwow.

The Walther match rifles are technologically sophisticated competition rifles combining superb accuracy with aesthetic elegance; standard Walther KK match action with adjustable trigger system; universal diopter sights (32.8 to 328 foot) range settings; anatomically compatible walnut stocks for left and right handed marksmen; variable stock length by fitting spacers; and vertical adjustment for buttplate drop.

On the UIT Match, UIT Universal Match and KK Match models, the sling rail is laterally offset. The UIT models are for the standard disciplines and the KK Match for the international events.

The following is a rundown on the various Walther match rifle configurations:

• UIT Special: The proven and economical weapon for the standard rifle event.

• UIT Match: KK smallbore system deeply inletted into the stock; rounded profile of stippled fore end provides excellent grip; high cheekpiece and dovetail sight bases give elevated sighting line, allowing natural, upright head position.

• UIT Universal Match: Top grade weapon for the discerning marksman; variable cheekpiece as described for the LGR Universal Match.

• UIT BV Universal: The special precision competition rifle with redesigned block action, mechanical trigger and variable cheekpiece; designed for all standard disciplines.

• UIT E Universal: A new, progressive design concept featuring fine-increment adjustment of the electronic trigger action and proximity

Walther KKJ Hunting Rifle
Walther KJS Hunting Rifle

Walther KK Match Rifle

Walther LGR Target Rifle

Walther LGR Match Rifle

Walther LGR Universal Match Rifle

Walther LGR Moving Target Rifle

discharge and faster than any conventional or electric pattern.

• UIT Moving Target: Specialized configuration for the Moving Target event, with 23.7 inch barrel and muzzle mounted counterweight. Trigger pull is preset to 17.9 ounces. Stock features thumbhole inletting. Potential adjustments include: cheekpiece height, buttplate drop, stock length, and pistol grip to trigger length. Extra barrel weight is 7.9 ounces. Optimal balance of this weapon enhances natural, rapid target acquisition. Telescopic sights and mounts are optional. Repeated international class scores highlight the uniqueness of this concept.

• KK Silhouette: A special competition rifle designed for shooting at metallic silhouettes.

• KK Match: New, international grade target concept, developed in conjunction with top flight marksmen. Advanced stock design permits maximum number of potential adjustments, including counterweights, hand shelf, palm rest, cheekpiece, hook buttplate, stock length and trigger action. Counterweights can be varied and balance modified as required. If the weapon is canted, the counterweight can be set vertical to the barrel axis.

Accuracy, high performance ammunition, automatic function and gas operation were the main criteria specified during the development of the new Walther Model WA 2000, designed around a high performance cartridge in order to achieve minimal impact variation. In comparative trials, the .300 Winchester Magnum provided the best results and was subsequently selected as the most suitable cartridge.

A highly accurate semiautomatic weapon, the target rifle model WA 2000 is available in .300 Winchester Magnum. The .308 Winchester

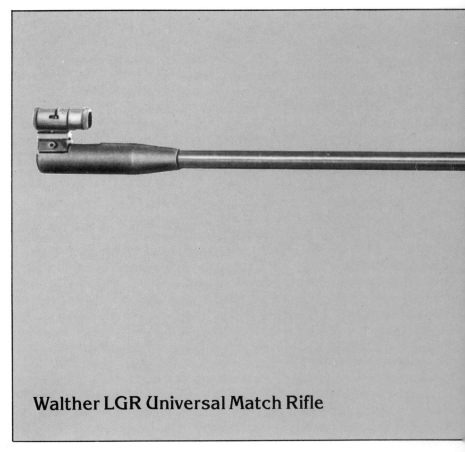

Walther LGR Universal Match Rifle

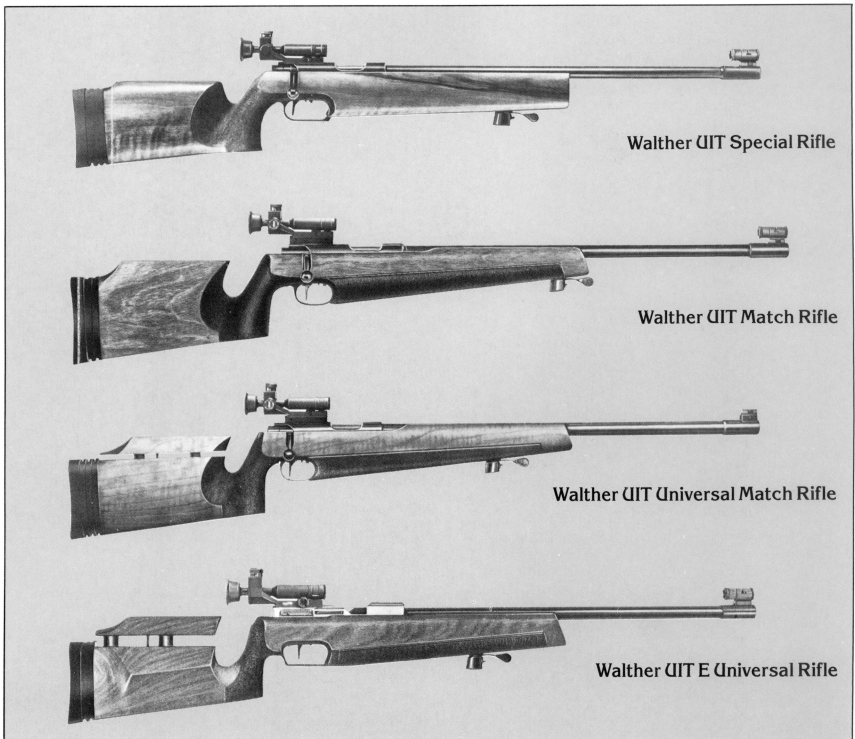

Walther UIT Special Rifle

Walther UIT Match Rifle

Walther UIT Universal Match Rifle

Walther UIT E Universal Rifle

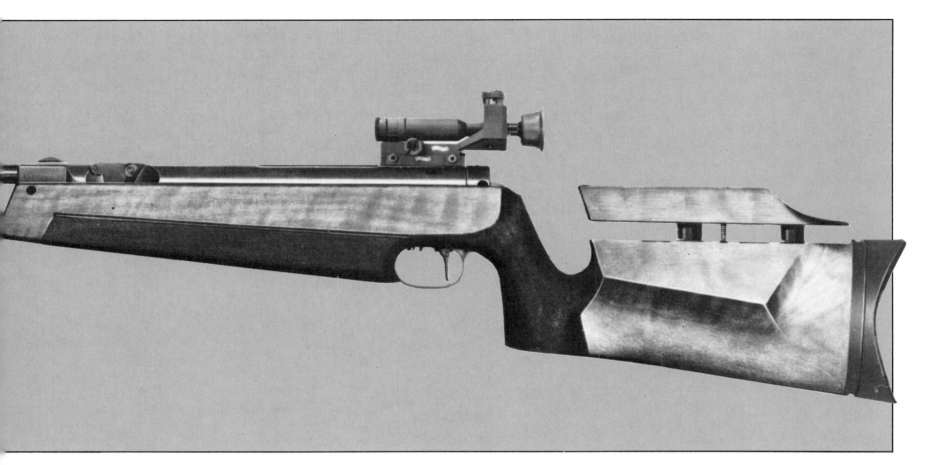

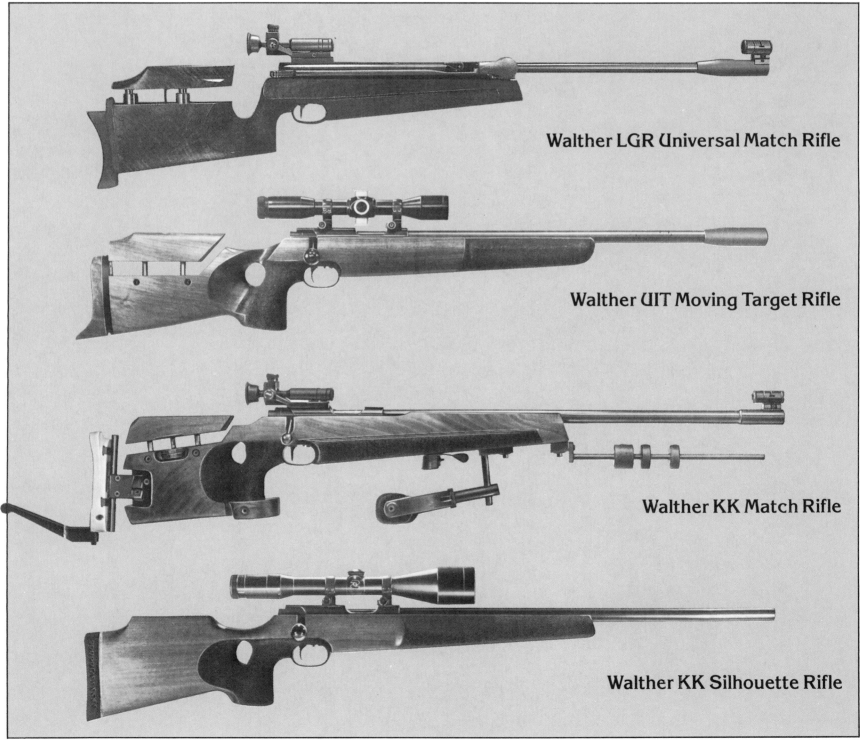

Walther LGR Universal Match Rifle

Walther UIT Moving Target Rifle

Walther KK Match Rifle

Walther KK Silhouette Rifle

chambering is also available as an option. All currently available precision rifles are derivatives of hunting or military weapons and, as such, invariably represent a compromise solution for the elite marksman who requires the ultimate in accuracy. The WA 2000 has been specially designed and built, and in combination with the .300 Winchester Magnum cartridge, it can be considered as a weapon system offering optimal performance.

The primary structure of the weapon is a framework made of profiled tubing. The rear of this framework is firmly secured to the receiver, which accepts the bolt and the barrel. Ahead of the receiver in the vicinity of the telescopic sight mounting, the framework is reinforced by intermediate plates installed on both sides. The muzzle end of the profiled tubing frame is stiffened by a special construction.

The reason for this design was to create a self-supporting element in which the barrel would be symmetrically retained and the recoil generated by the shot would be transmitted along the bore axis to the shooter's shoulder. With this construction there is no twisting movement and the weapon remains on target. Consequently, no time is lost through target reacquisition. Trigger mechanism, striking device, trigger, trigger guard and safety are installed in the lower rail and form one unit. As the most important part of the weapon, the barrel is the deciding factor for accuracy. Consequently, internal and external design is critical. Groove and land diameters, twist and chambering are carefully matched to the caliber and are held within close tolerances. A muzzle brake is attached to the muzzle.

The weapon is gas operated. Its bolt head has seven locking lugs and rotates through 60 degrees. Gas tapped from a port in the barrel

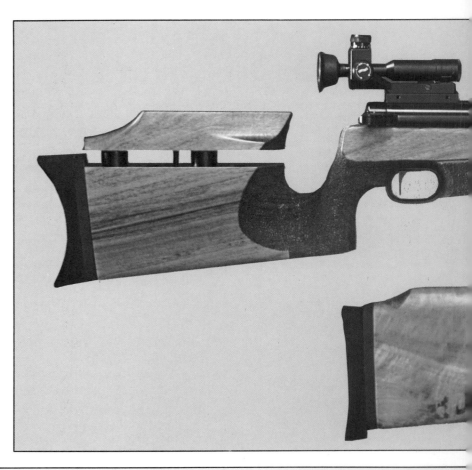

Walther WA 2000 Target Rifle

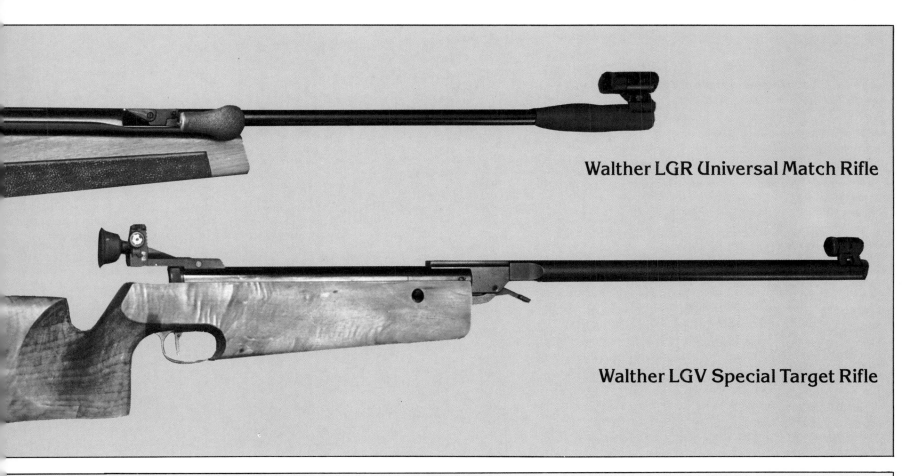

Walther LGR Universal Match Rifle

Walther LGV Special Target Rifle

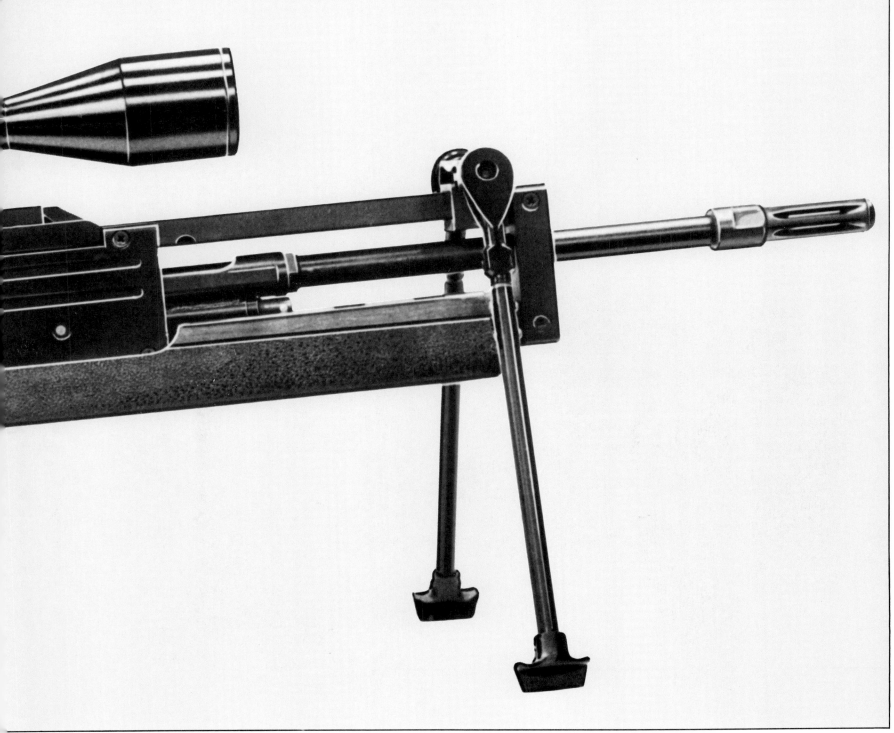

actuates a piston which initiates the unlocking cycle. The bolt stays open after the last shot. When the catch lever is thumbed down, the bolt runs forward and chambers a cartridge. Weapon ready to fire; the weapon has a detachable, single-row magazine. Cartridge feed is arranged so that the bullet tip is not damaged during chambering. This is achieved by two cams on the follower plate which also prevents the cartridge from slipping forward. The safety, which acts on the trigger and the sear, can be operated from both sides of the weapon.

This firearm comes equipped with a handy, adjustable bipod. Telescopic sights featuring rapid adjustment for ranges from 328 to 984 feet respectively, and from 328 to 1640.4 feet can be supplied in the calibers .300 Winchester Magnum and .308 Winchester, the rapid adjustment settings are calibrated with match ammunition to the respective optimal load combinations.

The scope mounts slide along a dovetail up to the forward stop and are retained by a clamping system. This makes sure that there is no wear on the mounts as actual retention only takes place when the clamping force is applied. A spacer block is supplied with each weapon to provide optimal eye relief for the individual shooter.

Unlike conventional weapons which have plastic or wooden stocks, the WA 2000's frame is designed to accept the other parts. All these parts are attached independently to provide individual stock layout and final adjustment for the shooter's personal preference. The rubber butt plate is adjustable to all shooters' tasks.

Walther also makes a submachine gun, the Walther MP in 9mm caliber. This submachine gun fires at a rate of 550rpm and its magazine holds 32 rounds. This firearm is available in two folding stock models.

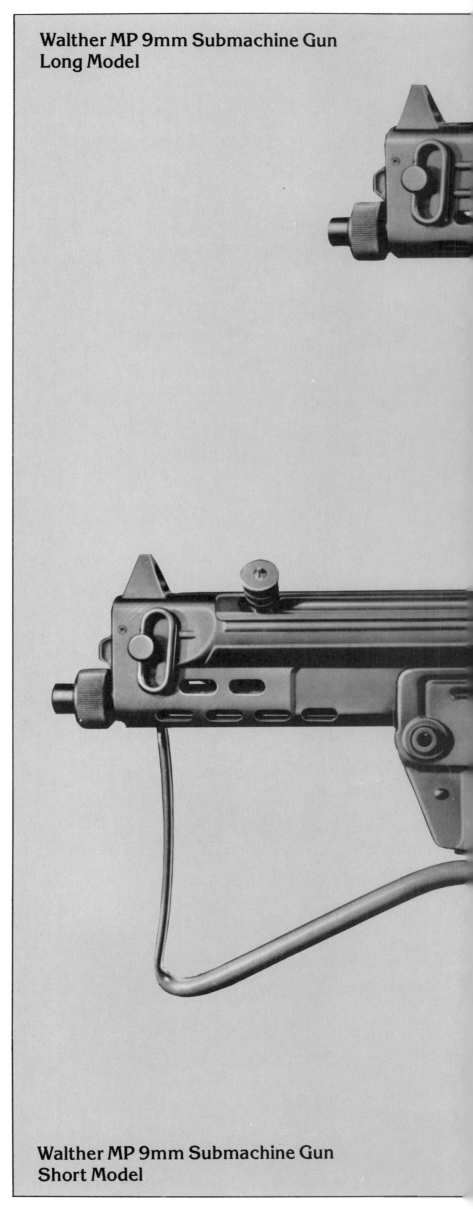

**Walther MP 9mm Submachine Gun
Long Model**

**Walther MP 9mm Submachine Gun
Short Model**

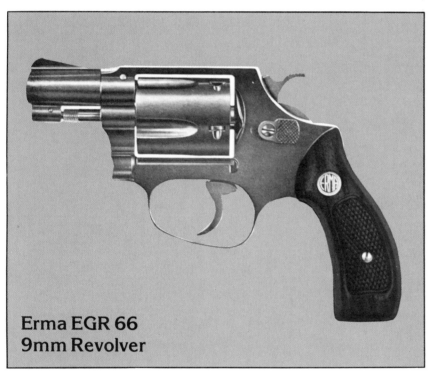

**Erma EGR 66
9mm Revolver**

ERMA-WERKE
Mod. EP 555 Kal. 6.35/.25

**Erma EP 555
6.35mm Semiautomatic Pistol**

The 'long model' is 29.4 inches with stock extended, and the 'short model' measures some 25.9 inches with stock extended. Folding the stock results in a dimensional saving on both models, of approximately 11.3 inches. This firearm features a full range of unique Walther design innovations.

Erma-Werke is proud of having more than 60 years experience in manufacturing firearms. The factory, founded in the early twenties in Erfut (now the German Democratic Republic), shifted to West Germany where the factory was newly founded. Erma gained an international reputation by making outstanding quality products and by modern technology and construction. Erma products are being exported nowadays to all five continents and enjoy great popularity thanks to their precision, styling and reliability.

The Erma EM 1 is a copy in .22 caliber of the history-making US M1 Carbine.

The EM 1 is a semiautomatic blowback-type firearm with a 10 to 15 round capacity. It has adjustable rear sights and has a grooved barrel for telescope mounts. The Erma EGM 1 is the sporting model of the Erma EM 1 carbine.

The EGM 1, aka 'Model 70,' features the same semiauto blowback operation as the EM 1, and at 5.6 pounds and 35.5-inch overall length, has the same handling characteristics as the EM 1.

The Erma ESG 22 is the first and, for the time being, only locked semi-automatic carbine in .22/Winchester Magnum in the world. Also available with original EM 1 stock and front sight (see illustration EM 1).

The ESG 22 is also available with the EM 1 stock and solid front sight. With open slide, fully adjustable rear sight, and five–12 shot

Erma 422 .22 Revolver

Erma 457 7.65mm
Semiautomatic Pistol

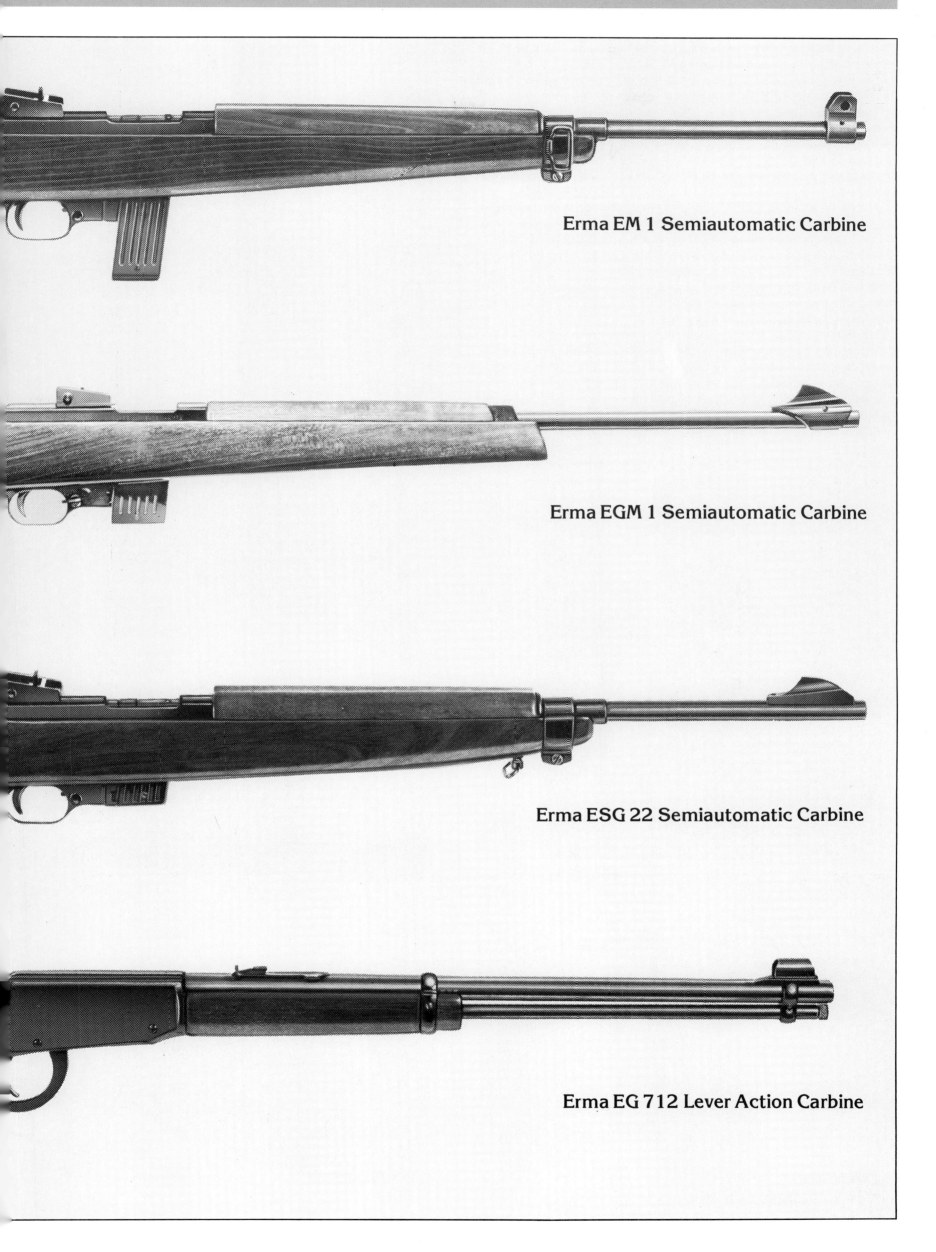

Erma EM 1 Semiautomatic Carbine

Erma EGM 1 Semiautomatic Carbine

Erma ESG 22 Semiautomatic Carbine

Erma EG 712 Lever Action Carbine

magazine capacity, this fine firearm comes standard with a sporting stock which features a handguard and sling swivels.

The Erma EG 712 is the latest Erma design of a lever action carbine for three calibers (.22 short, long and long rifle).

The EG 712 has a grooved receiver for telescope mounts and an adjustable rear sight. Of the pump-action Erma EG 722, it is said that 'when loading and repeating this ingenious carbine, it rests in firing position.' The EG 722 fires all standard .22 caliber ammunition, and its magazine is capacious enough to handle 21 shorts, 17 longs and 15 long rifles.

The lever action Erma EG 73 is a product of outstanding shooting performance and precision. In .22 Winchester Magnum, the EG 73 has all the Erma extras, and has a 12-shot capacity. The Erma EG 76 is the smallest of the Erma lever action line. This lever action model is also available under the type designation EG 294 for firing blank cartridges. The EG 76 fires 4mm longs, and has a grooved receiver for telescope mounting. The single shot E61 is a reasonably priced precision gun for the sports shooter.

The Erma Model 1860 is an authentic reproduction of the first black-powder breech-loading carbine of 1860, the Gallagher Carbine. In .54 caliber, this historic reproduction will return you to the days of yesteryear. The Model 1860 packs a punch with its 55 grain maximum black powder load! For a change of pace, the ELG 10 air rifle corresponds with the ever-popular Erma line of underlever models. The ELG 10 is a single shot, firing .17 caliber balls.

The Erma 772, 773 and 77 Sports Revolvers are sport weapons designed according to modern considerations, intended to appeal to the

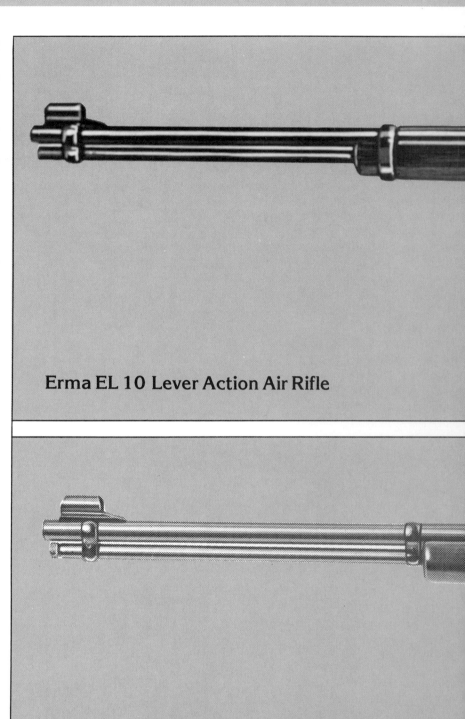

Erma EL 10 Lever Action Air Rifle

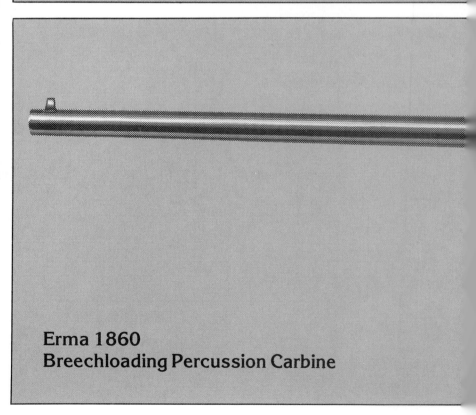

Erma GG 722 Pump Action Carbine

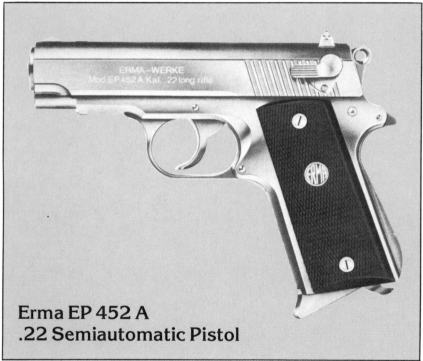

Erma EP 452 A
.22 Semiautomatic Pistol

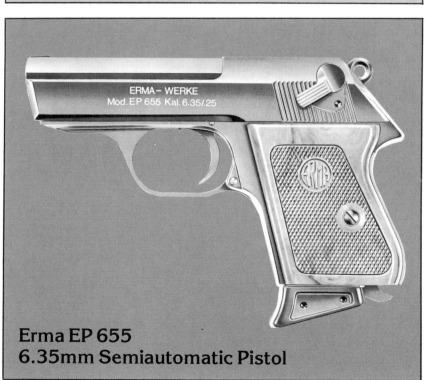

Erma EP 655
6.35mm Semiautomatic Pistol

Erma 1860
Breechloading Percussion Carbine

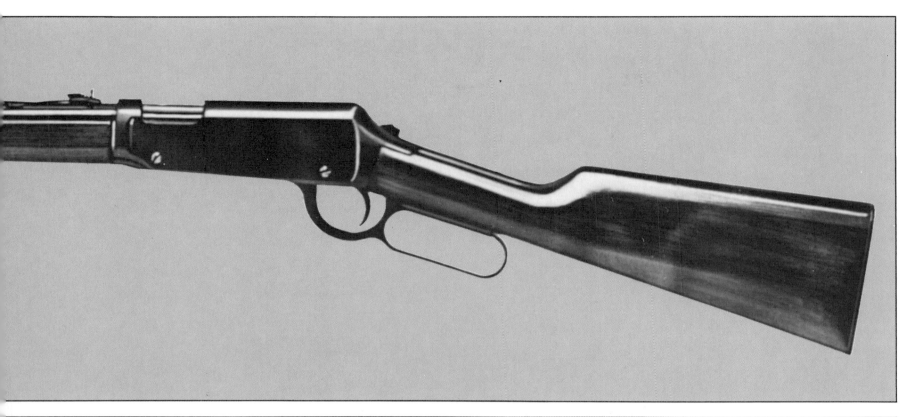

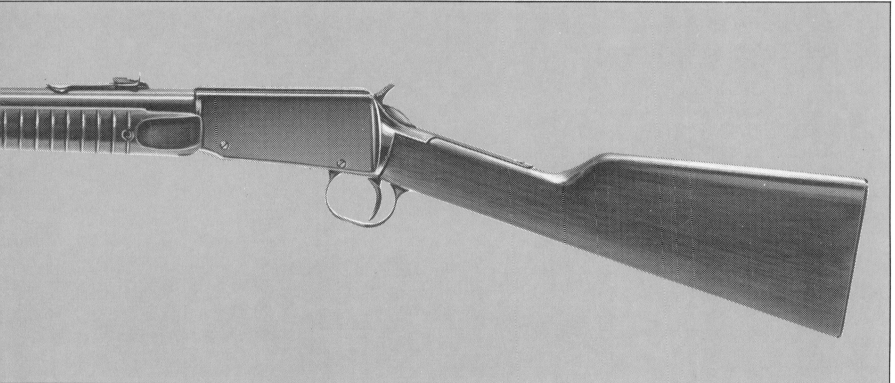

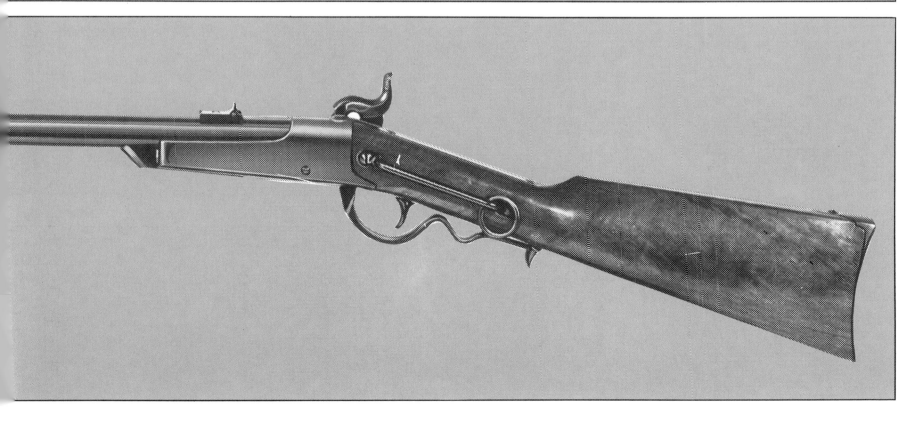

great number of dedicated hobby sport marksmen as well as top competing sportsmen. The ER 772 is in .22 long rifle caliber, the ER 773 is in .32 Smith & Wesson long and the ER 777 is in .357 Magnum. Each hold six shots and have adjustable triggers.

The Erma sport pistol ESP 85A is a weapon designed according to modern considerations. It is intended to appeal to the great number of dedicated sport marksmen as well as top competing sportsmen. The ESP 85A is available in .22 long rifle or .32 Smith & Wesson wadcutter long. The former has a 5–8 shot capacity, and the latter holds five shots. Front and rear sights are both interchangeable.

The Erma KGP 68A is a popular pistol of outstanding technical features for universal use. Available in .32 or .380 caliber, this 22.5-ounce Luger-style pistol is a handy firearm. The Erma KGP 69 is the ideal training gun for target shooting. The KGP 69 is an eight-shot toggle joint (Luger-style) pistol which weighs 30 ounces. The KGP690 is its classic brother in a gas-firing model.

The Erma ER 422/423/432 revolvers are ideal for sport shooting. All models are available with optional round or square grip butt. The ER 422 is available in .22 long rifle; the ER 423 is available in .22 Winchester Magnum; and the ER 432 is available in .32 Smith & Wesson long. The Erma self-defense revolver, the ER 440 is in .38 Special, and holds five cartridges.

The ERP 74 allows pistol-readiness under all conditions. In four mm, this 21-ounce automatic holds seven cartridges. The Erma EP 552/555 models are handy, reliable and practical automatic pistols with double action. Available in .22 long rifle, the EP 552 holds seven rounds. In .25 caliber, the EP 555 weighs just 14.7 ounces.

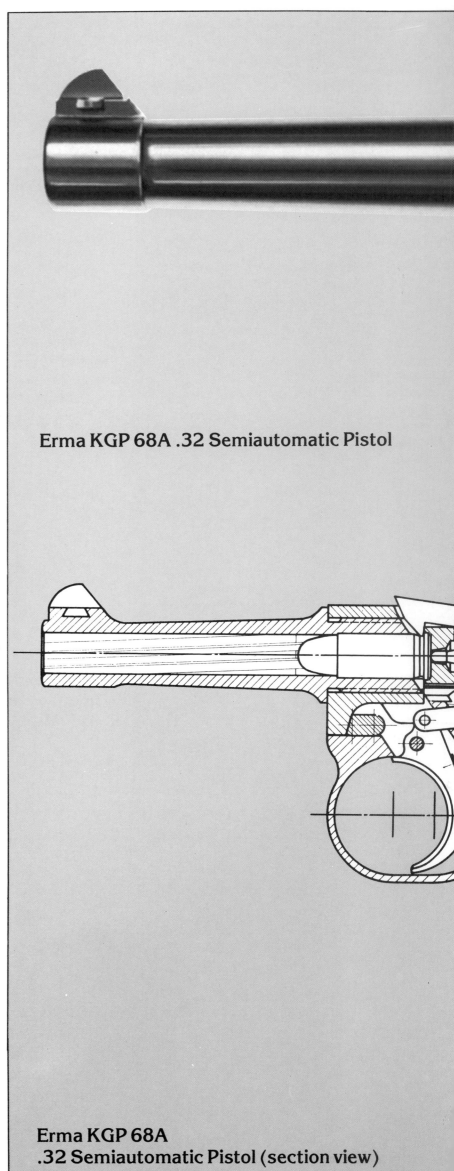

Erma KGP 68A .32 Semiautomatic Pistol

Erma EP 752
.22 Semiautomatic Pistol

Erma EP 452
.22 Semiautomatic Pistol

Erma KGP 68A
.32 Semiautomatic Pistol (section view)

Kal. 7,65/.32

0 2 3 4 2   ERMA-WERKE Mod. KGP 68A

F

The Erma EP 652/655 models are small self-defense guns of modern styling. At 13.9 ounces, the EP 652 is available in .22 long rifle, and the EP 655 is available in .25 caliber. The Erma 752 S is an automatic pistol with an additional ignition safety, in a modern design for self defense and sport shooting. In .22 long rifle caliber, the EP 752S holds eight cartridges. The EGP 55 is a small gas pistol with a double action trigger. This automatic fires five 8mm K gas cartridges. The Erma EGP 65 is another of Erma's fine gas pistols in 8mm, with an optional 15mm barrel. The seven-shot capacity of the Erma EGP 75S helps to round out Erma's line of fine gas cartridge automatics.

The Erma EP 452 is a .22 long rifle autoloader which holds eight rounds and weighs 21.8 ounces. It features an extra ignition safety and is excellent for sport shooting. The Erma EP 652 is a .22 long rifle, seven-shot autoloader which weighs a mere 13.9 ounces, as does its .25 caliber counterpart, the 5.3 inches long EP 655.

The EP 552 (in .22 long rifle) and the EP 555 (in .25 caliber) each hold seven cartridges and are double-action autoloaders. These pistols weigh 14.6 ounces apiece. Very similar in styling to the EP 552/555 is the EP 752 S, a 21 ounce automatic pistol with double action trigger in .22 long rifle. The EP 752S has an eight round capacity.

The Erma EGR 66 is a five-shot 9mm revolver with rounded grips and optional two or three-inch barrel. It weighs 20.3 ounces with the shorter, and 22.1 ounces with the longer, barrel. The Erma EGR 77 is a heavy-frame six-shot .380/9mm caliber revolver. With 2.5-inch barrel, the EGR 77 weighs 35.7 ounces. The EGR 77 has a double action trigger, and has a maximum length of 8.9 inches.

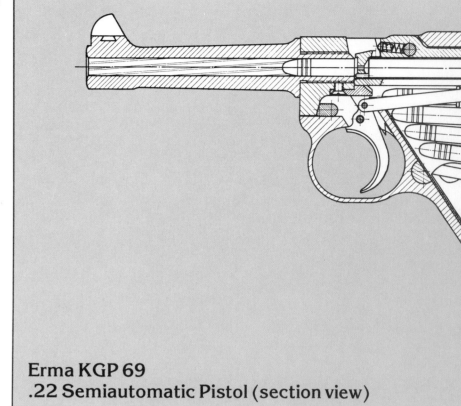

**Erma KGP 69
.22 Semiautomatic Pistol (section view)**

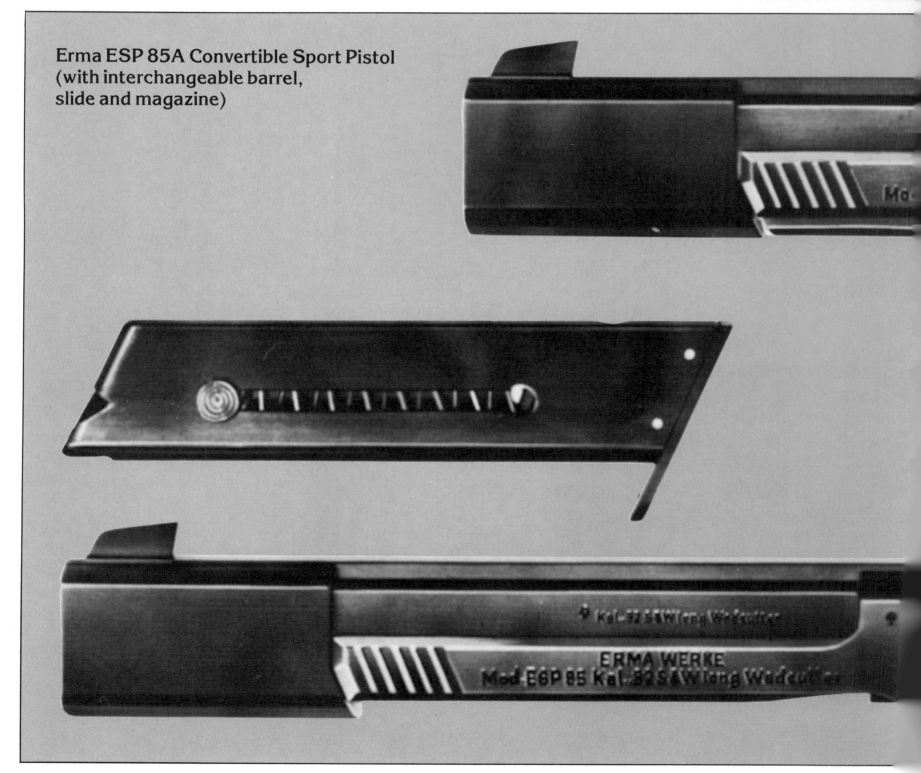

**Erma ESP 85A Convertible Sport Pistol
(with interchangeable barrel,
slide and magazine)**

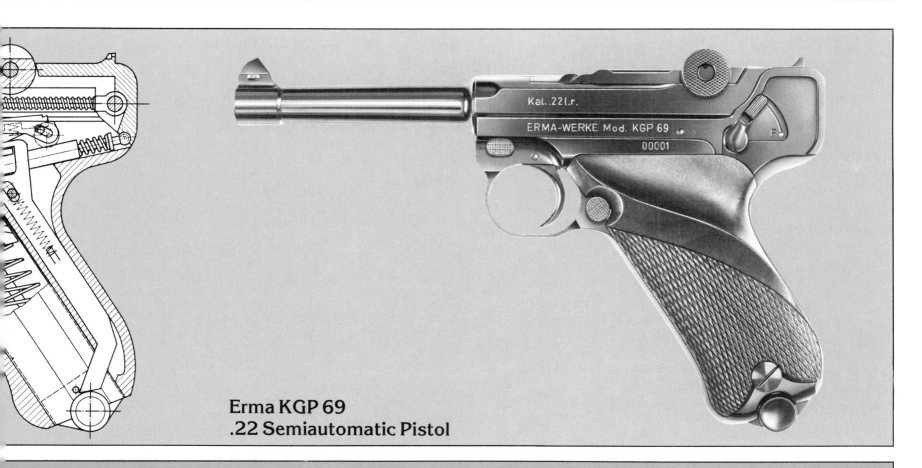

Erma KGP 69
.22 Semiautomatic Pistol

INDEX

Page 192: (left to right) Fox Model
Field Shotgun, Lefever Arms T
Shotgun, Browning Lightning Trap G
Shotgun, Springfield Model 1898
Crosman Model 114 Rifle, Remi
Woodmaster Rifle, Savage Model
Hornet Rifle, Noble Model 70J Sh
Stevens Model 1915 Rifle, Rem
Model 12C Rifle and Remington
600 Rifle.

B
rap
ade
ifle,
gton
23D
tgun,
ngton
Model

191